P9-ELQ-637

CONTINUOUS TESTING
FOR DEVOPS PROFESSIONALS

A PRACTICAL GUIDE FROM INDUSTRY EXPERTS

ERAN KINSBRUNER

INTRODUCTION

After experiencing great appreciation from the market following my first book, *The Digital Quality Handbook**, I decided to collaborate even further with industry thought leaders and vendors to complement the 1st book with this definitive guide to continuous testing for DevOps professionals. This book that is divided into the following 4 sections:

1. Fundamentals of Continuous Testing — everything DevOps teams need to know about CT from planning through metrics, coverage, DevOps pipeline orchestration and more.

2. Continuous testing for web apps.

3. Continuous testing for mobile apps.

4. The future of CT with emphasis on machine learning and AI techniques. Happy reading and huge thanks to everyone that was involved in this amazing project, that all of its profits will be donated to the proper cause of enabling kids to learn programming.

*http://book.perfecto.io/the-digital-quality-handbook/

Enterprise DevOps Recipe for Success

BY ROTEM KANER, ENGINEERING PROGRAMS AND OPERATIONS
MANAGER @PERFECTO

ROTEM KANER brings more than 20 years in software organizations with background in R&D, SaaS operations, product delivery and customer success. Leading and running release management, production management, responsible for processes and methodologies definition, planning activities and execution tracking and establishing the AWS practice both financially and technically. Rotem has vast experience in embedding Agile methodologies across engineering organizations as well as successfully leading DevOps transitions. Prior to Perfecto, Rotem held several program and SW development management positions in enterprise (HP SW, Convergys) and startup companies. Rotem holds an MBA and BA in computer science from Bar Ilan university, Israel.

INTRODUCTION

Striving to mature agile and DevOps processes for any organization is a great challenge. The complexity in developing such processes involves many moving parts, cross-functional team synchronization, continuous measurement of usage, efficiency and cost, automation of processes, continuous monitoring towards continuous improvement, and more. That's why recent surveys[1] from various sources shows that only 28–30% of the teams that aim to mature their DevOps practices are successful in doing so.

Driving the entire **DevOps process as a single engineering team** is an art form; once successful, it can meet its key goal: delivering maximum value from the product as fast as possible and with the highest quality.

This entire book is focused on recommended practices to eliminate bottlenecks and drive mature DevOps activities. This preface highlights the experience that Perfecto's engineering team gathered while transitioning to DevOps.

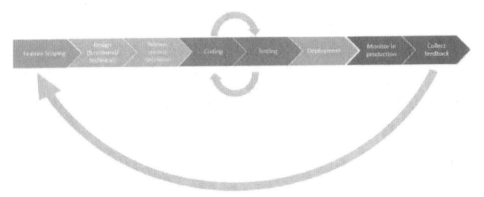

A transition to DevOps requires a combination of things that, as the book will clarify, involves People, Processes, and Technology.

KEY PILLARS FOR SUCCESSFUL DEVOPS TEAMS

Consider integrating these process-based activities into your DevOps practices. They require both the proper technology, the right leadership, and the individuals to make them work together.

✓ Ongoing collaboration with customers for validations of new functionalities and feedback.

✓ Following coding guidelines for tests and production code throughout the pipeline

✓ Continuous measurement, monitoring and analysis post-release

---

1   Practitest state of testing survey 2018 — http://qablog.practitest.com/state-of-testing/

✓ DevOps efficiency and cost analysis

✓ Governance and control

At Perfecto, we developed a unique *"Monthly Service Health Review Board"* to ensure and control these activities.

Perfecto's Monthly Service Health Review Board — to mature overall DevOps processes, and to continuously improve, Perfecto engineering leadership initiated a monthly review session per service, that investigates overall product health, service stability and quality, usage trends, operability and cost analysis to drive future steps, and to improve things that are in motion.

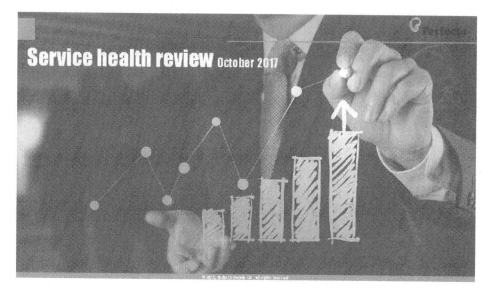

To drill down into the above checklist, and based on continuous delivery of features and value to customers, Perfecto has found success by including the following items as part of its *Service health review* checklist:

✓ **Continuous production monitoring** to identify usage trends and production issues — such activities drive consistent feedback to management and dev and help the entire team to adjust the service in various ways, based on customer needs.

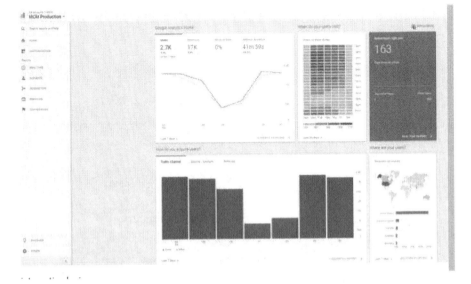

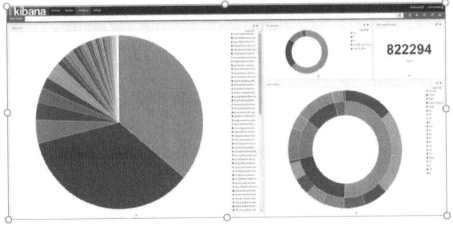

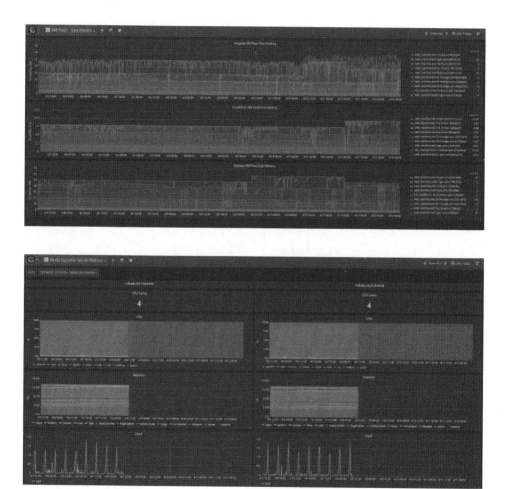

✓ **Cost analysis** — continuously measuring the cost of the product and being able to optimize it for efficiency impacts revenue and the success of the entire team. To analyze cost, there need to be tools in place that can measure and collect production analytics, usage trends, and available in-house knowledge of costs of development and support for the product.

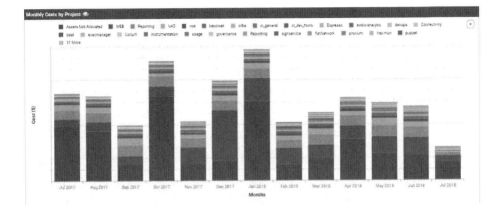

✓ **Conduct a customer base usability lab when applicable** — the value-add to this kind of activity is enormous. Usability labs with your customers will confirm or reject whether your feature spec meets their desired outcomes and that your implementation is easy to use and intuitive. During the usability lab, the R&D team and the UX expert will gather input from the customers that will help define the new products.

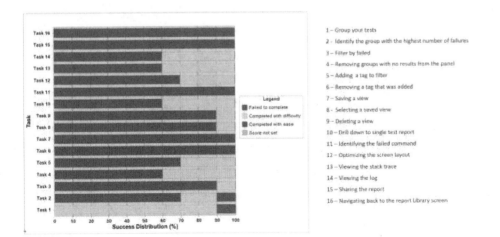

✓ **Define your feature rollout plans** — depending on the size of the feature and its value, the DevOps team will decide whether to gradually expose a feature, do an early access, or release it with an entire product iteration as is. Each path will have its pros and cons; therefore, the leadership team needs to make a calculated and risk-based decision. It's important to understand that for cloud-based products like Perfecto, having a gradual-exposure release requires a supportive product architecture such as custom feature flags per tenant, sufficient time for early feedback prior to GA, and good communication between customer management and R&D.

✓ **Build a solid test plan** — as the focus of this book is Continuous Testing, having a plan behind your overall DevOps activities is key for success. At Perfecto, the method of assuring quality involves various pillars, the important ones being:

- **Treating test code as production code** — with all this entails

- **ATDD** — Acceptance Test Driven Development as a key practice to assure quality

- **Strict code merge process** to assure master is always stable

- **Green CI** is a **must**

- **Continuous code reviews** throughout the coding life cycle — check for coding guidelines, memory leaks, peer reviews, and more.

- **Test for backward compatibility** across releases

- Assure that **Dev environment == Production environment** to reduce escaped defects and mitigate quality risks. An additional benefit of maintaining the above environments is the ability to release code to production at any time.

- Include testing — and especially **test automation** — as part of the MVP or feature **definition of done**

✓ **Match the technology stack to your product requirements** — build an efficient tool ecosystem that can support development, testing, and monitoring activities. When evaluating tools, consider both open-source as well as proven commercial tools. Perfecto uses a large set of technologies throughout its overall DevOps activities and continuously seeks additional solutions that can optimize and enhance its objectives.

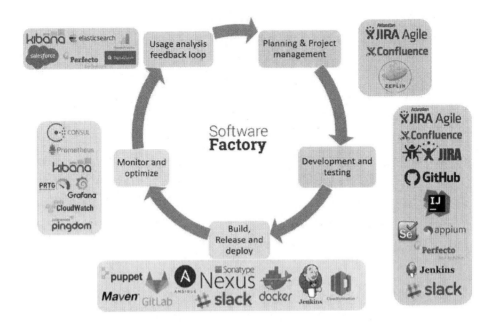

✓ **Leverage architectural MRC's (minimal required capabilities)** — consider things like horizontal scaling, multi-tenancy models, and others as part of your entire iteration planning.

✓ **Documentation** — while not always the coolest task, having robust documentation of features and test code helps when refactoring, debugging and enabling various personas.

✓ **Field enablement** — to ensure product adoption and delivery of high value to the customer, your field reps need to be on the same page regarding the core usage and supported functionalities of a new release to drive sales. Such enablement relies on existing documentation, demonstrations, and case studies, whenever possible.

SUMMARY

Maturing DevOps requires a mature team. Such teams need to follow processes and to be aligned around product objectives and goals. As described above, at Perfecto, the engineering team, which includes Dev, Test, and Ops, was able to implement a working process of releasing software fast, with high quality, and with ongoing visibility into usage and cost analysis. By following the process — and the aforementioned checklist — the whole company gains 3 advantages:

Accelerated software delivery	Balanced speed, cost, quality & risk	Reduced time to customer feedback
Faster time to value	Optimize velocity, planning	Improve user experience

In the following chapters, you will read more about how to implement Continuous Testing within a DevOps and CI/CD reality and learn specific best practices for web and mobile quality assurance.

TABLE OF CONTENTS

SECTION 1

Fundamentals of Continuous Testing

CHAPTER ONE

Fundamentals of Continuous Testing (CT) for Digital Apps

INTRODUCTION

According to a wide variety of research, most enterprises are either adopting Agile or have been practicing it for a few years already; however, only 35% of these enterprises have begun to mature DevOps as a complementary method to Agile. While the focus of these organizations was first on continuous integration (CI), and second on continuous delivery (CD), the required and **missing practice for maturing DevOps** was — and is — **continuous testing** (CT). The term CT should be as broad as possible from a test coverage perspective, and includes the areas of security testing, non-functional testing, production monitoring, and other testing types as well. These tests, which run continuously, must be reliable, fast, and automated as much as possible to increase team velocity and allow delivery of incremental value to customers, all while maintaining high code quality. CT is an important process that can help organizations respond faster to changes and market events and shorten time to value for customers.

DEFINING CONTINUOUS TESTING

To quote Wikipedia[1], continuous testing is *"the process of executing automated tests as part of the software delivery pipeline to obtain immediate feedback on the business risks associated with a software release candidate".*

To simplify the definition of CT, continuous testing is the **process of embed-**

---

1   Wikipedia's definition of CT — https://en.wikipedia.org/wiki/Continuous_testing

ding various types of software testing (unit, functional, non-functional) as a fundamental ongoing practice throughout the entire development *lifecycle.* Having the ability to verify the quality of software after each code change in an automated way in the CI process holds great benefits for all DevOps practitioners.

KEY CHALLENGES OF CT

Being able to deliver value at each software iteration, with high quality and continuous feedback to executives, is hard.

Maturing DevOps, and specifically CT, depends on continuous alignment between People, Processes, and Technology in the organization. Each of these three can become bottlenecks — or blockers — for CT.

People Challenges

The **people** element is crucial to the successful scaling of CT within DevOps.

In this context, "people" can be broken down by role or persona within teams — executives, developers, testers, ops, and security. Since each has a unique responsibility within the delivery pipeline, it is important to have perfect alignment between them. Also, having good methods and means of communication is important key to having all parties on the same page: some teams use tools such as Jira and Slack to stay in sync.

Executives need to step in and help drive change, from **measurements** and metrics to help identify issues throughout the various teams, to ensuring use of the right tools, to fostering practices such as including automation as part of the definition of done (DoD). As part of maturing CT, executives need continuous **quality visibility** for each build or iteration of their products. Also, leadership should push the "start small, then grow" methodology as a process. Just as teams develop their code in small chunks per iteration and stabilize them, so should testing grow and be stabilized through automation and CI; only then can you grow the test suite. In today's reality, there is a great focus on percentage of test automation and test automation suite size rather than test automation code quality, stability, and efficiency and its ability to provide valuable **feedback** to developers. Market leaders state that Agile and DevOps testing should be **FAST**: Fast, Actionable, Scalable, and reliable. Only then it can grow and expand. Leadership needs to make sure that the various individuals work as one and that they have the right set of tools, requirements, and continuous measurements to work towards. If there are skill set issues, the need to be addressed to avoid gaps due to lack of capabilities within teams.

Process-Related Challenges

Continuously releasing value to the customers, with high quality, mitigated risks, and efficient feedback and analytics that can be acted upon, is a challenging task in today's digital demanding reality.

Time constraints often get in the way of following common practices such as:

- Treating test code as production code, full version control etc.
- Including automation within the "definition of done" per iteration
- Committing new test code only when it shows consistent results ("3 strikes, you're out" rule)
- Continuously refactor test code to make sure it is still relevant and exclude redundant tests from CI/regression suites

Technology Challenges

Proper leadership and practices aren't enough to mature CT within DevOps without also having a great fit in technologies and test labs.

From what I've seen in my rich experience[2] in the quality space, whenever a test environment is unstable, insecure, not scalable enough, or not open to integration with various technologies and testing frameworks, that's when teams are blocked from maturing their DevOps objectives.

In an Agile environment where various developers and testers use different technologies and platforms, and sometimes with remote teams, having a

---

2   Dzone article on CT — https://dzone.com/articles/continuous-testing-principles-for-cross-brows-er-te

stable test environment to base all quality activities on is a key for success. It is not just about matching the test lab and the environment to the tools of the team but also matching these to the teams' skills and software methodologies, such as BDD, ATDD, TDD or others.

Test labs that don't fit seamlessly into development CI processes cannot serve the purposes of DevOps and CT. The stability and reliability of CI relies on the lab as its backbone.

Finally, especially in the era of DevOps and CT[3], there is much more test data being generated per execution. Having the ability to get great insight into large piles of test data and drill down into specific issues can be a key enabler to maturing CT. **Executives** are unable to reach a "go, no-go" decision without executive dashboards; developers and **release managers** cannot see whether their CI processes and builds are moving in the right direction and remaining within the time constraints. In many cases, pinpointing an issue feels like finding a needle in a haystack; test **engineers** and **test managers** can lack the necessary test artifacts to provide proper feedback to developers.

Prior to studying the pillars of success, it is a good idea to reflect on the well-known Agile Testing Manifesto.

---

3   Cloud Computing — making CI, CD and CT work together - https://www.cloudcomputing-news.net/news/2018/apr/11/finding-right-agile-formula-making-ci-ct-and-cd-work-together/

The Manifesto offers a great foundation for implementing CT since it forces DevOps teams to think with the end result in mind and focus on **delivering value fast and with high quality.** This is done by testing at all stages of the pipeline, proactively searching for quality issues vs. reacting to defects late in the process, and working as a team in order to deliver a best-in-class product.

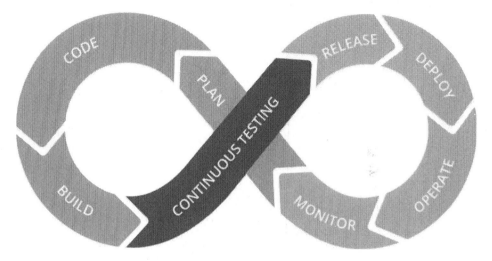

Successfully implementing CT in a DevOps reality is easier said than done. There are lots of moving parts in the pipeline that can slow down — or entirely disrupt — your quality release activities.

To create sustainable, ongoing CT, there are various pillars and a blueprint[4] that needs to be considered and maintained.

- Develop the right plan for your CT (Please refer to Chapter 2 by Joe Colantonio)

- Build a robust foundation that can support your planning

- Start small and grow your test scenarios and platform coverage (Please refer to chapter 8 in this book by Uzi Eilon)

- Manage and Measure your DevOps pipeline activities (Please refer to Chapters 3, 4, and 6 in this book to further learn about orchestrating the DevOps pipeline and measuring success)

- Leverage reporting and analytics to employ CT fast feedback to developers (see Chapter 7 by Tzvika Shahaf)

DEVELOP THE RIGHT PLAN FOR YOUR CT

Every success story has a great plan behind it. CT should be no different.

When trying to advance and improve DevOps processes, leadership should have a strong plan for all feature teams and individuals. Such a plan considers the following:

- Number of projects and their type (mobile, web, RWD, PWA, etc.)

- Team size — Dev, Test, Ops, SCM, etc.

- Team skill sets — development languages, testing framework familiarity

- Software development lifecycle methods — ATDD, BDD, etc.

- Technology availability — which tool stack is currently in use and what is missing?

- Market trends and analytics — to support new features, user stories, etc.

---

4   Perfecto's recommended blueprint for CT — https://www.perfecto.io/plan-with-the-blueprint-for-continuous-testing-success/

- Business maturity requirements

- Lab sizing and coverage requirements

- Define metrics for success — **smart** ones

To build a solid foundation — and to scale it — the previously listed requirements need to be set in advance and calibrated as a project evolves. Later in this book, we will define the pillars for a proper CT plan, with its relevant technology stacks and more.

BUILD THE FOUNDATION FOR YOUR CT PLAN

After setting goals and quality objectives for your projects, the different individuals in your team need a solid foundation to meet these goals. This foundation relies on a few important elements:

- Test automation framework and test authoring

- Test framework fit

- Risk-based test automation strategy

- Stable CI, maintained continuously

- Support for test data generation

- Stable lab and test environment

TEST AUTOMATION FRAMEWORK AND AUTHORING

Authoring test automation code should be no different than developing and maintaining code for your application features, such as login functionality, etc.

As the product evolves, so too should your test scenarios. When test code is not properly maintained with source code management (SCM) tools, it becomes difficult to make timely changes and build on top of them since there is a lack of proper documentation, traceability, and history of the test code.

In addition, when a new functionality is built into your mobile application or your web site, it may require changes to your test code, which may include writing new tests, modifying existing test flows, retiring tests, or even merging new tests into one large test. To be able to continuously address product changes, your test code always needs to be in sync with the product's evolution and carry with it relevant history and documentation.

Just as you treat your production code with ongoing analysis, refactoring, and more, it is critical that you do the same for your test code – this is an enabler for CT.

Developing your test code the right way from the get-go can be the main difference between a high-value test suite and a time-consuming, flaky, inefficient one. As mentioned above, treating test code as production code is a recommended practice; however, writing good, valuable tests is a different practice that involves various considerations:

- Having the right object identification strategy
- Having the right test framework to work with
- Measuring test efficiency within the CI
- Risk-based approach to test automation
- Continuous test data analysis and improvement

OBJECT LOCATOR STRATEGIES

As I described in my previous book[5], there are proven methods to identify the unique and stable objects for your application testing. It is recommended to work closely with your development team and ensure as much access as possible to the unique object IDs that will be used throughout your test code. Once these objects are identified, managing them within a page object

---

5   The Digital Quality Handbook — http://book.perfecto.io

model (POM) is another good and reusable practice from both a maintainability perspective and from a test-authoring time efficiency perspective.

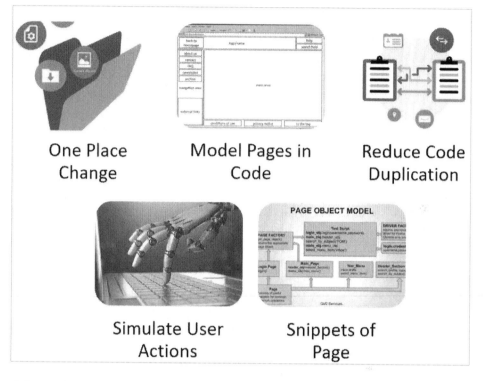

One Place Change

Model Pages in Code

Reduce Code Duplication

Simulate User Actions

Snippets of Page

CODE COMMIT BEST PRACTICES

One of the main reasons for regression defects and other quality issues within the DevOps pipeline is the lack of code commit validations by developers. Prior to each code change, small or large, there needs to be a process to enforce testing of that code. Such a process defines which testing types are developed and executed along with existing smoke or regression tests. A post-commit test suite should not be limited only to unit testing; it can — and in many cases should — cover API, UI, functional and non-functional test cases, as well as continuous code scanning for memory leaks, security, and more. This will guarantee smooth code delivery to the main branch. Once such a process is maintained by all developers, a merge that captures various code commits from individual developers in the team will be much safer and contain fewer regressions. This translates into a much more confident integration cycle and fewer escaped defects.

TEST FRAMEWORK FIT FOR THE JOB

I cannot overstate the importance of the test framework in the overall CT activities. A proper test framework(s) is at the core of test authoring, object management, test management, reporting, and various integrations and APIs for high test productivity. Many open-source test automation frameworks are great for test authoring but there are very few that combine all these required capabilities. That's why many commercial vendors embrace open-source frameworks, such as Appium and Selenium, and provide additional layers on top to complement the entire set of requirements a DevOps team needs.

RISK BASED TEST AUTOMATION STRATEGY

CT is all about fast feedback and offering high-value releases to the end users. These objectives should be considered when choosing which tests to automate and when to run them. One way to look at test automation strategy would to embrace Angie Jones' best practices, as shown in the image below[6]. In this example, deciding which tests to automate is determined by various scoring methodologies:

- What's the test engineer's gut feeling
- Risk calculated as probability to occur and impact to customers
- Value — does the test provide new information and, if failed, how much time to fix?
- Cost efficiency to develop — how long does it take to develop and how easy is it to script?
- History of test — volume of historical failures in related areas and frequency of breaks

It is important to use either this or another method that makes sense from quality, business, and time-to-market perspectives to drive efficient, ongoing CT processes.

---

6   Angie Jones slide share on what to automate — https://www.slideshare.net/saucelabs/which-tests-should-we-automate-by-angie-jones

ID	Description	G	R	V	C	H	Score
	Twitter Profile Scenarios						
1	Add a tweet	✓	25	25	25	0	75
2	View tweets	✓	25	25	20	3	73
3	Pin a tweet	✓	9	16	15	1	41
4	Follow a user	✓	20	25	25	0	70
5	Set handle/username	✓	20	25	25	3	73
6	Set location	X	1	10	25	25	61
7	Update handle	✓	3	9	25	4	41
8	Block a user	✓	20	25	16	0	61
9	View analytics of a tweet	✓	3	8	9	0	20
10	Balloons appear on birthday	X	1	5	15	0	21

SCORES

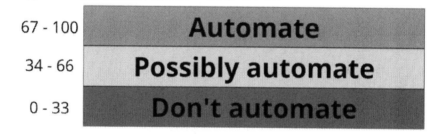

67 - 100	**Automate**
34 - 66	**Possibly automate**
0 - 33	**Don't automate**

TEST EFFICIENCY WITHIN CONTINUOUS INTEGRATION

CI is one of the keys to drive Continuous Testing throughout all DevOps phases. CI testing activities, however, are not the responsibility of the CI server that simply acts as a scheduler for job executions, but are instead the responsibility of test engineers, architects and developers who author the test code itself. The CI server is an orchestrator and scheduler of tasks and should not be running test code that isn't stable enough or that wasn't fully proofed.

Efficient testing within CI means

1. Reliable pass/fail results — zero flakiness
2. Fast execution and feedback to developers and testers — job, branch, and single test visibility
3. Meaningful results (printouts to console, logs, HAR files, screenshots, etc.)

ALWAYS MAINTAIN A STABLE CI

As explained earlier in the book, the 3 pillars for efficient DevOps are CI, CT, and CD.

CT and CD cannot succeed if the engine that drives them is flaky - and the engine that drives CT is Continuous Integration. That's why CI builds should always be green unless there is a real issue. To make your CI always green, teams need ongoing focus and processes that gate what gets into the CI engine. We will elaborate on continuous integration best practices later in the book; this is, again, a key to your overall DevOps maturity growth.

TEST DATA GENERATION

Depending on the market segment or vertical, test data generation has high value to both developers and testers. For banks, being able to continuously test against pre-generated banking accounts with various profiles is key to validating both functionality of their apps as well as performance in pulling account data. The same goes for insurance apps and healthcare apps. Such test data cannot be actual production data for a wide variety of reasons; therefore, as part of CT, teams need to have a way to virtualize and use this test data. Also, when the product evolves and test data becomes outdated, there needs to be a clear process for refreshing the data to include new fields or other advanced features.

24/7 STABLE LAB AND TEST ENVIRONMENT

Since the entire CI process relies on well-written test code, both test execution and CI stability depend on the availability and stability of the test lab. A stable lab means that all platforms connected to it, along with supporting test environments, 3rd party tools, and APIs, are working 24/7 with near-zero downtime. To create this sort of environment, in the DevOps landscape[7], there is no doubt that the "power of the cloud" has proven to be the only path to meet these objectives.

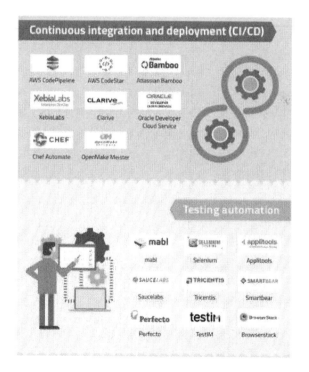

---

7   Mabl blog — mapping the DevOps tool chain — https://www.mabl.com/blog/devops-tools-orga-nized-by-category

START SMALL AND GROW YOUR CT WITHIN THE DEVOPS PIPELINE

Mastering CT within the DevOps pipeline means always having the right coverage, both from a test scenario perspective and a platform perspective.

There are different objectives within each phase of the DevOps pipeline that require different coverage principles. The early stages of developing a new functionality involve many unit test activities and back-and-forth debugging cycles by the developer. Typically, these activities happen on the developer's workstation and, to get fast feedback, the developer doesn't need a full-blown lab and may be satisfied with one or two relevant platforms (web and/or mobile). As development of the feature(s) evolves, there are different quality and development criteria that require an extended set of test scenarios and platforms to be executed; this requires a scheduled CI workflow, backed by a larger test lab — that will probably be cloud-based — to provide support for various users, various scales, and a more complex test environment.

As defined in the visual below, CT within the DevOps pipeline should be built according to each different phase, from early development through production monitoring. Each phase will include its relevant testing activities which will be triggered based on the activity and quality objectives via the relevant environment (dev workstation vs. CI server) — per commit, nightly regression, and ongoing monitoring. For each of the quality activities, and based on the team's process, skills, and CT plan, they will need to choose the right test framework for coding (Espresso, Appium, XCUITest, Protractor, etc.)

Also, CT triggers and environments do not define the testing scope; for this, each project will need to have a solid test plan and quality criteria that guide the correct balance between API, Unit, UI, Functional, and Non-Functional testing.

MANAGE AND MEASURE YOUR DEVOPS PIPELINE ACTIVITIES AND YOUR CI

You can't manage what you can't measure. As with so many activities related

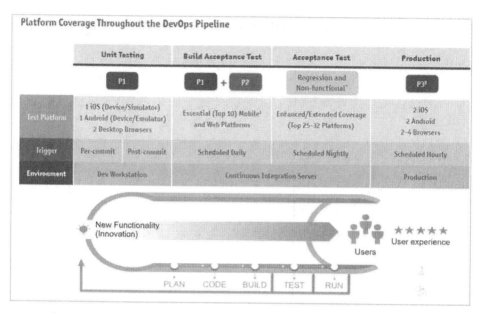

Platform Coverage Throughout the DevOps Pipeline

	Unit Testing		Build Acceptance Test	Acceptance Test	Production
	P1		P1 + P2	Regression and Non-functional*	P3²
Test Platform	1 iOS (Device/Simulator) 1 Android (Device/Emulator) 2 Desktop Browsers		Essential (Top 10) Mobile¹ and Web Platforms	Enhanced/Extended Coverage (Top 25-32 Platforms)	2 iOS 2 Android 2-4 Browsers
Trigger	Per-commit	Post-commit	Scheduled Daily	Scheduled Nightly	Scheduled Hourly
Environment	Dev Workstation		Continuous Integration Server		Production

New Functionality (Innovation)

Users

★★★★★ User experience

PLAN   CODE   BUILD   TEST   RUN

to continuous testing, there must be a clear definition of measurable goals, agreed upon as part of earlier planning, which can be referred to on-demand. Later in this section, there will be a deeper dive into what to measure and how; however, as a best practice, the following pillars need to be measured with pre-defined KPIs.

1. How fast are testing activities moving, and what is slowing down these activities?
   a. Test flakiness
   b. Test duration
   c. % of automated vs. manual tests
2. Application quality measurements
   a. # of escaped defects and in which areas
   b. MTTD — mean time to detection of defect
   c. Build quality
   d. Etc.
3. Pipeline efficiency measurements
   a. # of user stories implemented per iteration

    b. Test automation as part of DoD across iterations

    c. Broken builds with categories

    d. CI length trending

    e. Lab availability and utilization

    f. Etc.

4. Quality costs measurements

    a. Operational costs, lab availability issues

    b. Cost of hardware/software

    c. Costs of defects by severity and stage

    d. Etc.

Continuous measurement, while painful to both leadership and individuals, is imperative for continuous improvement of your DevOps practices. As part of your early planning, such measurements need to be agreed upon and selected; the foundation of your CT should be able to collect these and make them available on various dashboards throughout the process.

LEVERAGE REPORTING AND ANALYTICS FOR CT FAST FEEDBACK

As product quality is a 'moment in time' for an organization, so is a test scenario. Test code can quickly become irrelevant or outdated. To keep up with product pace and to continuously derive value from your quality initiatives, test code needs to be monitored and testing dashboards, both from functional test frameworks and CI, need to be reviewed by executives and team leaders.

Having actionable data from ongoing test executions can help teams author better tests and make valuable decisions. Later in the book, I'll dedicate an entire chapter to quality visibility best practices within the overall CT process.

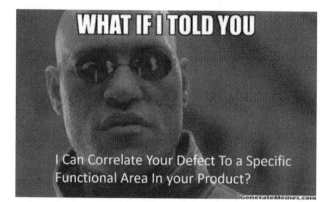

FAST FEEDBACK TO DEVELOPERS

As mentioned earlier — and this is at the heart of CT — fast feedback is imperative to maturing DevOps. Fast feedback in a CT context means that test engineers and developers author their test automation code on time and in parallel with feature development as much as possible. While that's a difficult objective to meet and often requires changes to existing environments, service virtualization, test data generation, and more, it is key to success. If a feature is implemented and the test code to validate it isn't ready in time to deliver feedback on quality, functionality, and user story matching, the iteration schedule will slip in the best case; in the worst case, a feature will be released based only on partial testing. As mentioned earlier, fast feedback also means that test results need to be as descriptive and informative as possible so that the MTTR (mean time to resolution) will be as short as possible.

SUMMARY

In this chapter, the key pillars of CT were defined with a drill-down into some recommended practices. Maturing Continuous Testing and keeping it working smoothly depends on the above-mentioned practices, which require collaboration between teams — as well as the understanding that CT can succeed only when People, Process and Technology are matched and fit your business objectives.

CHAPTER TWO

Build the Right Plan for Your Continuous Testing

BY JOE COLANTONIO

JOE COLANTONIO is currently a test automation architect for a large Fortune 100 company. He is also the founder of JoeColantonio.com[1], Test-Talks[2] and Guild Conferences[3] a blog, podcast and online conference platform dedicated to helping people and organizations succeed with creating automation awesomeness.

OVERVIEW

More and more industries and companies are running on software today. Most of the suppliers we subscribe to deliver their goods via online digital products and services. Yes, the saying is true — software is eating the world. So, would it also be accurate to say that testers are *testing* the world?

As an engineer in the trenches, you can see how software is consuming more and more and why our jobs as testers are more important than ever. It's up to us, as testers, to keep pace with the rapid growth. We are the quality champions and leaders of our software.

Will you allow software to become morbidly obese, with useless features or harmful side effects, or will you stand up for your users and help shape

---

1   Joe Colantonio's web site — https://www.joecolantonio.com/

2   Test Talks — https://joecolantonio.com/testtalks/

3   Guild Conferences — https://guildconferences.com/

your code to benefit your customers and society in general?

It seems like pretty heady stuff, but as teams push harder and faster to get features into the hands of customers, we are the last line of defense for educating our teams about the potential unseen consequences of our development decisions.

How do you prepare for this new world of testing?

The digital testing landscape is changing fast and, in this chapter, I will share some thoughts surrounding the new era of Continuous Testing as well as some key pillars to help plan for this transformation — People, Process and Technologies.

WHY ME?

First, why am I writing this chapter?

Because Eran is awesome and he asked me to.

However, the main reason is that I feel I'm in a unique situation that allows me a special insight into the current and future states of the digital testing landscape.

After interviewing over two hundred testing experts on my Test Talks podcast, as well as running multiple online Testing Guild conferences, I'm in constant communication with thought leaders in the space, which helps keep my finger on the pulse of the testing industry. Much of the information I plan to share has been gleaned from those interviews as well as my many years of experience working in automation.

So, where do we begin with Continuous Testing? The best way to know where we are going is to find out where we have been.

WHERE WE ARE NOW – AGILE

Rarely do I speak to a guest on Test Talks that hasn't worked in an Agile environment. Agile has been around for about seventeen years, but it didn't start affecting large companies until approximately six years ago. I think it's safe to say that Agile has now been adopted by the majority of organizations that are creating software. In fact, for some of you who are reading this book, Agile is all you've ever known.

This is clearly demonstrated in Google trends as well.

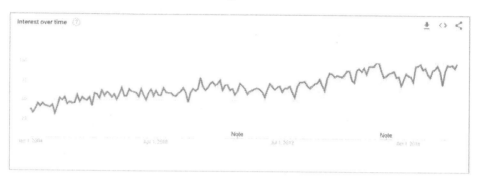

But pre-Agile, I remember working in the classic software development Waterfall model. Within that model, testers only began testing once the software requirements and development were complete, and we, as testers, had limited input and insight into them. It was basically a world full of silos.

Agile broke those silos down and brought everyone together as one team.

That change was a significant one because it meant teams could work for years on a project without speaking or getting any feedback from their users. As you might imagine, resolving issues found in production was almost impossible and fixing deep-seated architectural issues with the software required spending a great deal of time and money.

With customers' attention spans becoming ever shorter, an infinite array of software options, and tolerance for bad software at an all-time low, it's critical to find a way to get our users' input much sooner in the software development life cycle.

Agile was the first wave of modern software development I can remember that addressed the issues presented in the Waterfall development approach.

AGILE AND DEVOPS

Once Agile took root, the second wave — DevOps — began to appear.

Again, it took some time for it to gain acceptance, but it ultimately caught on even faster than Agile.

DevOps gave birth to the collaboration between software development and software operations, creating practices like continuous integration and continuous delivery to provide services and products at high velocity. This approach creates a mechanism that allows us to quickly get our products into the hands of our users, which means quicker feedback in order to determine whether it's delivering the value we've promised.

Like Agile did before it, DevOps broke down even more silos between teams, merging software operations with the rest of the team.

My company didn't start focusing on DevOps until late 2014.

If you look at Google and Indeed trends, you can see how it exploded around 2014. It's been increasing ever since, as seen in Google Trends and in the frequency with which it appears on job search sites like Indeed.com.

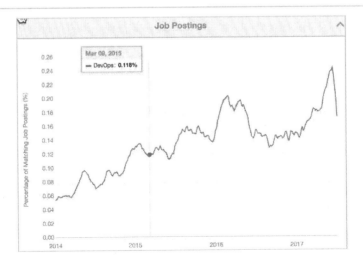

This is the second wave of modern software development.

So, what is the third wave?

I would say it's Continuous Testing.

CURRENT STATE OF TESTING – CONTINUOUS TESTING

Continuous testing is the ability to instantly assess the risk of a new release or change before it impacts customers. You want to identify unexpected behaviors as soon as they are introduced. The sooner you find or prevent bugs, the easier and cheaper they are to fix.

This approach is often accomplished by executing automated tests that probe the quality of the software during each stage of the Software Development Life Cycle (SDLC). The mantra of continuous testing is "test early, test often, and test everywhere in an automated fashion."

Testing begins not after everything is completed but from the start. Each step along the way serves as a quality gate, baking in excellence at each stage of the SDLC pipeline.

A popular term used for testing earlier and earlier in the software development life cycle is called "shift-left". However, I believe that making a shift-right with proactive monitoring and alerting after you release your applications into the wild is just as important. Both shifts and everything in the middle make up a continuous testing feedback loop.

In Episode 68 of Test Talks, Jeff Sussna, author of the *Designing Delivery: Rethinking IT in the Digital Economy* describes that loop thusly:

> "If you're doing continuous delivery, which means that you're delivering code changes on a continuous basis, suddenly it means that your software development life cycle is actually part of operations in a strange way. Then, finally, because you're continually processing feedback everywhere, you're continuously testing. Yes, it all becomes this continuous feedback loop — which is exactly why I started off the book by presenting this basic concept of Cybernetics, because that circularity and steering through feedback

starts to guide everything we do as a business and everything we do as an IT organization."

EVOLUTION OF AUTOMATED TESTING

As software methodologies change, software testing has to change as well. And just like going from Waterfall to Agile to DevOps, our approach to testing has changed along the way. This is critical to understand in order to get at the core of continuous testing.

Back in the 90s, most of my testing activities were manual.

Then, the second evolution of testing occurred with the introduction of test automation tools. The first iteration of testing tools was made available by vendors like Mercury/HP (WinRunner, QuickTest Professional), Seque (Silk Test), and IBM (Rational Robot). They all came out with solutions aimed at taking some of the manual end-to-end regression tests and automating them. The second iteration took place with the introduction of open-source testing tools like Selenium.

Back in the day, using vendor tools that were locked into their own proprietary systems and methodologies helped to feed the silo approach most teams found themselves in. This impeded the whole team contributing to the testing effort.

Not only has open-source technology injected new life into the software development community, it also has forced tool vendors to embrace open-source tools and create integrations with them as well.

This has helped create an environment in which every member of a team, from developers to testers, can use the same tools and technologies. This, in turn, supports more collaboration and better communication in software teams because everyone is now speaking the same language.

This shift has created a new era of continuous testing.

THE BIRTH OF CONTINUOUS TESTING

Now, with continuous testing, we're not only running tests in an automated fashion using the same tools and languages as the developers (and leveraging open-source libraries), but we're doing them continually all the way through into production — beginning with development. We're not waiting until the end like in the old "waterfall" days.

It's important to remember that continuous testing is not just about end-to-end, UI test automation. With the need to quickly release software, we can no longer rely on manual and automated UI testing only.

When we talk about automation in the context of continuous testing, it's the process of automating any manual task that is slowing down the process. It doesn't need to be a "test." For example, before my team could do continuous integration, we needed to have an automated deploy job for our software. Having folks manually install the latest build on the nightly automated test environment was not a scalable solution. These types of tasks are critical and need to be automated.

Continuous testing is not just a "testers" responsibility.

Developers' tools have matured enough that a programmer can get real-time test feedback on the effect of their impending change. Tooling is available that will automatically run their unit tests in the background to give real time info about the health of their code. For example, Kent C. Dodds (TestTalks Ep. 195) mentions he has used a tool called Jest that has:

> "... watch mode, which is like an interactive experience in the terminal. It's a real game changer for testing workflows — especially if you're really into TDD. For example, it's capable of only running the tests that are relevant to the files you've changed since your last Git commit, which is mind-blowing... really awesome if you have hundreds or thousands of tests and in a project that takes a long time to run it'll only run the ones that are relevant to your changes, or you can filter it and run specific tasks... or just run them all."

And although automation testing is a piece of continuous testing, it's not the only piece. It's also about a company having a true culture of quality and testing. Quality cannot be tested into a system. It needs to be added from the beginning. Continuous testing is a way to support this practice.

CHALLENGES OF CONTINUOUS TESTING

As we have seen, the challenge with moving toward approaches like continuous integration is that teams need to understand that the change towards continuous testing is not just about the need to create automated scripts.

Teams also need to fundamentally change the way they do development and testing to accommodate these fast feedback loops. Teams also need to adjust to moving code out into production in small pieces, rapidly.

For instance, many teams have begun breaking down their monolithic applications into smaller pieces using microservices. A microservices approach allows them to have those small, independent services that are independently deployable and independently testable. This architecture also opens up the possibility of moving away from long running, hard-to-maintain, UI-based automation to fast, focused, unit and API-based testing.

In continuous testing, the faster you can give your developer feedback on his or her code change, the better off everyone is.

This requires that most of the tests we create and run are at the smallest level possible to give the quickest feedback possible. I think most folks are familiar with the infamous testing pyramid by now, but at a high level, unit tests should be the majority of tests, followed by integration/API tests, with only a small percentage of your total test suite being UI-based automation.

Getting teams to recognize this testing shift can be a challenge that ultimately holds them back.

So, how do we succeed in the era of continuous testing? There are three main pillars to be aware of as your organization makes the transformation, and they are People, Process and Technology. I will go over these pillars at a high level, but some of the other chapters in this book will take a deeper dive into each area.

PEOPLE

If leadership isn't on board with quality, their teams' continuous testing efforts will fail.

Support for testing not only needs to come from the top down, it also needs to grow from the bottom up, with developers embracing testing and testers embracing development.

As I mentioned earlier, the power of Agile is that it breaks down the walls or silos that most teams used to work in within a waterfall development environment. Removing the separation between testers and developers forces teams to work together in the same sprint, developing and testing, and in the same iteration.

Everyone on the team needs to take responsibility for his or her contributions to the software development process.

This concept of working together, rather than having separate development and QA teams, can cause confusion when a firm begins making the move towards continuous testing. Developers need to be educated that "automation" doesn't just refer to UI tests. They need to be encouraged to embrace test driven development (TDD) approaches to make their code more testable — and testable in an automated fashion.

Testers need to help shepherd their teams along with testing. They should also be technically aware enough to be able to explain to the developers what their expectations are, and to know at what level a test should be done.

The phrase "technically aware" is one I've heard from Lisa and Janet Gregory, co-authors of the books *Agile Testing* and *More Agile Testing*. So, what does being technically aware really mean?

In *More Agile Testing*, Lisa and Janet describe technical awareness as something that covers the ideas of technical skills needed for testing and communicating with other members of a development team.

If your team really understands the whole-team approach of everyone working toward the same goal, then testers and developers can share a task — like the job of coding an automated test, for example. A technically aware tester can also collaborate with the programmer (whose life is programming and who is really good at it), and if your tests are written in the same language your developers use, it will help your testers to collaborate more effectively with your developers.

If testers can't articulate these things, it makes it difficult for them to, say, approach their managers and tell them why something can or cannot be automated — or why an approach the development team is taking is not the best option.

So, the burden for change is not just on the testers and the developer — it goes all the way up to the C-Suite. Quality needs to be embraced by everyone in order to succeed.

However, one major gap I've seen that is a big impediment for teams making this change is lack of proper training.

Companies and consultancies often omit technical coaching, leaving the teams to figure it out. In my experience, this is a bad idea.

Stephen Vance, the author of *Quality Code: Software Testing Principles, Practices, and Patterns* (and a past speaker at Guild Conferences) mentioned in his session that management often expects improvement without providing the support to ensure success. As a result, teams end up compressing their familiar processes, wondering why things aren't improving much. In fact, this need for continuous testing increases some of the traditional tensions between testers and developers.

With DevOps and Agile, we're all trying to create and release quality software quicker and more often, but I think simple things like training are sometimes overlooked. We can become so focused on velocity that we lose sight of things that may slow us down in the short term but, in the long run, will make things better.

Be sure you have a training plan in place for your folks before going "all in" on continuous testing.

Once you have your folks on board and trained, you'll need a process.

PROCESS

A typical continuous testing process consists of seven key elements:

- Develop
- Build
- Test
- Report
- Release
- Monitor
- Repeat

Ultimately, the process starts with testing the quality of a given feature.

Is it really what your customer wants? Has your team cleared up any confusion or misunderstandings before coding even starts?

I recently came across a study in *Crosstalk, the Journal of Defense Software Engineering,* which showed that 64% percent of total defect costs are due to errors in the requirements and design phases of the SDLC.

Getting clear on what it is you are trying to deliver to the customer can find bugs before a line of code is ever written! This is one reason some teams use acceptance criteria practices like Behavior Driven Development to help drive this communication and test the team's assumptions against what their customers really want.

Once the team agrees on what it is they are developing, testing approaches like TDD should drive the process and let you know if your code actually meets your business objectives.

Code that is checked in to your continuous integration process needs to be probed for quality. Automated style checks, security, performance and unit tests, automatic tests on check-in with a required pass/fail ratio needed before promotion to production, etc., will ensure that broken code is not promoted to production.

Once the code is deployed, production is monitored and data is collected to make sure it's actually meeting the customer's expectations. You can also proactively adjust to issues introduced by code changes before they impact your customers. All this feedback is collected and used to feed the process all over again. So, it's an iterative approach, with teams consistently acting and adjusting based on the data they are receiving from the feedback loop.

The goal is to deploy to production many times a day, measure impact, collect data, learn from small experiments that feed even more ideas, and the process starts all over again. This approach is a game changer. It's preferable to waiting months — or even years — to deliver something to your customers only to discover it's not what they really wanted, or that the architecture is completely wrong. You save time and money because you're able to weed out imperfections as soon as they enter production and self-correct based on quick feedback.

Remember, the key to the process is to create quick feedback loops.

If teams are ignoring what a test is telling them, delete it. The objective of continuous testing is not to create tests — it's to get actionable feedback as soon as possible. If a test is not providing that, keeping it around will just slow teams down by adding noise to the loop.

TESTING IN PRODUCTION

Testing in production is important because certain situations only occur in the wild and they are commonly ones that aren't anticipated. The problem with complex systems is that they can't be modeled very well. Even worse is that you can't know in advance how they're going to behave. The systems may be very resilient, but they can also be very sloppy and have a lot of failures that can't be avoided.

Most teams feel that the whole idea behind testing is to avoid failures in production. With such complex systems, you can't think this way. The mindset change you need to embrace is that you have to get comfortable doing some failure discovery in your production environments.

So, having a monitoring and alert system in place to find these unanticipated issues and having that tracing in production is critical.

For example, you want to know immediately if one of your services goes down or becomes unresponsive. By spotting an issue during production with the help of monitoring, you can often automatically roll back to the last-known good version of the service, often before your users even know there's an issue.

METRICS

The main part of the process is teams coming up with the metrics they will use to help measure the quality of their code at every stage of the SDLC and how to react to poor quality.

You need to understand the status, progress and quality level of each change you have in your pipeline. You also need to come up with some key metrics that capture how each of the changes will impact your end user.

Some examples of metrics I've seen teams use are:

- Application performance — you need to make ensure there is high availability of your services and application.
- Measure usage of the newly released or modified feature. Things to use as metrics could be Measure Usage, Request, Impact on Sign-up, Revenue.

For your people to put the continuous testing process in place, they'll need the right technology. With so many releases and changes in the pipeline, what tools and technology can your team leverage to handle the situation?

TOOLS & TECHNOLOGY

Tools need to be lightweight and easy to maintain as well as integrate with existing infrastructure. Once again, deciding what tools to use is a team decision. Some tools fit in better with certain teams. They need to evaluate and determine which one works best for them as a team and fits in with their own unique delivery process.

So, what tools support the continuous testing practice for a fully automated delivery platform? Our software needs to be functional, performant and secure. Tooling is needed to help with all these areas:

- Defining your users' stories
- Implementing your stories
- Creating builds and test runs
- Automation
- Infrastructure
- Production and monitoring

Here are some common testing libraries and tools and where in the Continuous Testing life cycle they would be used. (** This tools list is not complete; it is not an endorsement and is not ranked in any particular order.)

DEVELOPMENT

Developers need tools to assist them as they begin their coding efforts.

As I've mentioned, unit testing is a critical piece of continuous testing. Most development languages have a unit testing framework (or something similar) available. Here are some of the more common ones:

- JUnit
- NUnit
- Jasmine
- MSTest
- Mocha

MOCKING TOOLS

Unit testing is testing the smallest single amount of code or discreet behavior as possible, usually at a method level. A unit test shouldn't have any dependencies on anything external, such as other methods or APIs. The reason for not having dependences on anything else is that if the unit test fails, it's easy to know where it failed. To accomplish this, there are many mocking frameworks to mimic these services in order to allow the unit test to stay self-contained.

- JMockit
- EasyMock
- PowerMock
- Mockito
- Sinon.js
- Mockery

ACCEPTANCE CRITERIA TOOLS

To ensure the correct thing is being developed, here are some acceptance criteria tools:

- Cucumber
- Behave
- JBehave
- SpecFlow
- Fitness
- HipTest

CI SERVERS

Software needs to be in a constant working state and be available to ship to your customers at any time. Using continuous integrating tools, you can prove that your software still works as a whole with every new check in.

- TeamCity
- Bamboo
- Jenkins
- CruiseControl
- CodeShip

API TESTING TOOLS

If a test cannot be covered at the unit level, the next level to focus on would be the API layer. Luckily there are a bunch of tools, both paid and free, available for testing APIs:

- Karate-DSL
- Rest-Assured
- Postman
- Blazemeter API Functional Testing
- API Fortress
- RestSharp
- Citrus Framework

TEST DATA MANAGEMENT

One common automation pitfall some teams fall into when moving towards automation is not having a test data strategy in place. If you're a test automation engineer, you've probably faced test data dependency issues in your test automation suites that have caused all kinds of flaky test behavior. Not only can this be frustrating, it can also make your tests highly unreliable, which in turn can make your team lose confidence in your test suites. There are approaches you can use to help, but also there are some tools out there designed to tackle this tricky problem:

- Delphix
- Informatica
- CA Test Data Manager

FUNCTIONAL AUTOMATION TOOLS

There is a plethora of functional test automation tools available for your teams to choose from. Tools should be selected based on a team's needs, not what is the most popular one. Here's a quick sampling:

- Selenium

- Cypress.io
- QuickTest Professional
- Automation Anywhere
- Test Architect
- Test Complete
- mabl
- Watir
- Testim
- Protractor
- Test.ai
- Appium
- Applitools
- Eggplant

FEATURE FLAG SOFTWARE

Releasing a new feature can sometimes be scary, especially if you're not 100% sure how it will react in production. Using a feature flag lets you easily turn on and off certain features for a percentage of users. This allows you to experiment with new features and control how soon you roll out those features to all your users in production.

- LaunchDarkly
- Rollout.io
- Featureflag.tech

PERFORMANCE TEST TOOLS AND MONITORING

Performance testing, just like functional testing, needs to shift-left and shift-right. One exciting thing about having a full SDLC feedback loop is that when you understand your software's performance profile in production, you can then take that data back to your teams to make sure they're testing the right things in development.

- Neotys
- JMeter
- Gatling
- DynaTrace
- Flood.io
- Tarus
- Grinder
- New Relic
- App Dynamic
- DynaTrace

INFRASTRUCTURE AUTOMATION AND SYSTEM PROVISIONING

Another important piece of the testing transformation is to start treating your infrastructure like code. Provisioning environments in an automated fashion is also crucial to be able to quickly scale up test and environments. Here are some tools to help:

- Vagrant
- Docker
- Kubernetes
- SkyTap

DEVICE BROWER & OS COVERAGE

If you're developing a web or mobile app, you're going to need to test it against a variety of operating systems and browser combinations. Creating an in-house lab to handle all the devices and combination permutations that you need to test against can be expensive and time-consuming to set up — especially if you plan to share those devices across different team members. Cloud service providers get rid of all that complexity and cost by putting it in the Cloud.

- Perfecto
- Sauce Labs
- BrowserStack

TEST CASE MANAGEMENT

A Test Case Management Tool helps keep teams on track with how testing needs to be done. It allows teams to plan activities and report on the status of those activities to your management. Different tools have different approaches to testing and thus have different sets of features. You need a good system that will allow you to create a test plan and set yourself up in a way that you can be successful.

- TestRail
- QAComplete (Part of Tricentis)
- Zephyr
- PractiTest
- Jira

Once you have the tools in place to support the continuous testing practice, the next step is to optimize and make it better with each iteration.

What about the next wave?

THE IMMEDIATE FUTURE OF TESTING IS PREDICTIVE

As we strive to improve our process and gather and act on actionable metrics for improvement, I see AI/machine learning playing a larger role in the near future. It will enable us to continue moving towards a predictive model of each test cycle and release to identify risk even faster and earlier than we currently can.

If you're doing continuous integration and testing, you're probably already generating a wealth of data from your test runs. But who has the time to go through it all to search for common patterns over time? Wouldn't it be great if you could answer the classic testing question, "if I've made a change to this piece of code, what's the minimal number of tests I should be able to run in order to figure out whether this change is good or bad?"

Lots of companies are leveraging existing AI tools that do just that.

AI is a real thing and should not be dismissed by testers as another buzzword in the industry. I find it hard to doubt or bet against companies like Google who are heavily investing in this technology. For example, at a recent Google conference, CEO Sundar Pichai opened the event by stating that, "We're moving from a mobile-first to an AI-first world."

SOME KEY TAKEAWAYS (WHAT I LIKE TO CALL "AUTOMATION AWESOMENESS")

1. WHOLE-TEAM APPROACH

You want to improve the communication with your testers and developers and create a whole-team approach. In my experience, not having the right quality culture will ruin any continuous testing efforts you try to implement.

2. SMALLER IS BETTER

With continuous integration, your developers need to make their code testable. If you want to write test automation for your code, you need to be able to separate it into individual pieces.

The secret is to build small things that can be combined into larger things. The best way to build small things is to have a good test suite around the small things so that, first off, when you combine them into the bigger things, you have to write less tests on the bigger thing; second, it's also easier to test the bigger things because you already have guarantees about how the smaller things work.

You don't want to write code just for testing. You want to write code that is testable but doesn't do any more than is needed. What it often comes down to is breaking these things down into smaller pieces and testing the individual pieces.

3. AUTOMATION IS A MUST

You can't succeed in the world of Agile/DevOps without automation. Period.

4. PICK THE RIGHT TOOLS

There are a bunch of tools out there. Each team is unique and there is no one tool that everyone should use. Regardless of which automation testing tools are selected, I always recommend doing a two-week proof of concept (POC) to ensure the solution actually fits in with your team's development workflow.

5. LISTEN TO WHAT YOUR TESTS ARE TELLING YOU

Listen to what your continuous testing feedback loops are telling you. This is sometimes called "code smells." Code smells are indicators that something in your code or process isn't right. Being aware of indicators like these is the first step to improving your continuous testing process.

The whole point of performing tests is to get a clearer picture of where you stand in terms of being ready to release software. If your teams start ignoring and devaluing tests, it will be difficult for you to move forward to continuous testing.

TESTING STATE

So, that's my whirlwind tour of the way I see the emergence and future of continuous testing.

It's a great time to be a tester! Focus on your People, Process and Technology and constantly be adjusting how you develop based on your Continuous Testing feedback loop.

Keep in mind, however, that this won't happen overnight. It takes time for teams to get it right.

No worries. Start planning now.

Start small.

Create a small feature, run it through the process, and continually strive to make the process better. Listen to the feedback from your customers and teams; use it to help you build the perfect plan for your continuous testing process.

CHAPTER THREE

Continuous Testing: Charting Your Path and Tracking You Progress

BY WOLFGANG PLATZ

WOLFGANG PLATZ brings over 20 years of technology experience to Tricentis, http://tricentis.com. Wolfgang founded Tricentis in 2007 as a testing consultancy and laid the cornerstone for the development of our enterprise software testing product, Tricentis Tosca. Today, he is responsible for driving Tricentis' vision for making Continuous Testing a reality for enterprise DevOps. Platz also oversees the delivery of product-related support and services to our customers.

Prior to Tricentis, Wolfgang was at Capgemini as a group head of IT development for one of the world's largest IT insurance-development projects. There, he was responsible for architecture and implementation of life insurance policies and project management for several projects in banks.

Wolfgang holds a Master's degree in Technical Physics as well as a Master's degree in Business Administration from the Vienna University of Technology.

Let's face it. Businesses don't want — or need — perfect software. They want to deliver new, business-differentiating software as soon as possible. To enable this, we (development and testing teams) need fast feedback on whether the latest innovations will work as expected or crash and burn in production. We also need to know if these changes somehow broke the core functionality that the customer base — and thus the business — depends upon.

This is where Continuous Testing comes in.

Continuous Testing is the process of executing automated tests as part of the software delivery pipeline in order to obtain feedback on the business risks associated with a software release candidate as rapidly as possible.

Test automation is essential for Continuous Testing, but it's not sufficient. Test automation is designed to produce a set of pass/fail data points correlated to user stories or application requirements. Continuous Testing, on the other hand, focuses on business risk and providing insight on whether the software can be released. Beyond test automation, Continuous Testing also involves practices such as aligning testing with your business risk, applying service virtualization and stateful test data management to stabilize testing for Continuous Integration, and performing exploratory testing to expose "big block" issues early in each iteration. It's not simply a matter of more tools or different tools. It requires a deeper transformation across people and processes as well as technologies.

Continuous Testing has undeniably become imperative — especially now that 97% of organizations have adopted Agile and 71% are practicing or adopting DevOps (Sauce Labs). New Forrester research confirms that Continuous Testing is one of the key factors separating Agile/DevOps leaders from Agile/DevOps laggards. Nevertheless, most enterprises still don't have a mature, sustainable Continuous Testing process in place. Forrester found that even the organizations actively practicing Agile and DevOps have a relatively low Continuous Testing adoption rate: 26% (Forrester).

We know that we *should* be doing it...but the devil's in the details. How does your organization get there? Few companies have the luxury of building a new quality process from the ground up. And many need to address extremely complex systems and regulatory requirements — as well as avoid disruption to business-critical operations. So, how do you realign your well-established quality process with the unrelenting drive towards "Continuous Everything?"

This chapter will help you chart the most effective path to an optimized

Continuous Testing process as well as measure your progress in terms that the business cares about. It covers:

- The top 3 roadblocks to long-term Continuous Testing adoption in enterprise testing environments
- A phased strategy for building a sustainable Continuous Testing process that overcomes these roadblocks
- KPIs you can use to assess the progress made at each step of the Continuous Testing journey

The ultimate goal is to help you understand what specific steps are required to advance your organization's Continuous Testing initiatives and how to quantify progress in terms of speed, quality, and cost benefits.

Developer-level Continuous Testing (featuring unit testing, the foundation of the famous inverted test pyramid, as well as practices such as static analysis and peer code review) is certainly important. However, these "Development Testing" best practices are already reasonably well-documented and understood. The place where organizations inevitably get stuck is end-to-end functional testing.

THE TOP ROADBLOCKS TO SUSTAINABLE CONTINUOUS TESTING

Many organizations have experimented with test automation: typically, automating some UI tests and integrating their execution into the Continuous Integration process. They achieve and celebrate small victories, but the process doesn't expand. In fact, it decays. Why? Typically, it boils down to roadblocks that fall into the following 3 categories:

- Time and resources
- Complexity
- Results

Time and Resources

Teams severely underestimate the time and resources required for sustainable test automation. Yes, getting some basic UI tests to run automatically is a great start. However, you also need to plan for the time and resources required to:

- Keep notoriously brittle tests scripts from overwhelming the team with false positives

- Create tests for every new/modified requirement (or determine where to focus your efforts and what you can skip)

- Establish a test framework that supports reuse and data-driven testing — both of which are essential for making automation sustainable over the long term

- Keep individual tests and the broader test framework in sync with the constantly-evolving application

- Execute the test suite — especially if you're trying to frequently run a large, UI-heavy test suite

- Determine how to automate more advanced use cases and keep them running consistently in a Continuous Testing environment (see the next section for more on this)

- Review and interpret test the mounting volume of test results (more on this later too)

With Agile and DevOps, time for test creation, maintenance, execution, and analysis is extremely limited — but fast feedback is essential. How can you ensure that the most important things are sufficiently tested without delaying time to market?

Complexity

It's one thing to automate a test for a simple "create" action in a web application (e.g., create a new account and complete a simple transaction from scratch). It's another to automate the most business-critical transactions, which typically pass through multiple technologies (SAP, APIs, mobile interfaces, and even mainframes) and require sophisticated setup and orchestration. You need to ensure that:

- Your testing resources understand how to automate tests across all the different technologies and connect data and results from one technology to another.

- You have the stateful, secure, and compliant test data required to set up a realistic test as well as drive the test through a complex series of steps — each and every time the test is executed.

- You have reliable, continuous, and cost-effective access to all the dependent systems that are required for your tests — including APIs, 3rd party applications, etc., that may be unstable, evolving, or accessible only at limited times.

Moreover, you also need a systematic way to flush out the critical defects that can only be found with a human evaluating the application from an end-user perspective. Automation is great at rapidly and repeatedly checking whether certain actions continue to produce the expected results but it can't uncover the complex usability issues that significantly impact the end user experience.

Without fast, reliable feedback on how application changes impact the core end user experience, how do you know if a release will help the business or harm it?

Results

The most commonly cited complaint with test results is the overwhelming number of false positives that need to be reviewed and addressed. When you're just starting off with test automation, it might be feasible to handle the false positives. However, as your test suite grows and your test frequency increases, addressing false positives quickly becomes an insurmountable task. Ultimately, many teams either start ignoring the false positives (which erodes trust in the test results and Continuous Testing initiative) or giving up on test automation altogether.

When DevOps and Continuous Delivery initiatives come into play, another critical issue with results emerges: they don't provide the risk-based insight needed to make a fast go/go-no decision. If you've ever looked at test results, you've probably seen something like this:

What does this really tell you? You can see that ...

- There's a total of 53,274 tests cases
- Almost 80% of those tests (42,278) passed
- Over 19% of them failed
- About 1% did not execute

But... would you be willing to make a release decision based on these results? Maybe the test failures are related to some trivial functionality. Maybe they are the most critical functionality: the "engine" of your system. Or, maybe your most critical functionality was not even thoroughly tested. Trying to track down this information would require tons of manual investigative work that yields delayed, often-inaccurate answers.

In the era of Agile and DevOps, release decisions need to be made rapidly — even automatically and instantaneously. Test results that focus on the number of test cases leave you with a huge blind spot that becomes absolutely critical — and incredibly dangerous — when you're moving at the speed of Agile and DevOps.

If your results don't indicate how much of your business-critical functionality is tested and working, you can't rely on them to drive automated release gates. Manual review and assessment will be required... and that's inevitably going to delay each and every delivery.

THE PATH TO OPTIMIZED CONTINUOUS TESTING

Based on our experience guiding enterprise testing teams to steer clear of these common Continuous Testing roadblocks, Tricentis has developed a Continuous Testing Maturity Model. We've found that this is the most efficient path to rolling out Continuous Testing in a way that's sustainable for the team — and valuable to IT leaders aiming to accelerate delivery without incurring unacceptable business risk.

You can use this model to assess where you stand today and understand what's needed to progress from one level to the next.

Level 1: The Typical Starting Point

At this initial level, the key metric is the number of test cases. All test cases are designed based on tester intuition. Testing is performed manually or partially automated with a script-based approach (which results in a high rate of false positives that require constant maintenance). Testers must manually ensure test data suitability (e.g., by localizing and refining test data) and wait for dependencies to be provisioned in test environments. Any API testing is the domain of developers.

Anticipated efficiency gain: 1.3X

Level 2: Aligned

A risk assessment has been completed and Risk Coverage is now the key metric of test case definition and execution. Test automation still focuses on the UI, but now uses Model-Based Test Automation (MBTA), which significantly reduces false positive rates and maintenance efforts. Since there is still no comprehensive test data management in place, automation primarily focuses on new data object creation rather than complex administrative use cases.

Anticipated efficiency gain: 3X

Level 3: Managed

Session-based Exploratory Testing is introduced to expose risks that specification-based testing cannot find (e.g., in functionality implemented beyond the boundaries of the specification). Additional test cases are defined via combinatorial Test Case Design methodologies such as linear expansion. If functionality is exposed via APIs, API Testing is introduced at the tester level. MBTA-driven UI testing is extended in areas where API testing is not applicable or effective. Test automation is introduced into Continuous Integration through initial integrations with build and deployment tools.

Anticipated efficiency gain: 6X

Level 4: Mature

Test Data Management now provides the test data needed to enable continuous, consistent test automation. Service Virtualization ensures that testing can proceed even if dependent components are unstable or unavailable. The introduction of both TDM and service virtualization enables more sophisticated API testing, end-to-end testing, and continuous test execution. Tests can now be executed continuously as part of the software delivery pipeline, providing instant feedback on the business risk associated with the software release candidate.

Anticipated efficiency gain: >10X

Level 5: Optimized

Comprehensive test automation has been established and is supported by sophisticated, stateful service virtualization and test data generation/ provisioning. Metrics are in place to monitor and continuously improve the effectiveness of the software testing process. Continuous Testing is fully integrated into Continuous Integration and the Continuous Delivery pipeline. The transformation into "DevTestOps" via Process, People and Product is achieved.

Anticipated efficiency gain: >20X

KPIS FOR MEASURING YOUR PROGRESS

The best way to expand an initiative is to demonstrate the quantifiable gains achieved at each step and set realistic targets for the next milestone. Leveraging KPIs from leading company and industry best practices, you can quantify and demonstrate your progress in terms of accelerated innovation, reduced business risks, and improved cost efficiency.

	Accelerate Innovation (Speed)	Reduce Business Risk	Improve Cost Efficiency (Cost)
Why it matters	Digital transformation requires organizations to rapidly and consistently deliver innovative software. Legacy testing approaches are the primary bottleneck for delivering innovative software. No digital transformation initiative will succeed without transforming software testing.	Organizations cannot make informed release decisions without understanding business risk. Most organizations today lack visibility into the risks associated with a release candidate. With constant insight into business risk, teams can rapidly deliver software without compromising the end user experience	The prevailing method of validating software is outsourced, manual testing. This has proven to be time-consuming and costly—contradictory to Agile and DevOps approaches. Continuous testing not only reduces the overhead associated with traditional software testing but also minimizes production outages.

	Accelerate Innovation (Speed)	Reduce Business Risk	Improve Cost Efficiency (Cost)
Measure this to improve	• Release/delivery delays • Avoidable rework resulting from delayed feedback	• Unacceptable number of production defects • Unsound release decisions	• High cost of testing • Manual labor • Testing tool TCO • Test labs/environments
Measure this to assess...	• Time to market impacts • Quality process efficiency	• Business risk coverage • Test suite effectiveness	• Cost reduction • Budget freed for innovation

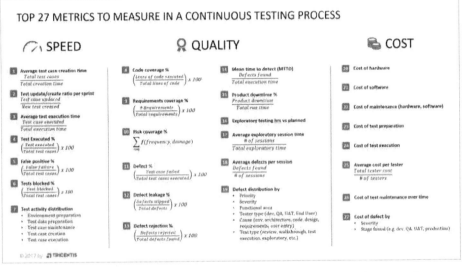

TOP 27 METRICS TO MEASURE IN A CONTINUOUS TESTING PROCESS

For an extended discussion of Continuous Testing and DevOps quality metrics, go to http://innovate.tricentis.com/forrester-devops.

YOUR JOURNEY TO OPTIMIZED CONTINUOUS TESTING

For a detailed assessment of where your testing process stands today and a map of your recommended path to Optimized Continuous Testing, sign up at http://innovate.tricentis.com/ctmm. The Tricentis Customer Success team will meet with you to review your existing practices, processes, technologies, test artifacts, and configurations. Based on those findings, they will help you understand your current maturity level, what you can gain by advancing, and exactly what steps are involved in attaining your goals.

CHAPTER FOUR

Orchestrating Quality Across DevOps Pipelines

BY BRAD JOHNSON, CLOUDBEES

BRAD JOHNSON has spearheaded product go-to-market as well as driven technical and channel alliances for market-leading enterprise software firms and cloud-pioneering startups in Silicon Valley for over 18 years.

He speaks and writes on executive level technical topics that span software development, testing, application performance management, and now DevOps. He is currently driving High Performance IT transformations as head of product marketing at CloudBees, the leader in Continuous Delivery.

Is test orchestration different? The answer is yes and no.

No, because the concept of orchestration in the agile software delivery process refers to the set of gates and controls that manage and optimize the flow of "stuff" through the entire process. From the ideas that are captured, to the user stories that are created, to the software code that gets written, to the non-code artifacts like logs and test scripts that are created, to automation that gets created, to the process models that are built to the execution rules...all the way to deployment and operations. Testing is just part of this.

Yes, because testing produces a subset of unique processes, artifacts and process flows that exist within the overall orchestration but are unique to testing. "Testing things" that fall into this subset include manual and automated test plans, test cases of all types, automation scripts, test environments and their definitions, test data, test results, execution logs and reporting output. The role of automation is critical in testing, and to manage and orchestrate the what, when, and why of the end-to-end test process is critical.

When considering the big picture of test orchestration, it is important to acknowledge both the similarities and uniqueness of test-related activities.

TOP CHALLENGES TO INTEGRATING TESTING WITH DEVOPS

Methodological

Agile methodologies frequently include testers on the team and even endorse Test Driven Development (TDD)[1], that is, starting with a failing unit test, then writing code to make it pass. But beyond unit tests, how and what kind of additional testing is done varies from organization to organization, team to team. To include appropriate levels of testing into efficient delivery pipelines requires the entire team agree to what tests are possible and necessary.

MAKING FUNCTIONAL TESTS A CORE PIPELINE FUNCTION

If you want to make testers laugh and developers cringe, suggest that all projects should have 100% code coverage with unit tests. Regardless of your thoughts on level of coverage, unit testing is universally recognized as necessary and effective in helping to assure the functional validity of software and, when run in an automated fashion, as used in Continuous Integration, is critical and effective.

Developers cringe about unit testing for several reasons:

1. They take time and mental effort to create, seemingly taking away from "real coding"

2. To run them, if not automated, takes time and effort

3. They may fail anywhere down the pipeline, which means possible rework

---

1   TDD definition — https://www.agilealliance.org/glossary/tdd/

The Jenkins Project[2] was created years ago by Kohsuke Kawaguchi[3] specifically with #2 in mind. He passionately believes that developers should never have to manually or repeatedly run tests when automation could do it for them. At its core, Jenkins has always been a flexible and extensible automation engine for eliminating unnecessary manual tasks.

However, many organizations stop at unit test automation and leave other non-functional testing to other teams or perform them out-of-band from the automated pipeline.

Integration Testing

While this is the "I" of Continuous Integration, many teams don't do it well.

This critical testing assures components and services work together and don't raise conflicts or regressions with one another.

System Testing

Typically a "black box" test of the complete end-to-end application or system, this non-functional testing can be done well with automation. It is time-consuming and often difficult, requiring different environments. As part of an orchestrated, automated flow, and in a "hands-off" manner, System testing can be executed as frequently as needed by automating the tests, as well as implementing and tearing down of integration environments. This can be done extremely well by utilizing cloud environments, containers, and configuration as code.

User Acceptance Testing

Long known as a time-consuming but necessary bottleneck, real users running manual tests to verify human perceived issues is a critical and important "gate" to production success! "Automation" seems impossible here — but it's not! For instance, notification, dispatch of test plans to users, automation and relaying of results are all parts of the manual process that can be managed within an automated pipeline. And, what's more, if the System Tests pass, UAT can be performed in the same ephemeral environments!

---

2   The Jenkins Project — https://jenkins.io/

3   Kohsuke Kawaguchi, Creator of Jenkins — https://www.cloudbees.com/team/kohsuke-kawaguchi

NON-FUNCTIONAL TESTING IS NON-NEGOTIABLE

Non-functional testing is the biggest challenge for truly Continuous Delivery. Of all testing, some of the quickest and most impactful wins can be made here.

Load Testing

Most developers don't think about what will happen when their code gets used by hundreds or thousands of users. For projects that may see high levels of usage, the fact that load testing is rarely executed at the unit level, and repeatedly thereafter, is surprising. There are so many good solutions, from free to commercial, to help. A team implementing automation with Jenkins and a cloud computing account can have a job create a test environment, execute "load" by simultaneously running unit tests, report results back and tear down the environment almost as easily as executing a single unit test.

Performance Testing

By adding some more measurement and monitors, as load tests progress, and particularly as part of integration testing, performance testing can be implemented earlier and less disruptively. Rather than requiring siloed performance teams late in the delivery cycle, their expertise can be dispatched in "upstream" iterations, so that the largest and most complicated tests that take place in staging or production have a higher success rate.

Security Testing

Forms of security testing range from scans for risky open source code to vulnerability tests. Strangely, security testing is still largely deployed manually and is rarely launched as part of the automated pipeline. Nothing about security testing requires it be left out, except perhaps the fact that there are dedicated teams. Another quick win for test orchestration is to have security team members added to agile teams and beginning to plug in security tests as pipeline components.

Technical

While many aspects of agile approaches disconnect technology from methodology, it is technology that has improved year after year and is now making automation, orchestration, deployment, scaling, and management much better. Applying technology to help with streamlining testing across multiple complex pipelines is a requirement to optimization.

Test automation is mature

There is no excuse for teams that skimp on building great automated functional tests to plug into their CI/CD. From great open source options like the time-tested Selenium to cross-browser and cross-device testing that lets dozens of tests execute in parallel in a fraction of the time, it's feasible and beneficial to add automation.

Orchestration is critical

Jenkins is running more than 19 million automated jobs[4] right now, many of which are automated tests. While this is a lot, Forrester reported in 2017 that only 23% of companies it surveyed had started with CI. With many great options ranging from free tools to CI/CD as a Service to end-to-end, governed CD systems, automation for the orchestration of all testing aspects of your pipeline is a requirement of companies moving beyond agile to DevOps today.

Deployment options are a revolution

Containerization is likely the largest boost to testing since web recording made creating automated functional tests as easy as clicking a mouse. The issue with many tests is the "not on my computer" syndrome. Containers, led by Docker, allow teams to create exactly the correct environment to test, save the configurations, and then re-deploy and tear the test system down as often or as rarely as needed. By doing this early and often throughout the delivery pipeline, by the time applications are promoted to production, they've been completely functionally and non-functionally validated, tested for load, performance and security, all within development and test environments that match product nearly exactly!

Organizational

"Change your thoughts and you change the world."

—Norman Vincent Peale

---

4   Jenkins Usage Statistics — http://stats.jenkins.io/jenkins-stats/svg/svgs.html

Driving change in thoughts and approaches to testing can be difficult among organizations with a history of siloed QA teams as well as engineering-centric groups who don't value the holistic and comprehensive range of testing available beyond the basics of unit and integration tests. The best way to face these challenges is with education; share experiences and schedule time in brown bag sessions, web meetings, or town hall gatherings on interesting "test" topics that tie to the goal of Continuous Delivery and DevOps.

IDEAS TO SPARK ACTION

Kubernetes for Quality

Learn the basics of Kubernetes and play with setting up a dev and test environment. All the major cloud providers have new services — Amazon EKS[5], Azure AKS[6], Google GKE[7]. When you're comfortable, share with your extended teams and get them excited to try standing up test environments.

Mobile Testing

Nearly every organization has a mobile app — and testing is usually an afterthought. Try out test services that enable you to replay tests on devices, learn how to automate the runs, and create a quick promo video to share with the team and garner enthusiasm. This may incite a new mobile quality initiative you can champion!

Create a testing pipeline and introduce Continuous Delivery!

Choose a CI/CD as a Service or download Jenkins to learn how to build your own automated pipelines. Many definitions of CD start after the development tests end. So, if CI/CD is new to your organization, be the catalyst and start with CD! It is relatively simple. If you have a suite of functional automation tests or performance test scripts, either attach to the repository where your test builds reside or move one to a new repository. Connect your tests, set up the CD system and RUN! Every product and service has documentation and video to help, so you will not be on your own.

Be the change! Let testing be the lead for CD transformation on your team.

---

5   Amazon EKS — https://aws.amazon.com/blogs/aws/amazon-eks-now-generally-available/

6   Azure EKS — https://docs.microsoft.com/en-us/azure/aks/

7   Google GKE — https://cloud.google.com/kubernetes-engine/

Scaling across diverse teams and projects

One of the challenges that teams face when transforming testing with DevOps approaches is how many models oversimplify the effort and time required. For new projects and small teams, of course, you can begin with a pure agile approach, utilize the best new tools, and glory in the lack of technical and process debt. However, most tech professionals work inside of large, established, diverse organizations. In this "real world", we need to pick battles, work within compliance guidelines, and interact across organizations, geographies and time zones.

Here are a few tips to consider while introducing the change of test orchestration to organizations of this sort.

Create a pipeline blueprint

A big mistake many people make is thinking they are not ready to start. They let "if only's" hold up progress.

"If only" our Jira system was more widely adopted.

"If only" the Dev team would run Jenkins.

"If only" my testing service provider would get trained on the latest UI test tool.

"If only"...

As with most big things, a good start is to choose what you have control over and start planning. A key concept of DevOps is instantiating a Deployment Pipeline[8].

"Pipelines", in short, are the fundamental pathway that delivery orchestration follows. They consist of all the tasks and deliverables that software delivery teams execute on the way to bringing ideas into production via software. The "continuous" aspect of DevOps pipelines considers the iterative and repeatable nature of software delivery. One methodology, SAFe, considers cyclical segments often owned by different teams interacting constantly along a pipeline (Figure 1.)

---

8   Deployment Pipeline defined — https://martinfowler.com/bliki/DeploymentPipeline.html

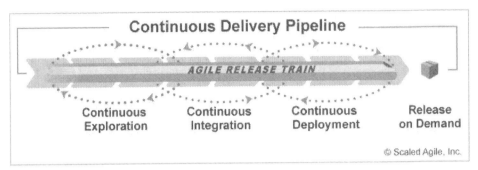

Figure 1.

Other pipeline views break out major stages of software delivery and emphasize technologies like source control and orchestration automation (such as Jenkins) as the engine that drives the pipeline. (Figure 2.)

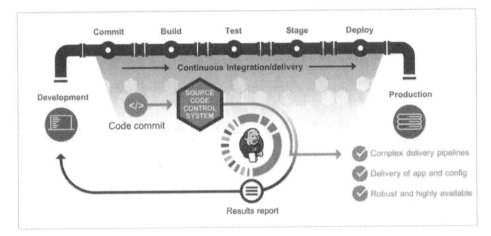

Figure 2.

Regardless of your choice of visualization or implementation, a critical first step is to identify and document your pipeline.

If you are delivering software, then you have a pipeline! It may be partially or poorly automated. It may be broken by organizational delays. It may be blocked completely for months at a time...perhaps by testing itself! However, it is still a basic pipeline and a good way to begin is to map it out.

Start with any flowcharting technique and lay out the steps of a basic flow that you either already do, or you see could be a beneficial set of steps to implement and automate. Figure 3 is a fast and simple example of a functional test stage that most companies do today. This simple model is a quick exercise any team can do. What this diagram indicates connected to steps are bubbles of "wasted time" to drive discussion. By identifying where you know time can be cut or improvements can be made, you can plan out how to build a CD pipeline segment by segment.

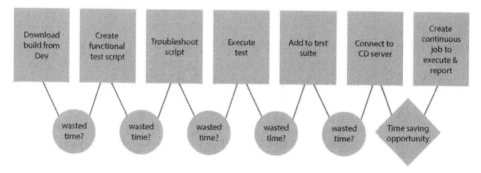

Figure 3.

Once you have even a small set of these pipeline blueprints vetted, with the areas of most time savings identified, it's time to begin pulling in automation and other techniques to drive your test orchestration pipeline, piece by piece.

Leverage cloud and proven automation approaches

Much can be — and has been — said about how cloud computing, with instant and disposable availability of compute resources, should be the first choice of development and test teams. With a track record of more than a decade now, teams who are not leveraging cloud are not only behind, they are at a disadvantage! Likewise, test automation, build automation, and automated orchestration and deployment have more than enough maturity to make the most skeptical testers confident.

SOME BASIC TESTING USE CASES FOR CLOUD:

Compatibility testing

Quickly spin up multiple operating system type or versions, simultaneously, with a command. Containers make this even easier as you can deploy to different clouds. Functional tests, for instance, could be run against many OSes. Similarly, you can perform multiple simultaneous browser tests, database types, etc.

Load testing

Using load generators to drive simulated traffic from multiple regions and up to large scale was one of the first use cases for cloud computing. Load tests can be triggered by a build job and results can be passed in an automated fashion as part of a performance regression suite.

User Acceptance Testing

AUT environments can be spun up as part of an automated process. Real users in any location and environments close to users (or far away) can be utilized to test the network impact of systems close to or far away from users.

Embrace Automation

A never-ending saga in the testing industry revolves around test automation. It doesn't matter how you feel about what is possible to automate, when you should start, how to manage test fragility, or who should create or execute tests; what does matter it that you plan to utilize test automation with your CI/CD orchestration.

If you aren't automating regression tests, you are wasting time.

Functional test automation has always been a great place to start with automation. For web, recording technology is mature and stable, so even junior level test engineers can reliably capture basic tests to replay. Once sets of automated functional tests are proven, repeatable, and combined into regression suites, it is a simple matter of ensuring the test environment is available — perhaps in a cloud instance — and running the suites as part of the build process.

Add mobile testing

Nearly every application has a mobile component and nearly every company has a mobile app. The need to test on many different devices and the pace of change of those devices is daunting. However, mobile testing has matured and recording or scripting tests to run on emulators or real devices can be highly automated. In turn, this automation can be triggered as a CI/CD orchestration job, to be run "hands free".

Load test, continuously.

Finally, load testing need not be the job of specialized teams. Using cloud or traditional servers, once load tests are created — at a single component test or even end-to-end — the CI/CD pipeline should include fully automated load test runs at various stages. The earlier teams start testing for scale and performance, the fewer problems they will encounter at the "Ops" end of the DevOps cycle.

SUMMARY: 3 KEYS TO TEST ORCHESTRATION SUCCESS

Starting strategically

Being successful in test orchestration is all about building a winning test strategy based on test automation that works. Test automation that works translates into a continuous CI jobs that are always green unless there is a real software defect. Where is the strategy, then?

If the entire DevOps plan bakes test automation that works into the entire pipeline from start to finish and treats the test code (functional, non-functional) as production code, that is a perfect strategic step toward success. When the overall test orchestration runs at scale, upon each code commit, the developers have much more time to focus on new features and to maintain high code quality that, overall, leads to faster release cycles. DevOps leadership ought to enforce test orchestration processes as a standard working flow and enable their direct reports to be successful in test automation authoring, execution, maintenance, and scale as needed.

Starting small

As in every complex challenge — and we agreed already in this book that continuous testing is a challenge — "start small and grow" is a great and proven practice. The key to continuous testing success in a DevOps workflow lies in building trust between the Dev and Test practitioners. To build trust, there needs to be a small and proven smoke or sanity test suite that runs automatically within CI (Jenkins) upon each code commit. Once trust is built for a small test suite, the next step is to scale the number of platforms that undergo these tests to "certify" these tests and make them an integral part of the DevOps pipeline.

Following this small proven and trustable suite will then be scaling the test suite to cover more essential test scenarios, as well as platforms. The important thing in scaling up a "trustable" running suite within CI is to continuously maintain the coding practices and test certification processes to maintain trust between the team members.

Starting now

The entire industry is implementing Agile development practices and aiming to scale DevOps and shift to CI/CD. Continuous testing is, to date, the biggest bottleneck from maturing DevOps due to trust, test flakiness, lack of best practices, and unstable orchestration methodologies.

Within this chapter, and the entire book, DevOps teams will find the necessary advice from industry leaders on how to shift toward continuous testing, scale such testing, and make it a reality as soon as possible. There is no other way to shift an organization to DevOps without assuring high quality iteration releases. If releasing a new piece of code takes too long, and at the end it's not covering sufficient platform and code, the entire pipeline is stuck, and that is not really DevOps.

CHAPTER FIVE

Testing Everything Every Day as Part of Continuous Testing

BY YORAM MIZRACHI

YORAM MIZRACHI is the Chief Technology Officer and founder of Perfecto — brings to the company a wealth of experience in networking, security, and mobile telecommunications. Yoram founded Perfecto Mobile after serving as the CTO of Comverse Mobile Data Division. In this capacity, he handled a variety of technological aspects in mobile applications, WAP, and location-based services. In 1999 Yoram was the CTO (and founder) of Exalink, which was later acquired by Comverse for $550 million.

Prior to founding Exalink, Yoram held several technology-related positions in the fields of communication and cryptography.

INTRODUCTION

The most recent World Quality Report by Sogeti[1] demonstrates both the depth of the pain of organizations trying to mature their test automation coverage and the great value this objective adds to their business. This value is easy to see, from early detection of defects prior to them escaping to production, to reduction of test cycle times and increased overall release velocity.

---

1   https://www.sogeti.com/explore/reports/world-quality-report-2017-2018/#tab4

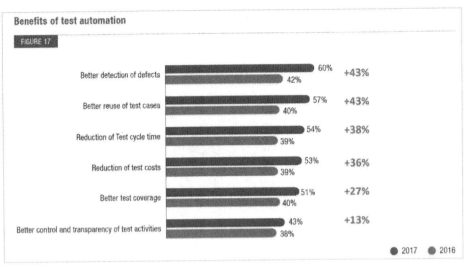

Fig. 1: World Quality Report insights on the benefits of test automation

In addition to the need for automation and the added value of automation, as organizations are maturing their DevOps processes and shifting towards agile testing methods, automating as many tests as possible — and as early in the build cycle as possible — is a key enabler for their DevOps activities.

Additional market research shows that while is it a part of DevOps and the shift-left testing trend that is growing across industries, QA currently oversees most of the testing.[2]

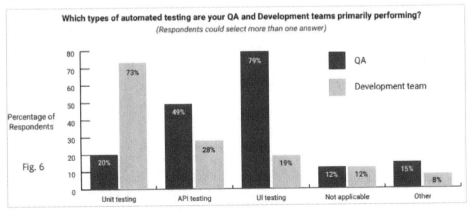

Fig. 2: Testing types by owner (QASymphony research)

---

2   QA Symphony research — evolution of test automation — https://www.qasymphony.com/land-ing-pages/report-the-evolution-of-test-automation/

From these figures, we can see that it is important that the testing structure in the organization is mature enough, has the proper lab and testing frameworks, and good insight into test data so it can provide the right level of on-demand feedback to executives as well as developers.

TESTING EVERYTHING EVERYDAY

Marching toward DevOps and continuous delivery of innovative product functionality relies on having an automated pipeline that is always stable, covers a sufficient number of test scenarios, and provides fast and relevant feedback to developers. In other words, DevOps teams that aim to fully scale their continuous testing need to employ the following equation: **full test coverage, executed via automation framework, once a day.**

Process-wise, testing everything every day in a mature continuous testing (CT) methodology aims to eliminate the following scenario (Fig 3) of late testing and escaped defects.

In the process shown below, developers typically implement required functionalities from a backlog of product feature requests and, while they integrate code daily into the source control management (SCM) system, most testing is developed and executed outside of the code integration process. In such a workflow, test automation isn't developed on time, defects escape to production, and the developer's attention is re-directed from the features backlog to defect investigation and resolution.

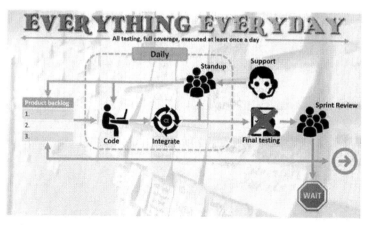

Fig. 3: Everything every day solving escaped defects and slow SDLC workflow

COST OF TESTING LATE: DEVELOPERS & TESTERS

As we've just seen, testing late and without code development synchronization introduces quality risks and slows down velocity. The impact is huge and, to help quantify it, Perfecto conducted research, also backed by market statistics, showing the implications of escaped defects in various phases of the DevOps pipeline, starting from same-day detection, through the end of sprint. The research results (Fig. 4) show that detection of defects the same day they were introduced into the software build allows developers to spend 47% of their business day on innovation and feature development when executing around 25% automated testing scenarios. Increasing test automation coverage to 75% would leave 77% of the time for developer to focus on innovation.

Bug detection	Time to fix
Same day	1 hour
Next day	2 hours
Next week	4 hours
End of sprint	8 hours (1 day)
Escaped defect	32 hours (4 days)

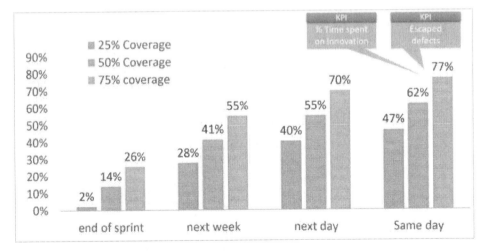

Fig. 4: Implications of escaped defects on developer productivity throughout the agile sprint/iteration

The math is simple: more automation, with more testing done daily, close to the code commit, translates into efficient defect detection, resolution, and more time to spend reducing the product backlog. This situation is a clear win-win for product and Dev/QA teams as well as the business.

THE PATH TO CONTINUOUS TESTING USING EVERYTHING EVERY DAY

What is required than from developers and test engineers to enable such efficiency?

As mentioned earlier in the book, it is the fit of people, process, and technology that enables CT within DevOps. It is also about scaling that synergy when there are multiple teams working in parallel and integrating new code each day across branches. Testing should be considered a development booster rather than a bottleneck, and therefore needs to follow the same rhythm, practices and timelines as developers set for their activities.

It's clear that testing everything every day is an ambitious goal — but it depends on how you define "everything". Testing everything requires a smart prioritization of the test code to allow best coverage with a minimum of test code. Test prioritization is not the only requirement here; test code stability is also important. Test stability earns teams' trust and allows them to move fast, get faster feedback, and act upon it. As this testing matures and scales, there also needs to be smart test reporting, as defined in this book, that provides on-demand quality visibility within CI, outside of CI, per team, per test type, and in various formats that fit various personas within the organization.

The path to testing everything every day goes through 3 pillars:

* Alignment
* Trust
* Growth

Alignment requires both dev and testers to always be in sync around the following

- **Status** — Where we are (e.g. we have 50% test failures, therefore execution is slow; classify issues by type)
- **Value** — Where we want to be (eliminate flaky tests, meet specific CI time window)
- **Resources** — Committed to make this work (test automation framework owner, developers)
- **Tools** — What's the framework?

Trust should address the following points:

- Remove Big Failure blocks
- Create small successes
- Create quick Visibility
- Achieve "All Green"

Growth should focus on the following objectives to allow teams to scale their CT and shorten their iteration duration even further:

- Be agile, add small "more" test steps
- Maintain all green status
- Continuous quick analysis

When all these steps are properly addressed with buy-in from management, alignment is in place on goals, tools, and resources, the velocity challenge within the pipeline isn't a broken mess.

In the first chapters about continuous testing fundamentals, mapping the path to continuous testing, andn tracking your progress to true CT, there are clear practices and recommendations regarding KPIs to measure progress, recommended tools for the job, guidelines on what tests to automate, and more.

When a test scenario fails, either as part of unit test, functional test, within CI or not, the assigned owner should be able, in just a few moments, to drill down into the test data and start the analysis rather than starting lengthy inquiries. From market research, typically — and especially with mobile test automation — test failures fall into 3 main buckets:

1. **Script/test code** issues (not following best practices around object locators, wrong wait method, not checking prerequisites of the test before launching it, etc.)

2. **Test lab** — whether a mobile device, desktop VM, or other target platform, if the platform is unstable, poorly connected, or poorly charged, thist will impact the overall stability and fail your objectives

3. **Test execution and orchestration** — when executing at scale and not managing CI/test executions wisely, the cycle takes too long. This could be due to the platform being unavailable, insufficient target platforms to test against, etc. In such cases, teams may often be tempted to take risky shortcuts which can impact overall quality. Sizing your lab properly, managing your CI and your parallel test execution every cycle, and ensuring that the platforms under test are in a ready state and available prior to triggering execution, are keys to smooth CT.

For most of these common pitfallse, having proper quality insight into various consumption methods per persona can make a huge difference. See the following visual, taken from Perfecto's DigitalZoom™ reporting, classifying failures by category and allowing teams to assign, analyze and fix these fast, and move forward.

SUMMARY

Achieving automation that works — and scaling it toward testing everything every day — is hard. It is harder when there are no clear guidelines behind these objectives. In this chapter, we touched on the implications on overall team velocity of leaving flaky or non-automated tests to the end of sprinty; we also offered a set of recommendations for testing what's important early in the development cycle, always aligning on quality goals, tools, and resources, and scaling and improving overall quality within the pipeline.

When you follow these guidelines, your pipeline should eventually look like this:

CHAPTER SIX

Avoiding the Big Bang in Your DevOps Pipeline

BY BRADBURY HART

BRAD HART is the Vice President of Product Management at Perfecto. He has over 20 years' experience specializing in software engineering process, design and implementation across the SDLC. Prior to joining Perfecto, Brad was one of the early founders of AccuRev in 2001, which was acquired by Micro Focus in 2013. As the VP of Product Strategy and Solutions Architecture, he worked closely with the PM, Engineering and Sales teams on the Borland suite of SDLC products. During AccuRev's growth, Brad built the Product Management, Product Owner, Sales Engineering, and Support teams and was responsible for all aspects of AccuRev's product strategy.

Previously, Brad held technical leadership roles at Nervewire Corporation, Eprise Corporation, and Rational Software, where he was responsible for the design, implementation and support of complex software development environments and processes. Brad also served as a Design and Mechanical Engineer at Texas Instruments, United Technologies and Stratus Computer, developing products for Airbag, ABS, Traction Control, Steering, and Transmission systems as well as Propulsion design for Aerospace systems.

Brad earned his B.S. in Mechanical Engineering from Worcester Polytechnic Institute in 1994 and his UNIX System/Network Admin, C, C++ Certification from Worcester Polytechnic Institute in 1998.

INTRODUCTION

Parallelization is key to making the entire DevOps pipeline run faster: parallel builds, parallel testing, and, for developers, parallel development across development teams. It is a very well understood best practice to "merge early, merge often" between developers on a given team to avoid late stage merge conflicts. Some teams have even taken the approach of using feature toggles to encourage real-time integration. Highly functional agile development teams tend to have this process well ironed out.

Team-to-team parallelization and integration pose a much more complex problem. Different teams use varying processes and may run at different cadences. All too often, organizations try to avoid the inevitable and push for a late-stage integration between teams resulting in the dreaded "stabilization phase/sprint" or the aptly named "release tail". This Big Bang approach to multi-team integration causes unnecessary release delays and a tremendous amount of overhead and pain for development teams and often forces the business to make poor decisions on time vs. quality.

There is a better way. This chapter describes methods used across multi-team DevOps environments to avoid the Big Bang, drive quality earlier in the process, and ship code faster! You will learn what the Big Bang is, what its negative outcomes are, how to avoid it, and what you'll gain from doing so.

WHAT IS THE "BIG BANG"?

You want to go fast. Parallel development eclipsed serial development decades ago. In any given development team, each member takes on their own tasks, stories, and defects, and begins coding. Years ago, before agile best practices took over, it was not uncommon for developers to work in isolation for weeks (or in some cases months) at a time. They were working in parallel with the rest of the team but, due to the complexity of yesterday's monolithic code bases, they had to stay isolated from other developers' changes in order to maintain a stable working environment. Fortunately, over the years, there has been a shift from monolithic codebases towards a micro-services approach. Each individual team owns its own piece of the pie. With the adoption of Agile/DevOps/Continuous Delivery, development teams are encouraged to integrate their code with the rest of the team members as soon as possible. Properly broken-down stories and defects allow for developers to merge their code with the main development branch on a more frequent basis. "Merge early, merge often" is now a second-nature best practice within any given development team.

WHAT ABOUT PARALLELIZATION BETWEEN TEAMS?

Taking any big project and breaking it down into manageable segments and assigning each to its own team is always a great way to improve production and velocity. There are some caveats, though. The further you break things down and separate them, the more work you have to do to ensure everything comes back together properly. Take the following example. You are responsible for building a bridge across a body of water. A natural approach would be to start on one side (say the left) and have the construction team work their way across the water from left to right. At any given point, a maximum of 10 people can work on the bridge. They can build 10 feet per day. If the bridge is to be 1000 feet long, it will take 100 days. The project manager wants to cut the construction time in half. Ideally, if they could add another 10 people they could go twice as fast. However, due to space constraints, only 10 people maximum can simultaneously work on the bridge. What's the solution? Run multiple teams in parallel! One team of 10 starts on the left side of the water, the other team of 10 starts on the right side and they meet in the middle. Since each team can produce 10 feet of bridge per day, they can finish construction in 50 days! That all sounds great on paper, but what happens if they meet in the middle and this happens (Fig. 1)?

Figure 1

Finding out that the two ends don't meet properly this late in the process will dramatically affect both the project delivery schedule and cost. It would have been much more advantageous to check earlier if they were on target and, thus, would have been able to correct any mistakes while they still had time. The goal of going faster is well understood but the path taken here proved to be error-prone and costly.

This exact scenario happens in software development all the time. To go faster, you must run multiple teams in parallel (even on the same codebase). These teams can be aligned to features, user journeys, product components, micro services, front end/backend, 3rd party, etc. Many complex enterprise applications have 50+ engineering teams working in parallel across all aspects of their product. Some are on the same delivery/release cadence and some are not. It is very common for the front-end teams to work in 2- to 3-week sprints while the backend teams work in quarterly release cycles.

At some point, all this code must come together to build a complete product. For organizations without stable, scalable continuous testing automation, this process is very painful. As one team incorporates changes from another team, how can they determine if there are resulting defects without robust test automation? Manual testing is too painful and time consuming. No team wants to slow down each week to test other teams' changes. The result is that everyone defers the inevitable. Each team runs independently from the other teams to accomplish the tasks they are responsible for and blindly moves forward. (Fig. 2)

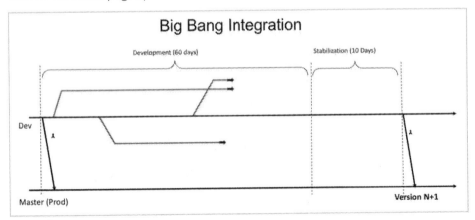

Figure 2

The plan is for each team to work on their own for 60 days' worth of development. The plan also accounts for a 10-day "stabilization phase" (aka code freeze). During this time, all the code from all the teams will be integrated and the end-to-end (E2E) testing begins. Whatever automation exists will be run, and the rest will be tested manually. Integrating at the end of the development cycle for the first time across all development teams is the "Big Bang". All the code changes from all teams are merged together all at once. Boom.

NEGATIVE IMPACT OF THE "BIG BANG"

The harsh reality of a "Big Bang" integration strategy is that it always results in delayed releases and/or reduction in quality (Fig. 3).

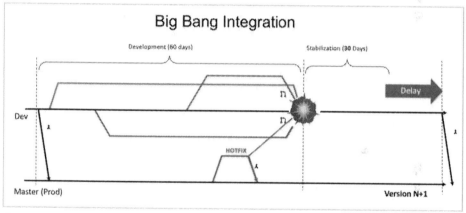

Figure 3

Bugs and incompatibilities are going to happen when working in parallel. It's the nature of the beast. For example, assume a developer on the front end team added a new feature that leverages the getCustomerInfo() API call on day 45 of development. However, on day 5 of development, the API team refactored the getCustomerInfo() API method and broke it up into multiple smaller methods and removed the getCustomerInfo() method all together. These types of things happen all the time. However, the team won't know the new functionality is broken until the Big Bang integration happens and they start testing. That is too late.

When working with many teams, these problems compound each other.

When you integrate 50 teams' changes all together, all at once, how do you determine whose changes caused the failure? It becomes exponentially more difficult to unravel the rat's nest, the complexity grows the longer you wait to integrate, and the more things you try to integrate at once.

The Big Bang approach is the worst outcome of the above time and amount of integration pieces. these. Waiting until the end of the development cycle and doing it all at once is a disaster waiting to happen.

What is the negative impact? Delays and/or reduction in quality. When the integration finally occurs, and testing begins, there will be a large number of defects and incompatibilities found. It takes time to figure out what caused the defects when they are all lumped together; this will require more and more test runs as defects are found and fixed. What should have been one E2E test cycle can quickly turn into 5–10 cycles. Each one takes a significant amount of time (especially if there are a large number of manual test processes). This forces one of two negative consequences for the business:

- Ship late
- Ship on time with known defects/lower quality

These are pretty painful decisions for a business to make. To maintain a high-quality product, the stabilization phase, or "Release Tail", will have to grow significantly. This will delay the release significantly, preventing customers from gaining the value of the new release functionality. This tends to be "crunch time" for the developers as well. Instead of working on the next release, they are working feverishly to fix defects in code they have already written. This prevents the business from going fast and delivering value to their customers.

Unfortunately, some businesses are forced to bow to time constraints and choose to ship closer to the original release date. Instead of fixing all the found defects, they assume the risk and release the product into the field. This inevitably results in poor customer experience.

HOW TO AVOID THE "BIG BANG"

There is a better way. You can avoid the Big Bang by:

- Integrating across teams **earlier**
- Integrating across teams **one at a time**

INTEGRATING EARLIER

There is no question about it. The earlier you integrate and find any potential defects, the easier and cheaper they are to fix. In fact, you will even avoid some defects before they have a chance to happen! Consider the above example regarding the API change. The change to the API was made on day 5 of development. If the new API code was integrated prior to the developer on day 45 building the new functionality, they would have known to use the new API methods from the get-go. The defect would have never occurred!

The less things have changed, the easier it is to determine the root cause of the problem. Trying to mesh 60 days' worth of changes is an exponentially more difficult task than meshing 5 days' worth of changes.

Let's say it takes 1 unit of time to resolve 5 days' worth of changes integrated between teams. Over 60 days, there will be 12 integration cycles, so that equates to 12 units of time. If you wait until the end of the 60-day cycle, it won't be 12 units of time. It will probably be more like 100. It is much, much harder to debug errors as time goes by and changes get piled on top of each other.

Of course, it doesn't make sense to integrate if you can't test. You can't test at this rate if you don't have automation in place that you trust.

INTEGRATING ONE AT A TIME

Let's use an automotive assembly line as an example.

The automotive assembly process is broken up into multiple teams. The body, engine, interior, electrical, and transmission teams all work in parallel on their own components. When the car is being built, they don't take all the

various components and slap them together all at once. Each team's work is added to the process in an orderly fashion. If there is a problem adding one team's piece, the line stops and the problem is fixed before other parts are added on top. Imagine finding out after the car was fully built that the car won't start and, after hours and hours of debugging, determining that the camshaft wasn't machined properly. That would be a very costly repair and would require removal and stripping of the engine. The problem was harder to find and harder to fix than it should have been.

The same is true for software development. Rather than integrating all the teams' changes at once, it is better to integrate the changes team-by-team.

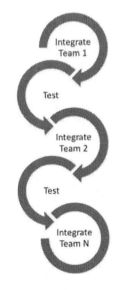

In this example, let's assume Team 1's changes are integrated first. Tests are run and confirm there are no issues. Next up is Team 2. Once their changes are integrated, the tests are run again. This time, they fail. There is obviously an issue with Team 2's changes being added. It might not be Team 2's fault (it could be a result of something Team 1 changed) but this doesn't matter. The time to figure out what went wrong is greatly reduced since you've isolated the difference between a successful test run and a failure to Team 2's changes. If, instead, you had integrated all 50 teams' changes at once, how would you know that it was Team 2's changes that caused the problem? You wouldn't. It would take a very long time to debug.

Again, this team-by-team integration methodology is only possible if you have a continuous testing automation suite that you trust to give you accurate results and that can be run on demand.

Here is an updated diagram showing an integration strategy across multiple teams that avoids the Big Bang by integrating team by team, early and often.

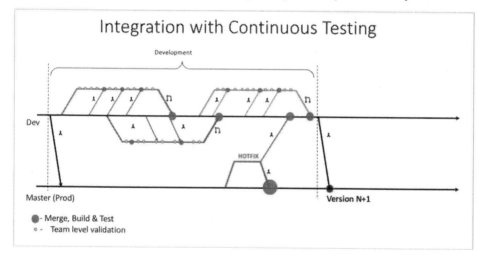

With this strategy, it is possible to dramatically reduce (and in some cases eliminate) the "stabilization phase" or "release tail". The result is that your development teams spend much more time coding new features and delivering value to your customers and much less time fixing defects. Higher velocity development alongside higher quality helps companies gain/maintain a competitive advantage.

SUMMARY

Going faster requires parallelization of efforts. Parallelizing your development comes at a significant cost and risk if not implemented properly. There is a natural tendency to avoid integrating changes between teams because it has traditionally been painful. The pain derives from a lack of continuous testing automation capability to verify integrated changes. Waiting too long to integrate, along with integrating multiple teams all at once, leads to significant release delays. "Stabilization phases" grow and organizations must choose between delaying a release or shipping lower quality software. The longer you wait to integrate, the harder it is to resolve issues. They become exponentially more costly. The secret is to integrate changes between teams early and often and to integrate changes one team at a time. This lowers the scope of change during each integration, making it easier to detect and fix any problems. Avoiding the Big Bang this way requires that you have a robust, stable, scalable automation test suite that you trust. It is worth the effort to build it. The increase in your development team's velocity, along with shipping higher quality software, provides tremendous advantages to your business.

CHAPTER SEVEN

Leveraging Smart Reporting as a Service Throughout the Continuous Testing Process

BY TZVIKA SHAHAF

TZVIKA SHAHAF is a Senior Director of Product Management at Perfecto, the market leading cloud-based platform for continuous testing of web, mobile and IoT software.

Tzvika is an Analytics expert and heads the DigitalZoom™ reporting and analytics product that is considered by leading market research firms as one of the most innovative solutions in the testing intelligence market.

Tzvika works with leading fortune 500 & global enterprises to optimize their Continuous Testing visibility and DevOps maturity

INTRODUCTION

Mountains of data slow down continuous testing

Releasing innovation faster to market means automating everything, versioning everything, and embracing continuous testing to provide fast feedback early and speed up delivery.

DevOps introduces a new reality of "Continuous Everything." This transformation is taking place to allow enterprises to meet frequent release cadences without compromising on any aspect of quality and user experience.

Continuous testing is key to qualifying new features and today's most efficient way to ensure smooth merging of simultaneous development threads. The high pace of commits through CI to master branches needs to be tracked; smoke test results, triggered automatically with every commit, need to be visible across the organization. In addition, making sure that the same tests are executed across all relevant digital platforms, such as different desktop web permutations, mobile device models/OS versions, and IoT platforms, dramatically increases the complexity of managing that test data.

Enterprises today are handling tens — sometimes hundreds — of thousands of test results per day. A team that was used to aggregating a relatively small amount of test data in the past is now required to deal rapidly with mountains of data that keep growing. The bottom line: among other challenges, continuous testing visibility is becoming a **big data** challenge.

Long testing data analysis

For leading enterprises today, it takes a test lead almost **2 days** to analyze regression test suite results. This wasted time could obviously be better devoted to more automation, innovation, and speedier releases.

The need for fast feedback is key to isolating and fixing problems identified during cycles. As suite size increases, there is always a risk of escaped defects to production. It is also important to emphasize that the cost of bug fixes increases over time.

Making the right release decision is a challenge for executives

With so many moving parts — product requirements, test scenarios, different technologies etc. — being used across feature teams and personas, reaching a go/no-go release decision is becoming an art.

Executives lack testing health control and visibility throughout their entire DevOps continuous delivery pipeline. This gap in visibility translates into additional noise and pressure directed toward practitioners (developers and testers). "Noise" translates as time being spent creating tailored reports for management (DIY) and manual data analysis to identify trends or issues related to a specific version of code, etc.

In many cases, these tailored reports are either late or very expensive due to the cost of tools and labor.

In short, there are a few key challenges related to Continuous Testing visibility which include:

- Ongoing limited visibility into the continuous testing health of the enterprise's digital services

- Navigating through big data to quickly scan large executions and zoom in on where the problems present huge challenges (especially from a time perspective — e.g. we need fast feedback)

- Releasing software fast relies on the developer's ability to quickly drill down and identify root cause issues of real defects

- Team collaboration mandates sync between processes and tools shared between different teams

APPROACHES TO GAINING CONTINUOUS TESTING VISIBILITY

Congratulations! Your automation framework is set up and you might even have a couple of suites ready to be triggered from your CI.

At this point, a couple of questions will be raised by the IT organization; the corporate tools strategy will shape the future of the organization's testing visibility. Considerations include aspects of DevOps maturity level, budget vs. objectives, as well as different philosophies of "build vs. buy" with regard to tools and IT.

Open-Source Built-In Reporting Tools — Some open source frameworks provide basic reporters (especially the Java frameworks: TestNG & Junit). These reports are effective as they cover the basic answers of test execution status plus a generic summary of the execution. However, like many other aspects of open source tools, it almost impossible to upgrade these reports to support enterprise-grade requirements. So, to manage the data generated by large-scale test execution (usually through CI), you will need to start combining and stitching multiple tools together. In the course of my work creating high levels of continuous testing insight, I met with the testing team at a large US-based HMO using TestNG; on top of TestNG, they customize the data in Allure and also link the reports to Jenkins. Unfortunately, their problem was that other types of tests running in the same regression cycle were speaking the same testing and reporting language; they had a couple of suites running from ALM over QTP (and the UFT report was not connected to the Allure dashboard — at this point, they considered uploading everything to ALM but that seemed like a heavy lift for the team and the longevity of ALM was questioned so they gave up on this path). In addition, the team had just added some responsive web design testing activities to their cycle. As a result, a new activity of desktop web browser testing was started using two JavaScript based frameworks: NightwatchJS and WebdriverIO. At this point, the team identified a market gap where a majority of the OSS JavaScript automation frameworks lacked sufficient reporting tools. This was the point where the team understood that they needed to upgrade the visibility requirement to an enterprise level and stop stitching reports together.

TestNG Reporter

Junit Report

Jenkins Pipeline Execution Test Summary Report

Allure Test Report

As an alternative to the previous question: "Can we build our own Reporting tool? We definitely know better than anyone else what our visibility needs are..."

Do-it-yourself (DIY) reporting tools — As described above, the variance of automation frameworks and tools — as well as the diversity of testing data types — makes an art form of "stitching together" work and reports.

The motivation of an enterprise to build its own homegrown reporting solution is usually brought on either by technical challenges (limited skill sets) or executive requirements that aim too high.

As for the first case, mixing and matching everything into a holistic (and yet effective) view of continuous testing sounds easy, but when each tool requires a separate authoring process and maintenance, it becomes clear that this is not scalable. At this point, the "we know better" attitude creeps in.

The other side of the house, which pushes for building an internal reporting solution, is usually aiming for a very high standard of dashboard views. There are very specific requirements of how the reports should look as part of the race for the ultimate report/dashboard. However, as is said of diamond lovers: they also have very expensive tastes...

If your enterprise is developing apps and services in the financial or health-care industries, my best advice would be to focus your efforts on testing your app and not on building the ecosystem around it — it already exists. Just as you do not develop the smartphone that runs your app, you shouldn't spend your best people on building testing infrastructure or reports.

As you have probably noticed, my product management nature forces me to spice up my story with real-world examples from leading digital enterprises (as I am fortunate enough to meet many of them around the globe). In this case, I have learned that maintaining a technical solution which is not positioned at the core of your business usually doesn't end very well.

At one of the global leading banks, the test result "report stitching" was conducted by a full-time employee (with the title of 'Data Analyst'); he was actually managing a Excel spreadsheet with the results of all tests running as part of the organizations regression job (I'll repeat myself: manual reporting for CI). Eight hours a day to build a report for a job that runs three times a day... by the time the first build manual analysis is conducted, the second one is already executed; no feedback from the first one can be considered to fix issues before the second is triggered. Feedback here is slow; this is exactly how bugs slip rightward.

In another case, with a US-based media company, a dev team was dedicated to building a reporting tool from scratch. A data repository was created, as were APIs for uploading data, UX planning & UI design, and so on. This was a successful tool but the backlog of requirements was growing and the team was diverted to the company's main business at some point. This move doomed the future of the tool and the company's dependency on the home-grown reporting concept.

Manual heatmap for Regression job

Chart	See children	Build Number → Package-Class Testmethod name ↓	16	15	14	13	12	11	10	9	8	7	6	5
☐	❖	org.common.samplea	FAILED	FAILED	FAILED	FAILED	FAILED	FAILED	FAILED	FAILED	FAILED	FAILED	FAILED	N/A
☐	❖	SampleATest	FAILED	FAILED	FAILED	FAILED	FAILED	FAILED	FAILED	FAILED	FAILED	FAILED	FAILED	N/A
☐		testA	PASSED	PASSED	PASSED	PASSED	PASSED	PASSED	PASSED	PASSED	PASSED	PASSED	PASSED	N/A
☐		testB	PASSED	PASSED	PASSED	PASSED	PASSED	PASSED	PASSED	PASSED	PASSED	PASSED	PASSED	N/A
☐		testC	FAILED	FAILED	FAILED	FAILED	FAILED	FAILED	FAILED	FAILED	FAILED	FAILED	FAILED	N/A
☐		testD	PASSED	PASSED	PASSED	PASSED	PASSED	PASSED	PASSED	PASSED	PASSED	PASSED	PASSED	N/A
☐	❖	org.common.sampleb	FAILED	FAILED	FAILED	FAILED	FAILED	FAILED	FAILED	FAILED	FAILED	FAILED	FAILED	N/A
☐	❖	org.common.samplec	PASSED	PASSED	PASSED	PASSED	PASSED	PASSED	PASSED	PASSED	PASSED	PASSED	PASSED	N/A
☐	❖	SampleDTest	PASSED	PASSED	PASSED	PASSED	PASSED	PASSED	PASSED	PASSED	PASSED	PASSED	PASSED	N/A
☐		testA	PASSED	PASSED	PASSED	PASSED	PASSED	PASSED	PASSED	PASSED	PASSED	PASSED	PASSED	N/A
☐		testB	SKIPPED	SKIPPED	SKIPPED	SKIPPED	SKIPPED	SKIPPED	SKIPPED	SKIPPED	SKIPPED	SKIPPED	SKIPPED	N/A
☐		testC	SKIPPED	SKIPPED	SKIPPED	SKIPPED	SKIPPED	SKIPPED	SKIPPED	SKIPPED	SKIPPED	SKIPPED	SKIPPED	N/A
☐		testD	PASSED	PASSED	PASSED	PASSED	PASSED	PASSED	PASSED	PASSED	PASSED	PASSED	PASSED	N/A

Continuous testing visibility is not just a dumb report... what should a smart report look like?

So, hopefully we now agree that visibility is key to a successful continuous testing process, that stitching together a combination of open source tools is not sufficient at an enterprise-grade level, and that DIY reports can be really good but are either expensive or impossible to maintain.

For teams that aim to mature their DevOps practices through advanced continuous testing, considering a Reporting as a Service (RaaS) solution is the most recommended and relevant way to go. Such solutions can not only be expanded as the company matures but they can also contain all CT entities in one single place. In addition, DevOps maturity is continuously evolving based on market and technology trends; therefore, having a scalable RaaS can be a key enabler for the continuous improvement of DevOps.

THE ESSENTIALS OF CONTINUOUS TESTING VISIBILITY

Let's look at the minimal requirements for resolving this market problem and provide a set of smart visibility components to shorten feedback loop cycles and increase value.

Insights into the CI pipeline — The post-execution phase naturally starts here. After a nightly regression cycle, for example, as a team lead or release manager, I need a high-level view that shows me the overall status of hundreds, if not thousands, of tests that were executed in separate builds. This executive-level view compliments my "plain-vanilla" CI views and helps me oversee the testing trends to support immediate decision-making processes towards release/ code checkout. To make the value proposition at this level as simple as possible: the desired view here should help me understand, both at a user's and a manager's level, whether we are headed in the right direction? Is my build stable over time? Did any of the recent commits create any type of regression? And, above all: are we good to go with the last build or should we revert and investigate?

Risk/focus area mapping — An aggregation of continuous testing results usually shows that there are specific areas that need deeper attention as they are unstable or keep failing. My experience with analyzing test results is that bugs usually come in buckets or categories, whether related to a specific type of operating system, a specific module of the service that keeps failing tests on the same functionality, or, in some cases, specific code that causes issues across different tests, device models, etc.

In this case, the most effective way to visually map and display the impact on different areas is with **heatmaps** — such executive summary views help managers and teams to quickly identify risk areas in their testing and focus on high level problems.

Different ways of visualizing the data to fit to different queries or responsibility areas will help teams isolate issues to a useful starting point: "I see that in the last 8 hours, my iOS tests are failing on two specific test scenarios." That's an improvement over "my iOS devices are on fire today..." which basically means nothing to the developer that will be required to investigate and debug the problem. It's all about basic conventions of "tell me where to start my investigation to fix the most critical issues."

I have started seeing more and more of these types of views displayed on TV screens for testing teams (any change of color immediately attracts the appropriate attention).

Summary report list — naming the problem and listing it (how big is the issue and where exactly does it impact my overall service health?) So, we know there is a problem; now we must investigate it in detail. Just like in an ER, DevOps teams conduct triaging activities to isolate problems. This affords the ability to slice & dice the data to build a dedicated view of the test, the platform, and more. This will help to understand if there is a test issue, a device issue, a backend problem, or something else. The granularity level of this view is usually a detailed list with test name, platform, status, tags (and other contextual elements that serve as identifiers for a test), and time-related info (date, time, duration etc.) On top of that, the ability to add comments during triaging serves as a powerful traceability tool.

Single Test Report — This is the best place to understand what failed in the test: a root cause analysis. This is also the place where testers and developers meet to fix bugs based on sharing the same views and artifacts. Cross-team collaboration is key to success at this level; this is the only way to fail fast and fix fast. Things here tend to get 'stuck in the middle' due to miscommunication or absence of facts that can confirm or reject a testing failure claim.

My best advice here is to base your process on evidence; this is not meant to be a way to prove that you're right but a way to resolve problems where everyone shares the same perspective and insight. Testing artifacts provide a jump start for developers to start the fixing phase on the spot. Artifact types may include video of test executions, screenshots taken at a critical command level, log files, network files (PCAP/HAR), device crash reports or vitals logs, etc.

This level of reporting is all about building a data-driven discussion around bug fixes and eliminating the common refrain of "It works on my machine, I can't reproduce the problem you're seeing — closing this case..." Reality demonstrates that many of these cases are discovered later after slipping into production.

Visual validation across application screens and UI helps developers and UX experts get faster feedback during the continuous testing triaging process; for this, teams need the ability to compare the UX of their responsive apps through visual validation across their digital platforms. The strength of such functionalities lies in their ability to identify differences as well as to make sure a new piece of code is rendering properly across all critical platforms. In the past, this was conducted manually as part of "looks good testing" — this was time consuming and error-prone. Keep in mind that such processes also should be scalable and meet the velocity of the product release.

COHESIVE TESTING INSIGHTS ACROSS THE ENTIRE DEVOPS PIPELINE

In today's reality, almost every type of testing activity data (UI, API, Performance, Accessibility etc.) is managed in a separate "silo." In most enterprises, data is not normalized and stitched together into a holistic view that provides a snapshot in real time.

This kind of broken process holds back a DevOps team's velocity. If an issue occurs during one of the tests, the developer assigned to fix the issue is required to collect the data from multiple tools/environments and conduct manual correlation activity that takes a lot of time.

Building a wider visibility is critical for an efficient Continuous Testing process. Both practitioners and executives should benefit from an extended opportunity to view everything through a single pane of glass.

A sustainable approach to managing and displaying data from multiple testing sources should include:

1. Basic tagging of events which are happening both on the front end (mobile device/browser etc.) and on the back end (specific service or API — remember, to find the needle in a haystack, first you need to define what a needle is)

2. Normalizing all test data to fit one report convention (preferably using an SDK or conversion tool)

3. Correlating events post-execution as part of the report (functional tests related to 3 relevant API tests, etc.) — this is the best way to save very expensive search time. As a developer, I expect to be very focused on the problem when I am required to fix an issue (not on the process of

fetching data).

4. Display (and also provide for download via API) all relevant artifacts for these activities — every good root cause analysis starts with evidence. You need to be able to provide these hints to the developer that fixes the issue; this could be a screenshot with the actual bug, a video that shows the app crash, or, of course, a log file that can be used for debugging purposes.

INTEGRATION

Fixing issues in DevOps is an art that depends on cross-team/tool collaboration and discipline. The test report serves as the junction where all practitioners "meet"; hence it should facilitate data-driven process (using evidence).

There are a few tool categories that the report should seamlessly feed into such as:

a. continuous integration hooks such Jenkins, Circle CI, and more

b. defect management such as Atlassian Jira

c. source control management tools such as GitHub, GitLab, BitBucket, and others

d. IDEs such as IntelliJ, XCode, etc.

e. collaboration tools such as Slack

GETTING SMART(ER) VISIBILITY OF YOUR CONTINUOUS TESTING

Noise reduction as a key to efficient defect triaging — The growing number of scenarios tested as part of a mature DevOps process also involves an increasing amount of noise. This noise is usually created by unstable or flaky automation. The majority of DevOps teams define these types of system failures as "false negative" test results.

When the test result triaging process starts, the developer's focus is to decrease the mean time to resolution (MTTR) for the inspected issues. To do that, here are some best practices to reduce noise and increase the developer's focus on finding the 'real' issues defined as failures:

1. **"Green is green so why bother?"** — this is a common refrain among many test automation teams that are looking to filter out the tests results with a "passed" status. As part of the initial defect triaging process, these results have no meaning. Later in the process, the need to compare the failing test to the last stable execution of the test ("passed") will arise. The bottom line: at this preliminary stage of finding big problems, it is strongly recommended to put aside the successful tests.

2. **Define the noise and "mute" it** — it is important to emphasize that nearly 80% of failures in test automation usually follow one or more patterns. **That is the most important advice in this whole chapter — find these patterns and you'll be on the fast track to automation success!** Putting aside functional failures which are related to scripting and framework issues, **industry figures show that 50% of the failures are related to system errors and thus should be marked as false negatives.**

Here is a breakdown and classification of these system failures:

- 25% of test results usually marked as failures are caused due to **lab** or **environment** stability problems. The main issues in this category are related to networking, stability, and different platform operations (device is disconnected or locked etc.)

- 25% of test executions fail due to **orchestration** issues. The main issues in this category are related to platform capability definitions — e.g. targeting a device that does not exist in the lab or has missing characteristics (such as operating system version) or targeting a device that is currently in use, and more.

FAILURE ANALYSIS – FOCUS ON TOP ROOT CAUSE ISSUES TO INCREASE PRODUCTIVITY

After the noise is reduced, the real game starts; it is time to start looking at actual functional failures. These are issues that are related to the app/service or to actual scripting/framework issues.

These failures can be handled by the relevant assignee whether it's a developer or tester, who have a great opportunity to improve their test automation code through following best practices.

Once failures are isolated within a single view, the next phase is to 'bucketize' them according to the actual reason. The big failure buckets (reasons) would typically include these common automation failures known in the market:

- Object handling — element.find commands that failed due to various reasons

- Time-outs and synchronization issues — page upload or search for elements that did not appear as expected — can be tied both to app performance issues and/or scripting issues.

- Scripting and coding best-practices pitfalls

By definition, coding will always involve bugs; therefore, the overall number of bugs will probably not be reduced by this analysis. The biggest lesson learned from this activity is about **focus:** being able to provide a prioritized top list of issues to the user will have a significant impact on project velocity and will allow the developer to immediately focus on the high-impact issues first.

Quick wins are needed in the DevOps mindset. Stick to the top five failure reasons and make sure you always fix those items first.

The highest maturity level for an organization that uses a RaaS involves implementing advanced technologies that leverage AI and ML/data mining techniques that reduce analysis time and boost software release velocity.

Among the capabilities that can be gained through ML and data mining, you might consider the following:

- Automated processes to retrieve information regarding commonality of failures

- Identifying trends/patterns for Continuous Testing "events" such as CI job duration, stability of activities over time, etc.

- Anomaly detection compared to a predefined baseline of continuous testing KPIs

- Smart risk & impact analysis for development code changes; for example, every time someone is conducting a change in specific GitHub repository, the failure rate rises for specific test cases or functional areas of the app

- ML-based predictive analytics regarding overall continuous testing activities throughout the product life cycle (in other words, if a failure occurs once, given that you're running the test under the same conditions, there is a high probability that such a test will fail again)

Implementing AI techniques as part of your Reporting-as-a-Service may include different levels of maturity (usually divided by the "level of freedom" that the artificial engine has):

- Tip me — highlighting a specific issue with a recommendation on how to fix it. This can be a link to an article, code snippet, video tutorial, and more

- Fix it for me (conditionally) — identifying the issue and suggesting the solution for the user to accept or reject. This still leaves a certain amount of control in the user's hands. For example, when identifying an issue as a defect, the engine will suggest opening a ticket in Jira; the user then needs to handle the next steps

- Fix it for me (automatically) — the engine identifies issue and handles them automatically (E2E) without any human intervention

SUMMARY

As more organizations are viewing velocity as the primary driver of — and objective for — DevOps, there is no doubt that having fast feedback capabilities after each product iteration is critical.

In this guide, we have outlined a recipe for success for building a smart reporting system as a service (RaaS). Make sure to invest the time to plan and design your Continuous Testing visibility objectives, which include the listed features and components as described in this chapter; this, in turn, will support your success metrics.

Planning in advance and considering a ready RaaS solution can save lots of wasted time on creating cool dashboards that, in the end, won't come near a tailored and stitched together reporting solution.

CHAPTER EIGHT

Guidelines for Matching Testing Tools to Your DevOps Pipeline

BY UZI EILON

UZI EILON is the CTO at Perfecto Mobile. He joined Perfecto in 2010 after a fifteen-year career as a software developer and manager at IDF, Netrialty, Comverse, and SanDisk. Over the past seven years, Uzi has grown the company by managing expanding R&D teams and leading Sales Engineering teams. His field of expertise includes mobile application testing, automation tools, defining customer projects,  and on-boarding, plus bringing in Agile methodologies into the equation. Uzi Eilon speaks regularly on behalf of Perfecto Mobile at events, such as AnDevCon, StarWest, HP Discover, and ongoing technical webinars.

INTRODUCTION

Mobile and Web projects are becoming more and more agile; "old-fashioned" manual regression testing methods are being replaced by automated processes, scheduled scripts triggered by other processes in the pipeline, and execution of specific tests verifying targeted application areas. There is no doubt that unattended automation in a DevOps pipeline is the foundation of successful development projects.

HOW TO CHOOSE?

But which tools should you use? Answering this question is critical to building the proper testing strategy and to the continuous testing activities within the SDLC pipeline. Before getting into too much detail, let's take a look at the two ends of the automated testing platform spectrum.

These tools can be divided into two major groups:

- **White-box**[1] — Tests written by the developer with access to the code, flows and native objects.
- **Black-box**[2] — Tests written by external test engineers without access to the code and using flows which simulate the user experience.

Espresso and XCUItest are the leading mobile white-box test automation tools, while Appium and Selenium are the leading black-box tools.

For mobile test automation, there is a big difference between these tools. White-box testing relies on an IPA/APK package that includes both the app under test and the test suite that is needed to test the app — these packages are executed on the device upon installation. Black-box test tools are executed remotely and communicate with the application via the network (mostly via HTTP).

White-box tests are executed on the device — this makes the execution time faster (up to 8 times faster). They have full access to the application code and thus have direct access to objects; this makes scripts much more stable.

This table highlights the major differences between the white-box and black-box tools:

Criteria	Black box — Appium	White box — XCUITtest/Espresso
Language	Any (mostly JS and Java)	Swift/Objective-C/Java
Created by	Open source	Apple/Google
Execution time	6T	T
Test Flakiness	High	Low

---

1   White-Box definition by Wikipedia — https://en.wikipedia.org/wiki/White-box_testing

2   Black-Box testing definition by Wikipedia — https://en.wikipedia.org/wiki/Black-box_testing

So, given its performance advantage, should teams stick to white-box testing only? The answer is a qualified 'no'; both black- and white-box tests should be used as part of the pipeline, each to serve different purposes.

Now that we understand the fundamental differences between the tool types, let's look at the DevOps processes.

MATCHING TOOLS TO YOUR DEVOPS

Organizations started to move into Agile so that they could release more features faster and meet customers' expectations of new digital experiences. This new velocity concept added complexity to the standard SDLC; DevOps is the software engineers' solution to that complexity.

The DevOps pipeline describes the actions from writing the first line of code until it is delivered to and used by customers. This process defines actions, stages, and when to move between stages. The foundation of an efficient pipeline is automation — automation of everything from building the software, copying, moving and deploying the app or micro-service, to automated testing to verify the artifact's readiness to proceed to the next stage, and more. The way to achieve this efficiency is by employing automated testing at each stage in the pipeline. Such tests have different targets, as will be described below.

Standard pipeline stages

- **Developer Local Build — component team:**
  The developers write their code and then must integrate it with other team members' code.

  After finishing a feature, before committing his or her code, the developer must verify that the component is still stable. This means getting the latest code, merging changes on the local machine, and executing **unit tests.**

  Unit tests are codebase tests which check basic feature flows without integration with other devices; all data in and out is controlled by the test. The goal of unit tests is to verify that the latest code did not break the team's code.

- **Hourly Build — component team:**
  Every hour, the latest component code has been built and all unit tests have been executed to verify the code is ready to integrate with other teams' code.

- **Hourly Build — application build:**
  Every hour — and if all the component tests pass — a full application build gets executed.

  This build contains all the applications' components and requires **basic functional testing** to verify that the app is stable and ready to move to **staging** and **regression tests** to verify the new functionally hasn't broken existing features, and to test it with other apps and services.

- **Nightly — integration test:**
  After verifying that the app is stable, it is moved to a staging environment; **full functional testing** has been executed on the app to verify that it works with all other services.

- **Pre-prod tests:**
  Last stage before release to production; this environment contains real production data and tests in this environment are focused on **coverage and performance.**

- **Monitoring:**
  After releasing the app, these tests verify the production service is up and running and available to customers.

The following table summarizes the different tests and stages:

	Local build	Hourly build component team	Hourly Build — application build	Hourly Build —regression tests	Nightly — integration tests	Pre-prod tests	Monitor
Tests	Developers Unit tests	Team unit tests	Basic functional testing	Regression tests	Full end-to-end testing	Coverage and performance- and other non-function tests (security)	

	Local build	Hourly build component team	Hourly Build — application build	Hourly Build —regression tests	Nightly — integration tests	Pre-prod tests	Monitor
Execute	Manually	Scheduler (CI server)	Scheduler (CI server)	Scheduler (CI server)	Scheduler (CI server)	Scheduler (CI server)	NOC tools
Environment	Local developer's machine	Build server	Build server	Build server	Staging	Pre-production	Production
Target	Verify the latest code does not break the component	Verify the code is ready to merge with the other teams' code	Verify the app is ready to be tested together with the other component/ services on staging.	Verify the new functionally did not break existing features.	Verify existing and new functionality. Works on "production like environment"	Verify the app is ready to be released. Support relevant platforms and required load.	Verify the service is available for customers
Pass action	Commit the code	Execute product build	Move to staging	Move to staging	Move to pre-production	Move to production	
Fail action severity	Low — developer fixes his code	Low – developers must fix the code fast and commit before nightly	Medium — developers need to analyze the integration bug	Medium — developers need to fix existing features and verify backwards compatibility	High — in this stage, bugs are more complicated and can affect the release date	High — load bugs are hard to fix For converge: severity is based on the platform bug	Extreme – production issues must be fixed ASAP

While considering these common frameworks, bear in mind that there are other popular tools and frameworks such as Protractor, Gauge, Galen, Nightwatch, and BDD frameworks like Quantum. All these tools are great test automation frameworks that leverage Selenium/Appium WebDriver configuration and execution, which allows the test developer to focus on application flow and tests.

In addition, such frameworks enable test developers to add unique test scenarios for specific technologies. For example, one might use Protractor for specific Angular-based application testing due to the unique capabilities the framework has for object identification support; in a different case, teams could leverage Galen to develop visual testing scenarios for their responsive web application testing.

Now that we've had a look at the different tests and tools, here is a map of the required test types and testing tools for each stage in the pipeline:

Responsive Web Apps (RWD):

	Local build	Hourly build component team	Hourly Build — regression tests	Nightly — integration tests	Pre-prod tests
Test type	Unit	Unit	• Basic functional testing • regression tests	Full end-to-end testing	Coverage and performance
Tools	Junit (white box)	Junit (white box)	Selenium RemoteWeb-Driver (black box)	Selenium RemoteWeb-Driver (black box)	Selenium Non-functional testing (security, performance)
Estimated execution time	Minutes	Minutes	Up to one hour	A few hours	A few hours
Resources	• Headless browser • Responsive viewer in browser dev tools	• Headless browser • Responsive viewer in browser dev tools • Mobile emulators	• Selenium grid (cloud) • Different browsers • Mobile Emulators • 2–4 real devices	• Selenium grid (cloud) • 4 Different browsers • 4–12 real devices	• Selenium grid (cloud) • 12 Different browsers • ~20 real devices

MOBILE NATIVE APPS (IOS/ANDROID):

	Local build	Hourly build component team	Hourly Build — regression tests	Nightly — integration tests	Pre-prod tests
Test type	Unit	Unit	• Basic functional testing • regression tests	Full end-to-end testing	Coverage and performance
Tools	Espresso, XCUITest (white box)	Espresso, XCUITest (white box)	Espresso, XCUITest Appium RemoteWeb-Driver (black box)	Appium RemoteWeb-Driver (black box)	Appium Non-functional testing (security, performance)
Estimated execution time	Minutes	Minutes	Up to one hour	A few hours	A few hours
Resources	• Mobile Emulator	• Mobile Emulator	• Appium grid (cloud) • Mobile Emulators • 2–4 real devices	• Appium grid (cloud) • 4–12 real devices	• Appium grid (cloud) • ~20 real devices

SUMMARY

As you can see from these tables, both black- and white-box tests can help improve overall pipeline quality. Keep in mind that different pipeline stages require different tools that provide relevant feedback at each stage according to the organization's quality and velocity objectives.

These differences between stages are required not only from a tool perspective, but also from a resource standpoint. A Headless Chrome browser may enough for unit tests but for full end-to-end testing, teams might need a complete Selenium grid with the full-blown browser UI and devices.

As you move to the pre-production stage, the same tests are still relevant and are still executed; however, the coverage, the environment, and the resources used are different due to the simple fact that the objective at that stage is to reduce the risk of escaped defects and improvement of the customer's digital experience.

CHAPTER NINE

Continuous Operations Within DevOps Processes

BY GENADY RASHKOVAN, AVP OF CUSTOMER SUPPORT AND CONTINUOUS ENGINEERING

GENADY RASHKOVAN brings 21 years of experience leading Support, Continuous Engineering and Service organizations in different product and cloud-based companies. Creating team environments to increase productivity, building organizational communication to improve collaboration and service, reduce costs, position products in the world market and increase maintenance revenue. Vast experience with strategic customer relationships and building customer confidence in technical solutions. Strong expertise in driving people, processes and technology. High level of production & competency, being elected to a "Ten Senior Managers Group" in a multi-Billion Dollar company for a line of product future road map definition. Built Support and Continuous Engineering organization from scratch.

INTRODUCTION

Continuous Operation[1] means your system and all its components are always operational. There can be a lot of pieces in this puzzle. How can we build a multidisciplinary and highly sophisticated system when it needs to remain

---

1   Continuous Ops byline — http://www.correlsense.com/continuous-operations-a-great-idea-but-de-tails-of-execution-still-matter/

operational? There are two main challenges that need to be addressed to make continuous operation a reality:

1. Planned and unplanned maintenance activities

2. A large variety of potential threats to systems' ongoing operations

Both challenges require proactive *and* reactive approaches; one takes preventive measures and the other utilizes proper system design to trigger different redundancy and HA (High Availability) mechanisms.

There are many moving parts to consider. Automated builds, provisioning, testing, and deployment are necessary. Choosing the right tools is critical to mission success; so are continuous feedback and information flow between all relevant teams.

CI CYCLE DIAGRAM

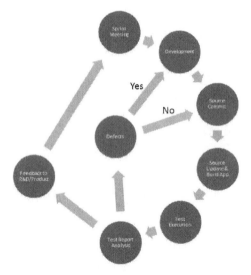

COMPONENT MONITORING

In ideal world of multi-component systems, everything moves in perfect synergy and nothing can go wrong due to flawless system design. All potential issues are prevented in the design and implementation stages and the system is completely self-sufficient. The system will automatically identify any potential problems and eliminate them as needed. As much as any organization would like to be in this position, there is still a way to go to reach that point. Today, with the growing trends of AI and machine learning, which aim to help industries get there, there is still a need to handle day-to-day challenges and keep perfecting the overall objective of Continuous Operation.

One of the crucial aspects of Continuous Operation is monitoring system health. Being able to know the current state of all critical components can provide control over system availability in general and, thus, support the journey to Continuous Operation. Monitoring — as well as your approach to monitoring — offers various options. Teams can monitor availability and functionality of all system components or focus on different behavioral metrics and/or changes that will allow them to predict certain upcoming patterns and stages of the system. The latter will open a new door into a proactive world — a world where teams handle issues and complications before they arrive. To build such a monitoring system, there needs to be a supporting platform, flexible enough to give DevOps engineers tools and abilities to build and define the measured thresholds and milestones that will be monitored by the **Automatic Detection System.**

AUTOMATIC DETECTION

One of the biggest challenges in building Automatic Detection Systems in a DevOps environment is the dynamic nature of such environments. Each build can bring something new: different release sizes, different execution times, resource utilization, etc. Such a variety of possibilities makes it very challenging to pre-define thresholds and expected system behaviors. However, this should not prevent an Automatic Detection System (ADS) from being implemented.

The design of an ADS should take this dynamic environment into consideration and have the flexibility to control thresholds and sensors based on environmental changes. Machine learning implementations can improve response times of the system to potential issues and extend the covered threats list.

Let's look at the example of managing a VM pool in AWS. Working with a static pool (a predefined number of VMs) can cause significant service degradation when running out of available machines — or overpaying when the majority of the pool is not in use.

In my company, we implemented a dynamic VM pool where the number of available machines is increased when a certain threshold is reached. The same behavior works in both directions and, when usage drops, the number of available machines in the pool is decreased.

An additional level of sophistication would be adding daily statistics analysis and auto-adjustment of thresholds. Say that every day, at the same time, system utilization is rising and a 90% threshold is consistently reached. That triggers the pool adjustment mechanism to increase the number of available VMs until utilization drops. The machine can learn the behavioral pattern and, after a predefined number of iterations, decide to increase the number of available VMs in the pool before the threshold has been reached. This mechanism will minimize the risk of running out of available VMs in case of instant utilization peaks where the time between 90% utilization and a 100% is too short. By minimizing the risk of running out of available VMs, we improve availability and create an auto-preventive mechanism.

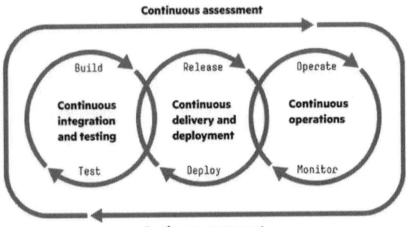

AUTOMATIC RECOVERY

Now that we've seen the importance of Automatic Detection Systems, let's focus on the next challenge. Detecting a potential problem is important; however, this is worthless if the system doesn't act immediately upon its findings. The simple model is to leverage a monitoring system that sends alerts that are all monitored by human beings; however, such mechanisms depend on human response and implementation times. In some cases, this will be sufficient and the problem will be prevented; sometimes, though, human factors can slow down the process and cause critical delays that eventually lead to system failure — this will invariably have an impact on the release cycle. To minimize such risks and make sure the system will receive immediate attention in case suspicious symptoms have been identified, a better approach would be an Automatic Recovery System.

The implementation of an Automatic Recovery System takes us one step closer to the ideal world. It minimizes response time as well as risks related to human error. Automatic Recovery not only improves system availability in general but reduces maintenance costs and eliminates errors by removing the human factor that, by nature, is error-prone.

A good example for such a process implementation would be an Automatic Mobile Device Recovery system. It is a given that during long and continuous test executions on mobile devices, we can run into device issues. Mobile devices are built and designed to be used by humans occasionally, during the day, and even then we sometimes have a need to clean the RAM or restart to get it running faster. Running automated testing requires continuous use and can lead to exhaustion of the device after a shorter period, at which point it must be recovered.

We analyzed a long series of device availability events and found a list of the most common errors that usually lead to device failures. By running a simple log monitoring process, we knew how to predict the phenomena and triggered device recovery procedures prior to actual failure.

The graph below that shows monthly resolution of how the growing number of automatic recoveries in a random large cloud minimized service disruption and impact on device availability:

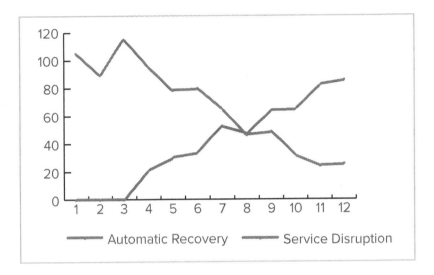

HISTORY LOG AND POST EVENT ANALYSIS

Automatic Detection and Recovery are focused on system monitoring in real time: proactive or reactive surrounds around current sensor readings and acting in real time. A different slant on the proactive approach is the Post Event Analysis process. Despite intense day-to-day pressures, it's crucial to find time to stop, look back, and check the statistics of recent months. Having this as a mandatory part of the process will force DevOps teams to look at the bigger picture.

"Let's analyze our last 20 outages and see what they have in common". Continuous feedback to the product owner is extremely valuable. Such feedback is even more efficient when it's backed by solid statistics that were done on a large number of recent events. Each component is compared to a baseline of this specific component, as well as to other components, to discover trends and the main threats to stability.

These statistics allow ops teams to maximize their impact and help promote improvements and fixes within the product. This approach enables a continuous proactive effort, feedback to R&D/QA/Product and other teams, etc.

Post-event analysis should be conducted not only in the case of human involvement, but also after an auto-recovery incident. It's crucial to log the auto-recovery event while dumping all relevant information for future analysis. This should be followed by a Root Cause Analysis (RCA) ticket creation, which may only be considered closed once analyzed and only after short- and long-term solutions are introduced. These RCA tickets can then be classified and monitored for quality and statistics purposes.

SUMMARY

At a time when organizations are shifting to higher DevOps maturity, it is essential to ensure that not only the dev and test sides of the process are progressing, but also to enable the ops side with both proactive and reactive approaches, as described above. The ability that DevOps teams have to address production issues when they occur — as well at the ability to prevent systems issues **before** they occur with advanced identification systems — translates into a great increase in DevOps team productivity. Today, advanced software is being designed with multiple micro-services and cross-software component dependencies that can cause issues with reliability and/or availability of the entire product; having the aforementioned solutions in the executive team's mindset will prove itself to be invaluable.

CHAPTER TEN

The Benefits of Exploratory Testing (ET) in an Agile Environment

INTRODUCTION

When thinking about Agile and continuous testing, the associated activity that typically comes to mind is automated testing: fast feedback and as little manual activity as possible. While this is true and it's the goal of moving fast, there is still room — and indeed real benefit — to employing exploratory testing practices as part of the overall CT processes. As defined by James Bach in his piece 'Exploratory Testing Explained'[1], ET is defined as "simultaneous learning, test design, and test execution." ET isn't new; in fact, it has been adopted by many Agile and DevOps teams. Based on a survey conducted by **Practitest in 2018**[2], 82% of participants are still doing more exploratory testing than scripted testing. These participants represent a group that is heavy on Agile (89%) and aiming to shift to DevOps (28% say that they are already practicing DevOps).

	2018	2017	2016
Exploratory Testing/Session-based Testing	82%	84%	87%
Scripted testing	68%	58%	60%
Bug hunts	42%	44%	45%
Coordinated user (beta) testing	29%	30%	24%
Pair testing	28%	24%	25%
User simulations	24%	35%	39%

---

1   James Bach Blog — http://www.satisfice.com/blog/archives/1509

2   State of testing survey, PractiTest — http://qablog.practitest.com/state-of-testing/

	2018	2017	2016
Mob testing	14%	17%	NA
Analytics of product telemetry	9%	NA	NA
Agile or agile-like	89%	87%	82%
Waterfall or waterfall-like	33%	37%	39%
DevOps	28%	26%	23%
TDD	19%	17%	18%
BDD	17%	16%	16%
Our own model or principle	13%	14%	18%
Context-driven	9%	7%	16%
Don't follow any structured model	7%	7%	6%

According to this definition, it can clearly be seen that by using such practices, teams can gain several benefits. When running exploratory testing in conjunction with other test practices, teams experience various test cases and scenarios and learn a lot about a product's functionality, maturity, and usability.

Such insights can be shared quickly with the various counterparts within the organization in the form of user feedback and, in this way, drive change faster and earlier in the process. In this context, it is important to understand that, usually, the persona that executes the ET is a product expert; this means that the value of his insights will serve both test automation engineers and developers.

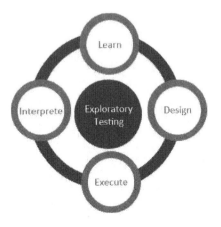

As the digitalization of the world continues to grow, all the various products being designed and developed are being changed, in many cases "on the fly". To be able to respond to change from a quality assurance perspective, teams often leverage exploratory testing for several reasons:

1. To understand if the current implementation makes sense from a user perspective — does the product meets his business objectives?

2. ET[3] can serve as a foundation for more advanced automated tests

3. To provide fast feedback to the developer and business prior to and/ or in parallel with test automation development

4. To complement use cases that simply can't be automated

To maximize the value of exploratory testing throughout the entire DevOps pipeline — and to match ongoing continuous testing efforts — it is important to fit these activities in the right stages or phases of the process.

Exploratory testing answers questions related to your features and/or your user-story's ability to meet business goals; does it meet these goals in a usable, consistent, and resource efficient manner? ET is not just about covering functionality; it is also able to address non-functional-related aspects of your implementation.

These inputs back to the feature/product team are critical and, as a result, ET is being used by many organizations in 3 different places:

1. Per each complete user story implementation — validating that the functionality is met and works as expected in parallel with automated tests

2. In parallel to full regression execution, to assess that not only user story functionality is working as expected, but, rather, that the entire product — from an ET perspective — has no regressions or issues

3. For a newly-introduced major functionality, teams will often open the ET tests to more than one or two testers to gather a larger set of feedback and raise the level of confidence[4] with the critical implementation

---

3   Exploratory testing by Satisfice — http://www.satisfice.com/blog/archives/category/exploratory-testing

4   Tricentis definition of ET within CT — https://www.tricentis.com/blog/2018/01/11/exploratory-testing-continuous/

EXPLORATORY TESTING APPROACH

Once you have understood the role of ET[5] in the overall process and the benefits it can offer, it is important to learn some approaches that are commonly used by the practitioners of this type of testing.

- ET inherits from the **heuristics** of the test engineer; such things guide the overall ET activities. The experience and the deep knowledge of the product architecture and capabilities allow the test engineer to perform efficient and impactful tests.

- When executing ET, think often about **additional test creation** and which areas are not covered by structured automated tests

- ET is hard to measure, and when done within an agile iteration, is should be time-bound. Employ **session-based ET** to both measure and stay within given time windows

- **Pair ET with other testers** and counterparts for efficiency and better-quality determination

- Follow product requirements while doing ET, but **think about the end-user**

- **Structure the un-structured tests** — While ET is not a guided testing activity, DevOps and CT follow methodologies, time boundaries, and automatic processes. Therefore, actions should be taken to reduce the negatives and the cons people might have with respect to ET:

  - Divide the product into areas and features and scope your ET based on these areas

  - Maintain a checklist of covered vs. uncovered areas from the above per iteration to help maintain quality coverage and feedback to the team

  - Follow coverage principles to address as many input fields, buttons, and product flows as possible — both positive and negative scenarios

  - Consider various testing techniques, such as integration tests and functional tests, while doing them as part of an ET activity. For example, validate integration of the system under test with other apps, check complex business logic scenarios, etc.

---

5   ET Tutorial, Guru99 — https://www.guru99.com/exploratory-testing.html

SUMMARY

In an agile environment, there is no doubt that the key velocity drivers are automation and continuous testing/continuous integration; however, due to the nature of modern digital apps, there is room for — and great importance in — performing expert-based exploratory tests at various stages of your DevOps pipeline in order to maximize product value, discover user-experience-related issues that cannot be covered by automation, or, when covered by automation later in the process, are too risky to handle.

CHAPTER ELEVEN

Benefits of Using Emulators and Simulators Throughout the DevOps Pipeline

BY ROY NURIEL

ROY NURIEL has over 15 years of experience in the quality assurance domain, specializing in Enterprise Software. Over the course of his career, his roles have spanned across engineering, product delivery and product management. Roy spearheaded complex projects as an innovation lead, growing ideas into market leading solutions, and is an expert in software quality, application lifecycle management (ALM) and end-to-end IT Management.

Prior to joining Perfecto Mobile, Roy held several senior positions at HP Software and Mercury, and was responsible for HP Software, ALM, and automation products. In his last role, he was responsible for building a new product line that addressed agile processes and other modern development practices.

Roy holds a B.Sc. in Computer Science from the Hebrew University in Israel.

INTRO

Agility and velocity force organizations to debate what the best platforms are for testing in each phase of their development lifecycle. There are options to choose from at each step, as well as which testing type to use, especially on mobile. Real devices, on the one hand, come with great value and benefits but also with their own set of costs. Emulators and simulators are also beneficial and can deliver unique value to both developers and testers, but also have drawbacks.

VIRTUAL DEVICES – EMULATORS AND SIMULATORS

In this chapter we will refer to emulators and simulators as "virtual devices". Both solutions virtualize mobile devices; however, there are differences between the two.

An **emulator** is a desktop application that completely virtualizes all aspects of a real device, both hardware and operating system. It allows the user to validate apps in as close a manner as possible to real devices.

Simulators don't mimic the hardware and the operating system. They provide an environment where the user can validate application flows; however, applications will not run in a true production environment.

A flight simulator gives you an experience like that of a pilot; however, it doesn't transport you from point A to B. For that to happen, you'd need a flight emulator.

While simulators and emulators aren't the same, in the mobile testing space, they are used (in most cases) for the same purposes and use cases. For simplicity's sake, we will refer to both as "virtual devices" in this chapter.

WHAT ARE THE ADVANTAGES OF VIRTUAL DEVICES?

To understand when virtual devices should be used, one should first understand their advantages:

1. **Variety** — One instance of a virtual device can virtualize a large variety of devices and operating system permutations. This capability allows users

to validate very easily on multiple platforms as well on cases requiring specific device/OS combinations. In addition, there are platforms that are only supported (for development and testing purposes), as of now, through virtual devices. An example of this situation is the Apple watch.

2. **Price** — Virtual device solutions are cheaper than real devices by a wide margin. This applies to both local and cloud solutions. The need to drive testing early in the development process requires teams to scale and test more. In large organizations, if each developer wants to run a set of validations pre-commit, this requires a large number of devices to execute on. The economics of running against real devices may not make sense at such a scale when virtual devices will allow the organization to scale and execute earlier in the process.

3. **Back to the same state and baseline** — With virtual devices, you can always start from the same device state. Achieving this with real devices may require doing a factory reset, which can take a lot of time and effort. The fact that the virtual device always starts from the same point helps, in many cases, to increase the reliability of automated test execution since there are no "surprises" and the device is always ready for execution in the way tests were designed; for example, the device will not be locked by another user.

REAL DEVICE ADVANTAGES

1. **The real thing** — While virtual devices are good for basic validations, to really validate that an application works, there is a need to run tests against real devices. While virtual devices can be very helpful to validate functional flows on the "happy path" (the main flow of the application rather than validations that try to see how the application handles negative and extreme cases) there may be cases of false positives, meaning that while tests may pass, in reality, there may be issues with the application (see examples below).

2. **User Interface (UI) validations** — User interface validation should be done on real devices to validate the accuracy and color of the UI (example below). In addition, there are usability issues that are very easy to find while working on a real device (unlike virtual devices). In most

cases, where there is a need to enter input from the keyboard, the latter overlays the app, unlike virtual devices where the keyboard is presented next to the device interface.

3. **Performance testing** — Real devices provide more accurate and reliable performance measurements on transaction times. In addition to the implications specific hardware has on performance, virtual devices also render the UI differently.

4. **Hardware- and sensor- related validations** — Common use cases that can be virtualized are ones that require interaction with device hardware and sensors (such as camera, accelerometer and biometrics); in some cases, the behavior of real and virtual devices may differ.

Mobile testing lab triangle

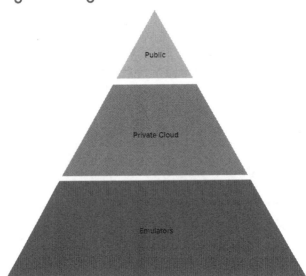

10% — Public Cloud

- Extend coverage — specific devices/models

- Burst testing — extend the private cloud solution

30% — Private Cloud — Real devices

- Complete functional coverage

- Performance testing

60% — Virtual devices

- CI test automation — scale in parallel

- Functional and unit UI tests

A few examples of differences between a virtual device (left side) and a real device (right side):

1. **Pixel 2 emulator vs. real Pixel 2 device** — differences in Twitter icon

2. **UI differences** — forgotten password page differences between real device and emulator

3. **Functional behavior differences** — Text box length limitation is ignored (highlighted in red) on emulator while blocked from exceeding 50 characters on a real device

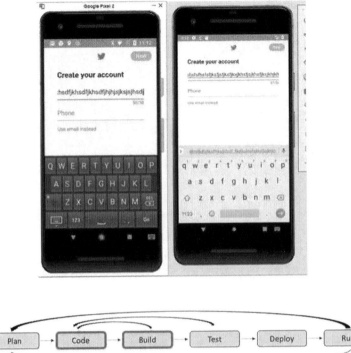

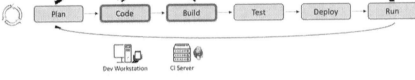

VIRTUAL DEVICES – MAIN USE CASES:

1. Local development and validation — Developers and testers use virtual devices on their local machines for development, debugging, and local validations. In the last case, most common IDEs for native applications come with virtual device tools as part of the basic installation. Xcode comes with simulator functionality while Android Studio comes with an emulator; both became stable and mature in the last few years and each has a large variety of capabilities for advanced validations.

2. Continuous Integration testing — The major use case for virtual device labs is for continuous integration (CI) testing. The increasing adoption of

DevOps and agile methodologies drives teams to test more in the early stages of the development process. New test automation frameworks that are more aligned to developers' skills and tools, such as Espresso and XCUITest, help development teams to increase their test automation coverage; however, to run these tests there is a need for a proper execution environment — a lab for those tests to run against. These automated tests can run either in the pre-commit phase, executing a set of tests for fast quick validation prior to committing or merging code, or triggered through the CI a few times a day, providing quick value to development teams on recent code changes.

WHAT IS THE RIGHT MIX?

Since test activities happen from early development stages all the way to deployment and monitoring of the application, there is a need for both types of platforms — real and virtual.

Below is a proposal on how to build the right mix for each one of the phases in the application lifecycle.

Code —

* Local validation — Developers should validate code during the development phase, either with a local device or virtual device (which in most cases are part of the developer's IDE). In the case of UI validation, it is recommended to validate the new UI on real devices rather than virtual ones to make sure that the outcome looks as expected.

* Pre-commit validation — Execution on Unit and UI Unit tests should run, in most cases, against virtual devices (90%). In addition, there are cases where the developers make changes in components which, based on their knowledge and experience, will behave differently on real devices — in those cases, it is recommended to give developers on-demand tools to select which tests they want to run and select the platform to run against — either virtual or real.

Build —

Depending on team maturity, teams run the CI process one or more time a day. The goal is to build a mix that allows scalability while providing good coverage and insights on end user experience. To allow scale of execution and parallel validation for multiple developers and teams at the same time, a typical CI mix might look like this:

- Commit job — Will run for every commit a developer makes, executing a basic sanity check to make sure the change didn't break the build or introduce a significant regression. Due to the need to run this job at scale (every commit), these tests should run on a virtual device.

- Multi-merge validation — Job that validates the last X commits and tests if one of them broke the build or introduced a regression. Usually, this type of job will run every few hours/X number of code commits. This job runs more tests to provide larger coverage; here, we start to introduce real devices into the CI — the mix should be 70% virtual and 30% real devices

- Night job — This job runs regression tests and extends coverage. In this case, tests will run against real devices.

Test — Additional test activities that run outside the CI process will run on real devices. Here, the goal is to validate and get the complete end-user experience, functional flow coverage, UI validation, and performance testing. All tests (100%) should run on real devices.

Monitoring — While there are organizations that have Real User Monitoring (RUM) solutions that run on real devices, there is also value in synthetic monitoring: execution of single-user automated tests that measure app performance running every 10–15 minutes. In this case, to get the most accurate results, the best practice is to use real devices.

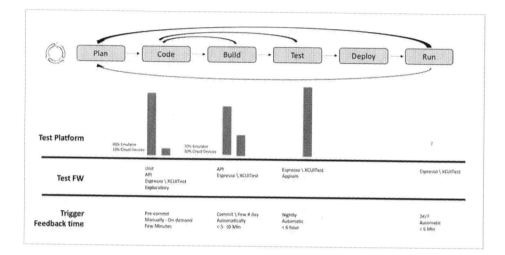

SUMMARY

The key to implementing continuous testing and maximizing velocity in the mobile space is to have the perfect balance between emulators, simulators and real devices. Each of these extremely different platforms brings unique values and benefits to the developers and testers; however, these values are maximized when used in the right phase of the development life cycle. Ensure that you properly plan the test coverage, the platform under test, and the testing tools throughout your continuous testing activities and continuously monitor the mobile space since new devices, as well as new versions of emulators and simulators, are released constantly to the market.

SECTION 2

Continuous Testing for Web Apps

CHAPTER TWELVE

Recommended Practices for Testing Responsive Web Apps (RWD)

INTRODUCTION

When was the last time you visited a website on your mobile device and it didn't render correctly? Maybe the page wasn't laid out right or the text was too small to read? Probably recently, right? You are not alone. According to Criteo's State of Mobile Commerce report, today, 4 out of 10 web interactions take place on multiple devices — but nearly half of internet users complain that the websites they use aren't optimized for mobile.

One of the primary problems with mobile browsing regards the lack of responsive web designs (RWD). For organizations, RWD can make or break their business. It provides trust, authority and brand awareness, and helps firms meet that elusive goal: an engaging and seamless mobile experience.

Borrowing a phrase from Ethan Marcotte's book *Responsive Web Design*, "the best websites respond to changes in browser width by adjusting the placement of design elements to fit in the available space[1]." For example, if you open a responsive site on a desktop and then change the size of the browser window, the content should dynamically arrange itself optimally for the screen.

---

1   Responsive web design book — https://abookapart.com/products/responsive-web-design

Unfortunately, this process is not as easy as you may think; it is the web developer who is tasked with making this process seamless. It's his or her responsibility to ensure that the performance, functionalities, and visual layouts of websites are consistent across all digital platforms and various user conditions. When you factor in the continuous testing of new features and guaranteeing your website is working optimally on all browsers, devices, operating systems (OSes) and carrier networks, RWD can be a daunting task. Any glitch can significantly affect the user experience and negatively impact a brand.

THE KEY TO TACKLING THE CHALLENGE

DevOps teams should start their journey towards good RWD by embarking on a fact-finding mission. Obtaining the most recent mobile and web traffic analysis provides teams with data about popular locations, browsers, and mobile OS/devices that were used to access their website. Once you understand traffic patterns across your browsers and mobile platforms, you can start to consider a coverage plan.

This is a good start; however, it does not factor in the larger market, your competitors, or the newest platforms and configurations. Instead, a more comprehensive program is required: one which prioritizes continuous testing across multiple platforms.

DevOps is a key enabler for continuous delivery (CD) of innovative features and products to end users. To make it work continuously, teams must automate their entire process as much as possible — from development, through build acceptance testing, functional and non-functional testing and deployment to production. In this context, RWD projects should apply the same rule: maximum automation coverage.

To succeed, DevOps should automate what's right and continuously execute it upon any code commit. Here are 6 recommended practices DevOps teams can take to ensure their sites are optimized:

Test Scenario	Test Description
Visual Testing	Assure RWD content looks right on any screen and platform.
Client side performance testing	Test and measure the time it takes your website's objects to render on screens and optimize the content size accordingly.
Navigation testing	Assure that the site performs the expected function correctly (i.e. Log-in functions well across web and mobile platforms).
User condition testing	Test your site across platforms for real user conditions such as incoming calls, ads, popups and other interruptions.
Accessibility testing	Comply with the accessibility standards across mobile and web, and assure that your RWD site adheres to the guidelines through voice, visual and other engagement methods.
Platform coverage	Use analytics to test your website against all relevant devices, browsers and OS versions covering screen sizes and resolutions in various conditions and locations.

ADD VISUAL TESTING TO YOUR TEST AUTOMATION CODE

A responsive website will display content differently when screens resize and user conditions change. To account for this extra layer of complexity, app development and testing teams should combine various validations to ensure that when the context changes, the viewports also change. Doing this will also make sure that the content being displayed is accurate, not condensed, and that it does not cause usability glitches.

In addition, add relevant UI checkpoint validations that can compare the visual display on the screens when events occur. This will quickly highlight issues and shorten the feedback loop to the developers, resulting in faster resolution and quicker release.

Some important check points to consider, from a visual standpoint, when testing responsive websites:

- Alignment of text, controls and images
- Text, images, controls and frames do not run into the edges of the screen
- Font sizes, styles and colors are consistent for each type of text
- Typed text (data entry) scrolls and displays properly
- Pages should be readable on all resolutions and screen orientations
- Content defined 'important' needs to be visible at all breakpoints

EXECUTE CLIENT-SIDE PERFORMANCE TESTING

Web performance is a key aspect of a RWD test plan that ensures a great user experience. Remember that RWD targets a variety of combinations such as Safari on specific Mac OS versions, Edge on Windows 10, etc. As such, DevOps teams should continuously test the time it takes content and images to load on the various viewports. Teams should also look carefully at overall website performance and how it varies on different platforms and under specific network conditions.

Two of the most common issues with RWD sites are:

- Lack of large content compression in the website, which causes slow page load times
- Failure to measure object sizes and make sure they are customized to the screen sizes on which they appear

There are methods of measuring client-side performance, such as load timer measurement, reviewing HAR files, DOM object tree scanning across platforms, and more.

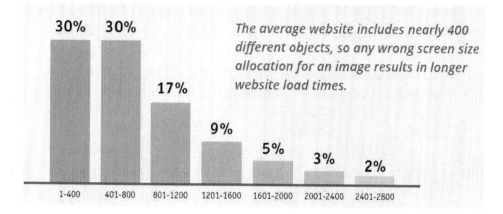

The average website includes nearly 400 different objects, so any wrong screen size allocation for an image results in longer website load times.

PERFORM NAVIGATION TESTING ACROSS PLATFORMS

The ability to track the journey a user takes when they interact with a brand online is paramount. They may start from a smartphone, move to a tablet and then to a desktop browser, or sometimes even reach your RWD site from a non-responsive site. From a testing perspective, these kinds of user paths need to be covered.

Navigation testing ensures that a user can successfully complete a full end-to-end run through your site. Testing screen orientations and other navigation elements, such as shortcuts, menus and other web elements, can improve the user experience when users access the site from a smaller screen. Remember, you need to make sure that the screen orientations on both mobile and desktop work well so that nothing breaks when moving from portrait to landscape and vice versa.

Google recommends the following practices when moving between screen sizes and devices and resizing windows:

- Create breakpoints based on content, never on specific devices, products or brands
- Design for the smallest mobile device first, then progressively enhance the experience as more screen real estate becomes available
- Keep lines of text to a maximum of 70–80 characters

Another tip is to test what happens when users transition between responsive and non-responsive web environments.

INTEGRATE REAL WORLD CONDITIONS INTO TESTING

Since RWD testing covers multiple mobile and desktop combinations, you need to guarantee that these environments[2] also mimic your users' daily, real-world conditions. It's recommended that you start by collaborating with marketing and business groups on target user data, including insights into who your target user is, where he/she lives, and what their network conditions are. Testing ideal "happy path" scenarios (i.e. strong Wi-Fi, full battery, no competing apps) will provide very limited insight into how your app will behave under real user conditions, so consider creating personas (profiles of your target customers) that account for complex, real world environments. Instead of running only functional tests such as log-in, search, payment and checkout under generic conditions, also test responsive websites against user conditions including location, preferred device(s), network coverage, and other apps running in the background. This will help ensure that your content is laid out correctly on any viewport.

RWD requires a constant network connection, so it's key to test real-world conditions both with internet connectivity and without, and test for the poor connectivity that occurs when moving through tunnels and switching to airplane mode. In today's competitive landscape, websites are also exposed

---

2   Perfecto's Wind Tunnel — https://www.perfectomobile.com/solutions/perfecto-wind-tunnel

to interruptions caused by web add-ons and adware pop-ups. Pop-up interruptions are one of the most common web "user conditions" to test for as they can block user flows within the web page and cover up important content. In such cases, dev and testing teams need to assess the user impact of pop-ups. We all know they can be quite disruptive. Unfortunately, blocking ads does not solve the problem because the ad vendor will sense that ad blockers are on and will pop up on a different page. As part of user condition testing — especially for mobile — we recommend mimicking pop-ups and add-ons as well as incoming events such as calls and security alerts. Assess their impact on user experience and make sure they do not cover any critical web content.

PERFORM ACCESSIBILITY TESTING ACROSS MOBILE AND WEB

Web accessibility means opening up the web to everyone, especially those with disabilities, allowing them to perceive, understand, navigate and interact with the web. This includes all types of disability, including auditory, physical, speech, cognitive, and neurological. Most websites have some sort of accessibility barrier that makes it difficult for a person with a disability to use their site. Web accessibility helps by making sure that people do not face these roadblocks when accessing the web, regardless of their disability.

Today, organizations are struggling to automate and perform, per each release cycle, the accessibility tests which are necessary according to WCAG[3] as well as other requirements. Whereas there are tools for web such as WAVE[4] (and others), for mobile, which involve more advanced interfaces such as voice and sensors, it is much harder to comply and automate testing for all requirements. Despite these automation challenges, it is critical to perform — at least manually — most accessibility tests on your RWD at critical product milestones to assure no regressions are found when a new browser OS is introduced, or a new mobile OS is released. It is also important to follow innovations in the marketplace and open-source community and identify

---

3   WCAG reference — https://www.w3.org/WAI/WCAG20/quickref/

4   Git example by Amir Rozenberg on how to use WAVE accessibility with chrome — https://github. com/AmirAtPerfecto/ChromeAccessibilityTestWithWAVE

new tools that can help reduce some of the manual testing. An example of this kind of tool is the Chrome's built-in developer tool, called Lighthouse[5]. Using this tool to perform audits on your web page can produce useful accessibility and quality reports related to your RWD site.

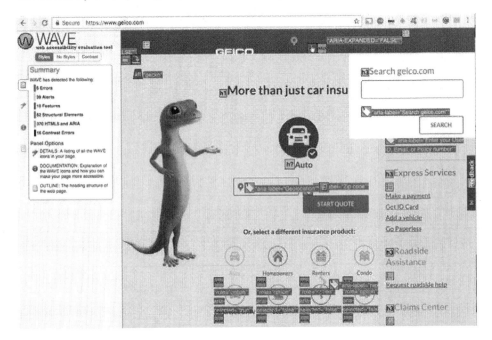

DETERMINE THE RIGHT PLATFORMS FOR TESTING

The mobile landscape currently includes a nearly eight-device-long list of leading smartphones. What's more, with the extensive use of tablets, which have unique screen sizes that impact content layout as well as site load times and performance, teams need to incorporate relevant iPads and Android tablets into the mix to maximize mobile coverage. As a result, determining the right platforms to test on can be challenging.

---

5   Google Lighthouse — https://developers.google.com/web/tools/lighthouse/

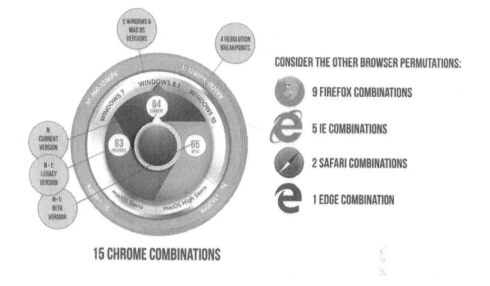

CONSIDER THE OTHER BROWSER PERMUTATIONS:

9 FIREFOX COMBINATIONS

5 IE COMBINATIONS

2 SAFARI COMBINATIONS

1 EDGE COMBINATION

15 CHROME COMBINATIONS

To help mobile teams properly mitigate user-experience issues and ensure high quality across all platforms and geographies, they should take advantage of reference guides[6] that outline the requirements for digital quality testing. This will help them build an up-to-date device lab that covers the latest market platforms and operating systems (OS).

Summary

Coverage Levels	Mobile Device Coverage	Desktop Web (Only) Coverage	Responsive Web Design Coverage
Essential	Top 10	Top 10	Top 20 (Essential Web + Mobile)
Enhanced	Top 25 (Essential +15)	Top 22 (Essential +12)	Top 47 (Enhanced Web + Mobile)
Extended	Top 32 (Enhanced +7)	Top 33 (Enhanced +11)	Top 65 (Extended Web + Mobile)

RWD is a challenge, but in a hyper competitive market — where user experience so often wins the day — it's vital. "Mobile First" is often the rallying call of web designers, meaning that they design first for mobile, then for other

---

6   Perfecto's Factors Magazine — https://info.perfectomobile.com/factors-magazine.html

platforms. The truth is that we should be designing for 'users first' — and that's where RWD comes in. Ensuring a superior user experience, regardless of the platform they're using, can be make-or-break for brands.

SUMMARY

Expanding your digital footprint across every browser, device, and user scenario depends onfollowing best practices and using the rights tools and processes. In this chapter, I've covered some best practices, but delivering great responsive websites goes beyond these. Don't discount the importance of correct image formats, best CSS and other coding practices, and proper page design. These alone require a great deal of planning and execution.

Add Visual Testing to Your Test Automation Code

Do Client-Side Performance Testing

Test Your Navigation Across Platforms

Integrate Real User Conditions into Your Testing

Implement Accessibility Testing Continuously

Use Analytics to Establish Your Digital Test Coverage Plan

When it comes to testing, a successful RWD release begins with an optimized test plan that covers the right platforms. Once a digital quality test plan is in place and teams are actively managing and maintaining it, teams should adopt a continuous quality strategy that relies on robust test automation, including both visual object analysis and DOM native object identification. Teams that have access to a test report for all digital platforms will be able to address RWD issues and maintain the RWD code to support new features, new platforms, and other market changes as they occur. If you have the right test environment, your responsive web journey will be a rewarding one for both you and your users.

CHAPTER THIRTEEN

A Complete Guide for Testing Progressive Web Applications (PWAs)

INTRODUCTION

The digital space continues to reinvent itself with the objectives of advanced user experience, simplicity, and seamless deployment across platforms. This area is quite mature with respect to 3 types of digital apps:

1. Native iOS and Android apps

2. Traditional web and mobile web apps (.com, m.dot)

3. Responsive web (RWD)

As of the writing this chapter, Google's continuous leadership in the market is reflected in the evolution of a new type of app called the PWA (Progressive Web App). The goal of progressive web applications is to bring the RWD experience to the next level regardless of the platform on which users consume it — mobile or web.

There are more early adopters than usual for this new app type, such as Mozilla, Google and Microsoft[1], while Apple is lagging a bit with the Safari support.

This chapter will provide insights into questions such as: What is a PWA? How is a PWA built? What are the benefits of developing a PWA? And finally — how are these apps tested? Read on.

---

1 Microsoft app store support for PWAs — https://www.windowscentral.com/first-batch-windows-10-progressive-web-apps-here

THE MOTIVATION TO DEVELOP A PWA

When organizations moved from .com and m.dot web sites to RWD, their goal and belief was that it would be the "final" cross-platform solution they would need to develop and maintain. As mobile technology continued to grow, end-user experience expectations grew as well. Suddenly, RWD seemed like an incomplete solution.

To highlight a few gaps between RWD and native mobile apps, we can include most sensor-based use cases such as camera, network dependency, mobile notifications, and more.

Trying to sustain a digital business that includes a mix of native mobile apps *and* responsive web is quite difficult, expensive, and often fails to offer a synchronized experience between the 2 types of app.

PWAs[2] aim to build some key mobile native capabilities on top of a web application to merge these two digital channels into one. The benefits of such a change are numerous:

- Consistent user experience across mobile and web for any form factor (same as RWD)
- Single code base to maintain and develop (same as RWD)
- **Enhanced web user experience** when consumed from a mobile device (push notifications, sensor support and more)
- **No need to install** an app on the mobile device through the app store. This saves deployment time and certification time.
- **Enhanced load** times and responsiveness of the PWA[3] when used from a mobile device (app shortcut, caching)
- **Connectivity independence** due to offline mode and service workers (see next section)
- Highly **discoverable** due to the PWA manifest file and service workers, which facilitates indexing by search engines

---

2   Dzone Blog — The rise of PWAs — https://dzone.com/articles/the-rise-of-progressive-web-apps-and-the-impact-on

3   Google developer guide to PWA — https://developers.google.com/web/progressive-web-apps/

- **Shareable app** via link vs. a need to install a native app from the app store

PROGRESSIVE WEB APP ARCHITECTURE

To understand a bit more about the new technology, let's look at how a PWA is built.

PWAs leverage two main architectural features: service workers and manifest files.

Here are some basic technical details that need to be known by both developers and testers of a PWA.

- **Web App Manifest** — this is the file within the PWA that describes the app, provides metadata specific to the app such as icons, splash screens, and more. Below, see an example Google[4] offers for such a descriptor file (JSON).

---

4 Google PWA App Manifest — https://developers.google.com/web/fundamentals/web-app-manifest/

```json
{
  "short_name": "Eran K.",
  "name": "Eran Kinsbruner PWA Manifest",
  "icons": [
  {
  "src": "Erank-icon-1x.png",
  "type": "image/png",
  "sizes": "48x48"
  },
  {
  "src": "Erank-icon-2x.png",
  "type": "image/png",
  "sizes": "96x96"
  },
  ],
  "start_url": "index.html?launcher=true"
}
```

Once you have defined a manifest.json file for your PWA, there needs to be a Start URL indicator to tell the app what to do when launched.

Defining a start URL typically looks like this:

```
"start_url": "/?utm_source=homescreen"
```

Google allows PWA developers to customize their app and change background colors, add a splash screen, enforce a specific orientation, such as landscape, and more. In addition, it allows the developer to set whether the app will launch from within the device's native browser or as a standalone app, hiding the browser UI.

```
"display": "standalone"
```

Once the manifest file is developed, Google and Mozilla enable developers and testers to test the validity of this important file. As can be seen in the screenshot below, when using the Google dev tool (Lighthouse), developers can load their manifest file from the Application tab and verify that all properties are correctly set and that theme colors and other properties are as expected. In addition, Google specifically offers a full PWA checklist to cover the specific functional areas of these apps.

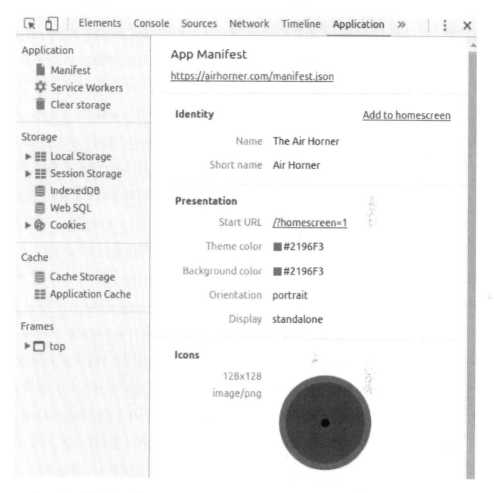

- **Service Workers**[5] give developers the ability to programmatically manage the caching of assets and control the experience when there is no network connectivity.

Here is how Google's development portal defines a service worker script — "A service worker is a script that your browser runs in the background, separate from a web page, opening the door to features that don't need a

---

5 Google PWA service worker definition — https://developers.google.com/web/fundamentals/primers/service-workers/

web page or user interaction. Today, service workers already include features like push notifications[6] and background sync. In the future, service workers might support other things like periodic sync or geofencing. The core feature discussed in this tutorial is the ability to intercept and handle network requests, including programmatically managing a cache of responses."

```
// Check that service workers are supported, if so, progres-
sively
// enhance and add push messaging support, otherwise continue
without it.
if ('serviceWorker' in navigator) {
navigator.serviceWorker.register('/service-worker.  js')
.then(initialiseState);
} else {
console.warn('Service workers aren't supported in
this browser.');
}
});
```

TESTING 101 FOR PWAS

In this section, we will drill down into the specifics of testing a PWA and what test types are required as a superset to existing RWD apps.

The uniqueness of PWA requires an additional focus on specific components such as the manifest file and service workers. Once these two components are validated, testing the app across different devices and form factors for the functionality of offline, push, and other features supported by the app, is obviously required.

---

6   Service worker push notification — https://developers.google.com/web/updates/2015/03/push-no-tifications-on-the-open-web

Here is a recommended checklist for a PWA test plan

Step 1: Perform complete validation of the **manifest.json** file — check for load on supported browsers (Opera, Firefox, Chrome, soon Safari)

Step 2: Test and debug your supported **service workers.** This can be done through the Chrome internals page[7] (see next image taken from Twitter PWA). In this section, enable and disable each service worker and ensure they behave as expected. Commonly, service workers enable things like offline mode and registering the app for push notifications — perform these validations across mobile and web.

---

7   Chrome internals service worker page URL — chrome://serviceworker-internals/

Step 3: PWA mobile-specific **capabilities.** PWAs add support for camera (scan QR codes e.g.), voice injection (record a memo), push notifications, and more. Make sure to cover these use cases based on your app across mobile devices — these will be an additional set of functional tests only relevant to mobile devices.

Step 4: Since a **PWA** is a superset of a **RWD,** all the RWD testing pillars apply here. This means you need to consider:

1. UI and visual/layout testing across multiple form factors

2. Performance and rendering of the content across platforms (load the proper code and images to the correct platform — mobile vs. web)

3. Network related testing — in addition to the offline mode that is covered by service workers, make sure to cover the app's behavior under

various network conditions (packet loss, flight mode, latency %, 3G, 4G, 5G, etc.)

4. Functionality of the entire page's user flows across platforms, screen sizes, and resolutions

Figure 1: 1st Step in Creating a PWA Native Mobile Extension on Android

Figure 2: 2nd Step once Shortcut Added, Launch Twitter Lite (Android)

Figure 3: Android application (APK) installed on the device, ready for automation

Apple iOS, with its Safari browser, started supporting PWAs in iOS 11.3; however, as in reference 7, the maturity is still low, and compared to iOS native apps, there are a few limitations and quality issues that require attention. Some of the issues reported across apps are due to PWA teams' lack of testing; others are attributed to the maturity of PWA support on iOS.

In addition — and this is a very important distinction from Android — for iOS, there is no installable IPA per PWA, as opposed to Android, which installs an APK file (not through the App Store). An iOS PWA is installed as a subset of the Safari browser with extended web and mobile permissions. Still, with this in mind, a test automation engineer needs the ability to launch the PWA from the iOS device home screen, something that Selenium cannot do on its own — only Appium can.

Here are some of the limitations iOS PWAs have compared to iOS native apps:

- The app can only store 50 Mb of offline data and files
- If the user doesn't use the app for a few weeks, iOS will delete the app's files. The icon will still be there on the home screen and, when accessed, the app will be downloaded again
- No access to certain features such as Bluetooth, serial, beacons, Touch ID, Face ID, ARKit, altimeter sensor, battery information
- No ability to execute code while in the background
- No access to private information (contacts, background location) and no access to native social apps
- No access to in-app payments and many other Apple-based services
- On iPad, no ability to work with side or split views sharing the screen with other apps — PWAs always take up the whole screen
- No push notifications, no icon badge or Siri integration

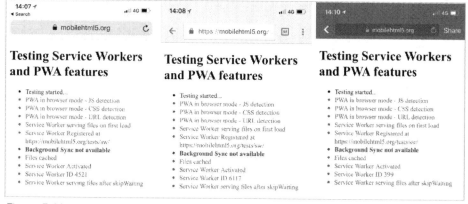

Figure 4: Apple iPad running Trivago progressive web app[8]

5. Differences between browsers and platforms must be covered as well. If you consider iOS vs. Android, Samsung's browser vs. Facebook's built-in browsers, etc., these have implications on the number of instances or copies a PWA app can have on a device[9]. With this in mind, caching, service workers per app instance, and overall user experience needs to be validated.

Figure 5: Various instances of a web page across in-app browsers and native browsers.

8   Medium article covering Apple support for PWA — https://medium.com/@firt/progressive-web-apps-on-ios-are-here-d00430dee3a7

9   PWA on iOS quality concerns https://medium.com/@firt/pwas-are-coming-to-ios-11-3-cupertino-we-have-a-problem-2ff49fd7d6ea

Step 5: Handle **test** automation code and **object** repository. PWAs are JavaScript apps that have different deployment output on Android vs. iOS. On Android devices, the "Add to Home Screen" of a PWA will install an Android .apk file to the device application repository. On iOS, the "Add to Home Screen" will add a web shortcut that is actually a hybrid application running in an iOS environment without the Safari browser.

To test both iOS and Android PWA apps, the developers and testers will need a proper object spy that can identify both the app shell objects and the WebView objects within the app; launching the .apk and the iOS PWA needs to be handled outside of the Selenium test code since this is impossible to do with Selenium. As of publishing time for this book, Appium's object spy for Android and IOS is not yet able to properly automate PWA apps. Perfecto was able to create an extension to Appium that allows launching the app on real iOS devices and identifying and interacting with the app objects.

From a test automation strategy perspective, there is a clear way of automating PWA apps.

Leverage **Selenium** for most web portions of the app and extend via **Appium** to the mobile native pieces, such as launching of the app, handling pop-ups, push notifications, and other mobile native activities. In some cases, it is also recommended to leverage visual-based testing tools to either launch a PWA or validate the UX/UI across the different platforms. This strategy is a new way of thinking about web and mobile app test automation. Until PWA technology arrived, practitioners had a clear tool strategy that stated **web testing = Selenium, mobile app testing = Appium;** now, PWA combines both frameworks and means engineers need to think **PWA testing = Selenium + Appium.**

For an application named 'Smaller Pics,' as an example, a test automation engineer will need to add the following code:

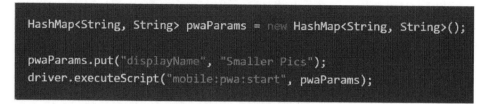

```
HashMap<String, String> pwaParams = new HashMap<String, String>();

pwaParams.put("displayName", "Smaller Pics");
driver.executeScript("mobile:pwa:start", pwaParams);
```

Once testing is complete, to close the PWA iOS app, a user would need to use this command:

```
driver.executeScript("mobile:pwa:stop");
```

From an object locator strategy, since iOS PWA is a hybrid app, all internal objects are WebView (DOM) elements while the native wrapper consists of native elements which for iOS, for example, are XCUIElementTypeWebView

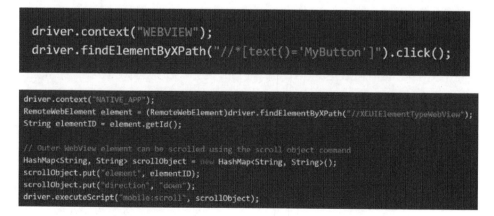

```
driver.context("WEBVIEW");
driver.findElementByXPath("//*[text()='MyButton']").click();
```

```
driver.context("NATIVE_APP");
RemoteWebElement element = (RemoteWebElement)driver.findElementByXPath("//XCUIElementTypeWebView");
String elementID = element.getId();

// Outer WebView element can be scrolled using the scroll object command
HashMap<String, String> scrollObject = new HashMap<String, String>();
scrollObject.put("element", elementID);
scrollObject.put("direction", "down");
driver.executeScript("mobile:scroll", scrollObject);
```

For Android PWAs, the story is quite similar. Developers and testers for these apps can leverage Android Studio's device monitor to address object identification. From a test automation strategy, teams need to consider 2 methods for automating the PWAs on the mobile front:

1. Leverage visual testing, as shown in the screenshot below, along with Selenium (Perfecto offers these capabilities)

2. Develop a dedicated layer or set of commands that can handle the over-lay of the PWA on top of the iOS Safari browser and the Android APK, as mentioned above. See the Appium test code below as an example.

Step 6: Make sure to cover, step by step, Google's recommended checklist[10] for PWAs since it includes a lot of the core functionalities of these apps and can ensure not only good functionality when followed, but also great SEO and high rankings in Google's search results. See below a sample result from auditing the PWA Twitter app using Google's Lighthouse tool.

---

10 Google PWA testing checklist — https://developers.google.com/web/progressive-web-apps/ checklist

Progressive Web App

These checks validate the aspects of a Progressive Web App, as specified by the baseline PWA Checklist.

(64)

4 Failed Audits

▾ Does not respond with a 200 when offline   ✕
If you're building a Progressive Web App, consider using a service worker so that your app can work offline.
Learn more.
WARNING: You may be failing this check because your test URL (https://twitter.com/ek121268) was redirected to
"https://mobile.twitter.com/ek121268". Try testing the second URL directly.

▾ User will not be prompted to Install the Web App   ✕
Browsers can proactively prompt users to add your app to their homescreen, which can lead to higher
engagement. Learn more.
Failures: No manifest was fetched, Service worker does not successfully serve the manifest's start_url.

▾ Is not configured for a custom splash screen   ✕
A themed splash screen ensures a high-quality experience when users launch your app from their
homescreens. Learn more.
Failures: No manifest was fetched.

▾ Address bar does not match brand colors   ✕
The browser address bar can be themed to match your site. Learn more.
Failures: No manifest was fetched, No '<meta name="theme-color">' tag found.

▸ 7 Passed Audits

▸ Additional items to manually check

Accessibility

These checks highlight opportunities to improve the accessibility of your web app. Only a subset of accessibility
issues can be automatically detected so manual testing is also encouraged.

(50)

Elements Use Attributes Correctly

These are opportunities to improve the configuration of your HTML elements.

▸ Image elements do not have [alt] attributes   ✕

SUMMARY

PWAs are a new and advanced type of application that is emerging to enrich end user experience and provide additional mobile-specific capabilities on top of web sites. While the objectives of such apps are clear and the rush to adopt these apps is beginning, it is important to understand that with any new technology there are growing pains. Based on my experience, these apps have a great future ahead of them; however, the community, along with the browser vendors — Google, Apple, Mozilla and others — need to close key gaps with respect to test automation, standardization of PWA development across platforms and browsers, and implementation of sensors that are currently missing, in order to make these apps ready for prime time.

Rich and mature mobile native apps support AR/VR, face recognition, fingerprint login, and more; as PWA catches up in terms of functionality, it becomes an obvious choice for organizations to make the switch. Finally, for organizations that already have an RWD site in place, it should be quite easy to make the leap towards a PWA by developing the app shell, manifest file and relevant service workers; therefore, it is a good business decision to move in that direction today, just as many other organizations have done already.

There are a few online resources on top of the ones mentioned earlier in this chapter that can provide mobile feature support[11] on desktop browsers — these are worth tracking as the technology evolves.

---

11   Mobile supported features in web — https://whatwebcando.today/

CHAPTER FOURTEEN

Intuitive Automation Framework Development

BY NIKOLAY ADVOLODKIN

NIKOLAY ADVOLODKIN is a seasoned IT Professional, Test Automation Expert, and Quality Assurance Innovator whose dedication to innovation and progress has earned him the reputation as a strategist in the information technology space. Throughout the span of his technical career, he has not only cultivated a wealth of experience, he has received extensive acclaim for his continual success. Most recently, he was  named one of 33 Test Automation Leaders to follow in 2017 by TechBeacon.com; according to Udemy.com, he is also the #1 Selenium Webdriver Instructor across the globe, educating 50,000+ students on the ins and outs of test automation from 120+ different countries.

Currently, Nikolay proudly serves as the CEO and Test Automation Instructor at UltimateQA (www.ultimateqa.com). Furthermore, he is a frequent contributor at SimpleProgrammer.com and TechBeacon.com. He has also been a speaker at multiple conferences.

When he isn't teaching people how to be automated software testing masters or revolutionizing the test automation world as we know it, Nikolay Advolodkin enjoys exercising, self-development, and travel. He is also an avid entrepreneur with an unquenchable thirst for knowledge.

INTUITIVE AUTOMATION FRAMEWORK DEVELOPMENT

Have you ever struggled to create an automation framework for executing automated acceptance tests? According to a recent survey of 650+ Automation Engineers, the number two problem for these engineers is the ability to create an automation framework. The number one problem is that they don't have enough knowledge to do automation well. In fact, 81.3% of engineers struggle with these two problems.

What if there was a way to solve both problems — at the same time — with a simple technique? Well, there is a way: a technique known as Acceptance Test Driven Automation (ATDA). This approach can solve the top two problems that automation engineers struggle with when developing automation frameworks.

When used appropriately, ATDA will help you to:

- Create an automation framework quickly — in less than an hour
- Remove the insane learning curve required to create an excellent automation framework
- Make test automation much easier

In this chapter, you will learn why the number two reason that automation engineers struggle with automation is framework design and development. Next, you will learn what Acceptance Test Driven Automation is, how to use it, and how it can solve the problems that 81% of automation engineers face. You will leave this chapter with an ability to create a production-ready test automation framework in under sixty minutes.

Why is it so hard to create an automation framework?

This is a critical question to analyze. I will take you through multiple scenarios to convey why creating a robust and long-lived automation framework is just not intuitive.

Keep in mind that the examples below are not intended to criticize any single person. The problem is not the developer of the code but the fact that framework development is not intuitive if you don't approach it from the correct point of view. Scrutinize the code and ask yourself "why does this happen"?

Below is an example of an automated acceptance browser test from an automation engineer with several years of experience.

```
 1   [Test, TestCaseSource(nameof(DataSource))]
 2   [Category("LL"), Category("Cog")]
 3   public void RespondToAllItems(string accNumber, string dataSubject)
 4   {
 5
 6       #region Parameters
 7       //if (accessionNumber.Contains(TestContext.DataRow["AccessionNumber"].ToString()))
 8       //{
 9       accNumber = accNumber;
10       string subject = dataSubject;
11       string loginId = DataLookup.GetLoginIdByAccessionNumber(accNumber);
12       string username = DataLookup.GetUsernameByLoginId(loginId);
13       string password = DataLookup.GetPasswordByStateCode(
14           DataLookup.GetStateCodeByLoginId(username));
15       string schoolName = DataLookup.GetSchoolNameByUserAndLogin(username, loginId);
16       string sessionNumber = DataLookup.GetSessionNumberBySchoolAndLogin(schoolName, loginId);
17       int lineNumber = DataLookup.GetBookletLineNumberByLoginId(loginId);
18       #endregion
19       #region Test Steps
20
21       Assessment assess = new Assessment(
22           UseAdminPageToGoToLocation(accNumber, loginId).Driver, true);
23
24       try
25       {
26           assess.AnswerNonReadingWritingItem(subject);
27           Reporter.LogTestStepAsPass("Responded to accession number " + assess.GetAccessionNumber()
28               + " for Item Type " + assess.itemTypeString);
29       }
30       catch (Exception ex)
31       {
32           ePScreenshot.SaveContentScreenshot(assess);
33           exceptionString = ex.ToString();
34           throw new Exception(exceptionString);
35       }
36       //    if (assess.itemTypeString == "Comp" ||
37       //        assess.itemTypeString == "CompR")
38       //    {
39       //        assess.PageWait(0);
40       //    }
41       //}
42       #endregion
43   }
```

What is this test case actually testing? It seems like it's trying to answer something that is not reading or writing. So, is it answering Spanish, Math, Geography or something else? You cannot answer any questions without inspecting the actual code.

Furthermore, this test also seems to pull in data, interact with the web application, create reports, and capture screenshots. If any of these responsibilities change, every single test that performs these actions will also need to change. Let's not even mention the fact that there are commented-out 'if' blocks in random places.

So, how did a "professional" automation engineer create such a confusing and poorly-written automated acceptance test?

This next piece of code is an example that I received from a test automation engineer with over 9 years of experience.

Sorry for the bad image, this is what I was given as a code sample from a "professional."

Do you have any idea what this automated acceptance test is actually validating? What requirements are satisfied with this test case? As with the previous example, you cannot answer these questions without spending a ton of time digging through every single method to understand what it is doing.

Even worse is the fact that this test exposes all of the web interactions inside the test. This means that when the inevitable change to the HTML page happens and you need to perform one softValidate() less or one click() more in some other step, you need to update every single test to reflect this change. This could mean several hundred updates due to a single change in the application under test.

As you can tell, it's not easy to write a robust, well written, durable automated acceptance test. Imagine how bad the test automation framework is if this is the state of the tests. How much value does this automation really provide to the employer?

WHAT IS THE FIRST STEP THAT YOU WILL TAKE TO CREATE AN AUTOMATED FRAMEWORK?

Just start automating test cases

This is a very common solution for automation engineers that have never designed an automation framework. If you are taking this approach, you are probably picking some manual test and trying to automate it. This is absolutely the worst approach.

First, you are reinventing the wheel. In today's time, there exists a test automation framework for every language binding. These test automation frameworks have been developed by very talented and experienced individuals with decades of experience. It's a massive mistake to assume that you can recreate something better.

Second, you need a test automation and framework development strategy. Test automation is extremely similar to software development. I would argue, in fact, that it's exactly the same. As a result, test automation must follow all of the design patterns and principles that software developers use. You cannot just start cowboy-coding and expect positive automation outcomes.

What if you have some experience with test automation frameworks?

Copy a framework you previously created

After years of experience on the job, as a wiser engineer, you will just copy the framework structure that you previously created at other jobs. Then, you'll modify the framework according to your new environment.

But how did you get to this framework architecture in the first place?

After years of doing this myself, working with other automation engineers, and teaching others test automation since 2013, I'll tell you how. You fail, for years at a time, through trial and error, stumbling onto an automation framework that you are actually happy with.

You can see that there's a reason why over 80% of automation engineers struggle with design and development of automation frameworks. It's a seriously complicated problem.

Acceptance Test Driven Automation

Acceptance Test Driven Automation (ATDA) is a technique for creating automation frameworks at light speed. ATDA will help anyone to intuitively build a test automation framework without requiring any previous knowledge. After learning this technique, you will be able to create a production-ready automation framework in less than an hour. Afterwards, you can push this framework into your CI system and start providing immediate value to your employer.

When used appropriately, ATDA will help you to:

- Create a production-quality automation framework quickly
- Develop extremely readable acceptance tests
- Design a logical framework architecture

I developed ATDA after learning how to use Test Driven Development (TDD) for the development of software systems. In TDD, you use unit tests to drive the development of the system that you want to design. Using TDD allows you, the developer, to create a system that is easy to test and that limits over-engineering. Since the tests — aka requirements — drive the design, it's harder to over-engineer. ATDA applies the same idea.

Using ATDA, you write acceptance tests to drive the development of your test automation framework. Acceptance Test Driven Automation, get it? If you are familiar with TDD you will notice the similarities. However, instead of using unit tests to develop your system under test, you will use acceptance tests to develop a test framework that will execute automation against your software under test (SUT).

This is different than Acceptance Test Driven Development (ATDD) because your automated acceptance tests aren't actually testing the system that you are developing. Rather, the acceptance tests drive the creation of the automation framework. This automation framework is then executed against some external application to test that application against requirements. However, we use those acceptance tests as a guide to framework design.

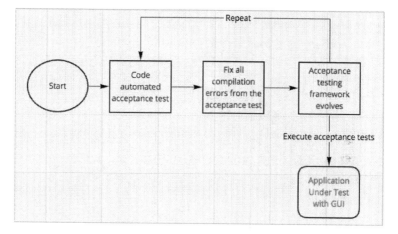

How to apply ATDA to framework development?

In this section, I will teach you the exact steps that you must follow to create the fastest production-ready acceptance automation framework that you have ever seen.

You will use this application for testing http://bit.ly/SimpleWebApp

It looks like the image below. A super-simple example just to keep the lessons easy.

Sample Application Lifecycle – Sprint 1

Sprint 1

First name:

[   ]

Submit

Go to the next sprint

I will be using C# to write my code. However, you can do the same thing with any programming language, IDE and browser automation tool.

Rule 0: Use page object model

There is only one rule that you must follow throughout the development of your code using ATDA. Use the page object model to code your tests. If you are unfamiliar with the page object model, go to http://bit.ly/SeleniumWithC to learn it in depth in the Complete Selenium WebDriver course.. Discussing the merits of page objects is beyond the scope of this chapter.

Step 1: Red

In this step, you need to code your acceptance test in plain English. If you have a compiler, it will complain; don't fix these errors yet. Simply code your test exactly as you want it to read and look. If you run your test after this step, it will fail, so it's Red.

Here is a sample of my code after I am done with this Red phase:

```
[TestMethod]
public void RedPhase()
{
    var Driver = new ChromeDriver();
    var sampleApplicationPage = new SampleApplicationPage(Driver);
    sampleApplicationPage.Open();
    var ultimateQAHomePage = sampleApplicationPage.FillOutForm("First name").Submit();
    //Should().BeTrue() is FluentAssertions Nuget package, not code I designed
    ultimateQAHomePage.IsVisible.Should().BeTrue();
}
```

Please note the red squiggles. The compiler has no clue what ChromeDriver or SampleApplicationPage are. Don't worry, we will resolve this soon.

Step 2: Green

Now it is time to fix all the compiler errors by implementing all of the logic for this test.

The goal here is just to get the test to pass as fast as possible. It must perform all of the actions in the browser when you are finished. The end result will be a passing test, meaning it's Green. So, you must execute your test to call this phase complete.

Here is how the code looks after I implemented the automated acceptance test.

Here is one finished page object.

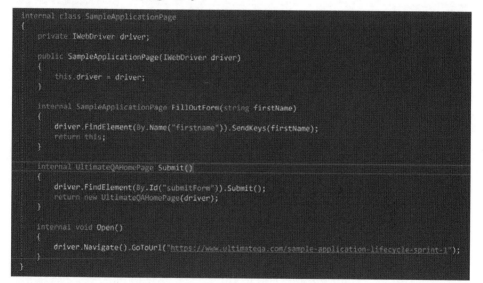

```
internal class SampleApplicationPage
{
    private IWebDriver driver;

    public SampleApplicationPage(IWebDriver driver)
    {
        this.driver = driver;
    }

    internal SampleApplicationPage FillOutForm(string firstName)
    {
        driver.FindElement(By.Name("firstname")).SendKeys(firstName);
        return this;
    }

    internal UltimateQAHomePage Submit()
    {
        driver.FindElement(By.Id("submitForm")).Submit();
        return new UltimateQAHomePage(driver);
    }

    internal void Open()
    {
        driver.Navigate().GoToUrl("https://www.ultimateqa.com/sample-application-lifecycle-sprint-1");
    }
}
```

This is the second page object.

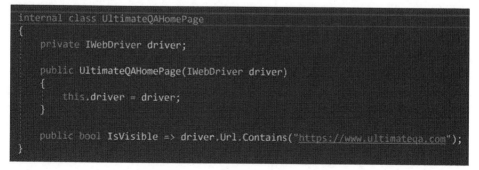

```
internal class UltimateQAHomePage
{
    private IWebDriver driver;

    public UltimateQAHomePage(IWebDriver driver)
    {
        this.driver = driver;
    }

    public bool IsVisible => driver.Url.Contains("https://www.ultimateqa.com");
}
```

Here is the final outcome of this step to call it complete.

Step 3: Refactor

At this point, you have a working automated acceptance test: excellent! Technically, you can now push this test into production and have it start testing your application. However, ATDA is focused on quality and maintenance, so there is one more step, called Refactor.

In this step, the goal is to clean up the mess that you created when implementing your automated acceptance test. The goal here is to remove all code duplication and make sure that all components of your system maintain a single responsibility.

This is a critical step if you want to keep your automation framework living for years at a time without needing to be rebuilt. However, since this is the first test you created, the code is pretty clean. For exemplary purposes, I will show you what some refactoring would look like.

In this case, I simply added some methods to execute before and after the test method executes. This is a very common type of refactoring that you might want to do when you see duplication.

Once your code is clean and you are proud of it, the Refactoring phase is finished. Furthermore, your automated acceptance test is also finished. Now, you just repeat ATDA for every single automated test that you write.

```
[TestClass]
public class SampleAppTests
{
    public ChromeDriver Driver { get; private set; }

    [TestMethod]
    public void TestWrittenUsingATDA()
    {
        var sampleApplicationPage = new SampleApplicationPage(Driver);
        sampleApplicationPage.Open();
        var ultimateQAHomePage = sampleApplicationPage.FillOutForm("First name").Submit();
        //Should().BeTrue() is FluentAssertions Nuget package, not code I designed
        ultimateQAHomePage.IsVisible.Should().BeTrue();
    }
    [TestInitialize]
    public void RunBeforeEveryTestMethod()
    {
        Driver = new ChromeDriver();
    }
    [TestCleanup]
    public void RunAfterEveryTestMethod()
    {
        Driver.Quit();
    }
}
```

Framework ready for production

Congratulations, you just automated an acceptance test in less than thirty minutes. I did, at least! Let's look at exactly what happened using ATDA.

First, this test is production ready and you can start executing it immediately. This means that your employer is already seeing a return on their investment in you. Seriously, there is nothing at this point that should prevent you from pushing this test into your CI system and have it start providing value.

Second, this test is clean, without duplication, and without over-engineering. The test meets the current requirements of the test case: that's it, nothing more. Doesn't the test read almost like plain English? It is extremely easy to understand what this test is actually doing. Even more pleasant is the fact that if you open a method, it does exactly what the method says it does.

```
internal UltimateQAHomePage Submit()
{
    driver.FindElement(By.Id("submitForm")).Submit();
    return new UltimateQAHomePage(driver);
}
```

Above is an example of a method called Submit that performs a Submit action on some element. How pleasantly unsurprising is that?

Furthermore, you have a fully functional test automation framework that's ready to be executed in production. I understand that this framework is not yet finished and that you might want to add some enhancements. So, add enhancements when you need them. Don't over-engineer for something that you don't need. I have seen automation engineers create automation frameworks with Excel spreadsheets and complicated HTML reports before they have even run their first test. In the end, nobody used the reports or the spreadsheets; it was a waste of money. Nobody can predict the future, so let's write test automation code for the present.

As a result, using acceptance test driven automation, you meet all current requirements in the fastest possible time. Your employer benefits since your acceptance test is ready to work in less than an hour. You have a test that you can execute and start validating the system. This is, ultimately, the point of test automation: to test the system and ensure that it's free of defects. The best part is that you don't have to think about what to do next. Just write your test and Red, Green, and Refactor your way to success!

CHAPTER FIFTEEN

Advantages of Headless Browser Testing as Part of a Cross-Browser Testing Strategy

INTRODUCTION

A common test plan for a web application, whether it be .com, m.dot, responsive, or progressive, consists of various pillars, each executed at the appropriate stage in the DevOps pipeline. These pillars typically include unit tests, functional tests, accessibility, security, performance, and potentially a few others.

Executing all these tests on real desktop browsers like Chrome, Firefox, Edge, Safari, IE, and other mobile browsers takes time, setup, and ongoing maintenance. The question is: **"Do we really need a full-blown desktop browser with a full user interface (UI) for all testing activities?"**

Modern cross-browser testing practices prove that in various stages of the development life cycle, and for specific testing purposes, teams can get the full value of a real desktop browser — and even more — using a headless browser solution. While not the same concept, consider mobile emulators' and simulators' roles in an overall testing strategy — they are not completely able to cover all testing requirements and do not fully mimic the real end-user environment, but they add unique value to testing teams and developers in many ways.

HEADLESS BROWSER DEFINITION AND BENEFITS

Before we can define when to use a headless browser and what the benefits (and drawbacks) are of doing so, let's first understand what it is.

Based on Wikipedia's definition, a headless browser is *"a web browser without a user interface. Headless browsers provide automated control of a web page in an environment similar to popular web browsers, but are executed via a command-line interface or using network communication. They are particularly useful for testing web pages as they are able to render and understand HTML the same way a browser would, including styling elements such as page layout, color, font selection, and execution of JavaScript and AJAX which are usually not available when using other testing methods."*[1]

In much simpler terms, a headless browser is a solution that allows developers and testers to test their website without the need to launch the full UI.

The key benefits[2] of using such solutions are:

1. At least 3 times faster execution; therefore, quicker feedback for functional web tests[3]

2. Zero setup and maintenance of a Selenium grid with various browsers and versions

3. Tests can be developed and executed from the development environment without setting up a full-blown test environment

4. **Some** of the leading browsers support headless testing[4] — Chrome headless, Chrome Puppeteer, Mozilla Firefox[5]

5. Various test framework solutions are available to drive headless browser testing (Puppeteer, Nightmare, CasperJS, SlimerJS, and more)

6. Fast and automated web data scraping[6] from websites

---

1   Wikipedia definition for headless browser — https://en.wikipedia.org/wiki/Headless_browser

2   Benefits of headless browsers — https://www.keycdn.com/blog/headless-browsers/

3   Introduction to headless browser testing — https://blog.logrocket.com/introduction-to-headless-browser-testing-44b82310b27c

4   Headless browser testing — https://github.com/dhamaniasad/HeadlessBrowsers

5   Firefox headless browser — https://developer.mozilla.org/en-US/Firefox/Headless_mode

6   Web scraping — https://www.webharvy.com/articles/what-is-web-scraping.html

7. Advanced testing capabilities such as screenshots, HAR file generation, security testing, and performance

Some key limitations of headless browsers:

1. Can only be executed against 1 browser (e.g. Puppeteer or Chrome) — does not allow parallel testing of 1 test code across multiple browsers and permutations

2. Limited reporting capabilities compared to solutions that run across full browser UIs

3. Does not test the full UI across platforms — nor from a user perspective

4. Edge and Safari don't support headless mode

5. Limited to tests that require the user to see the browser UI

WHEN TO USE A HEADLESS BROWSER?

Headless browsers come with some useful benefits, as outlined above, but they cannot serve all quality and development needs.

It is recommended to include headless browsers as part of your testing strategy in various phases of the development life cycle. Certainly, use such platforms in the early stages of your development of a web feature to develop and run **unit** tests, and **basic UI** tests through screenshots. In addition, for any functional tests, such as **network** traffic analysis through **HAR** files, **performance** validations, or **security** testing, which don't need to "see" the entire specific browser (Chrome, Firefox etc.), you can target your tests against a headless browser.

WHEN NOT TO USE A HEADLESS BROWSER?

Now that we've defined what you *can* test on a headless browser, this is an easy question to answer. All cross-browser **functional end-to-end** testing should run against full browsers with their complete UI in a Selenium grid or in the cloud[7]. In these cases, the test frameworks used will be a bit different,

---

7   Perfecto's cloud solution — http://www.perfecto.io/platform/the-cloud-based-testing-lab/
cross-browser-testing/

and will include Selenium, Protractor, WebDriverIO, and others. In some cases, headless browser test automation can also leverage Selenium, as mentioned in the references, but it's not a must; as will be shown later in this chapter, the various dedicated tools[8] for headless testing have different syntaxes.

Compare a test written using Nightmare API:

```
nightmare
  .goto('http://yahoo.com')
  .type('form[action*="/search"] [name=p]', 'github nightmare')
  .click('form[action*="/search"] [type=submit]')
  .wait('#main')
  .evaluate(function () {
    return document.querySelector('#main .searchCenterMiddle li a').href
  })
```

with a similar CodeceptJS test:

```
I.amOnPage('http://yahoo.com');
I.fillField('p', 'github nightmare');
I.click('Search Web');
I.waitForElement('#main');
I.seeElement('#main .searchCenterMiddle li a');
I.seeElement('//a[contains(@href,'github.com/segmentio/nightmare')]');
I.see('segmentio/nightmare','#main li a');
```

Fig 1: Sample code using Nightmare and Codecept.JS against headless browser

GETTING STARTED WITH HEADLESS BROWSER TESTING

Setting up a headless browser local environment and developing a JavaScript-based test is simple. In this section, you can learn how to get started with 2 different solutions: Nightmare and Google Puppeteer. You can also read about headless Firefox[9] and Selenium's Gecko driver and use them as well.

Nightmare Headless Testing

Nightmare, by Segment[10], is a browser test automation library.

The goal of this tool is to expose a few simple methods that mimic website

---

8   Java script browser testing tools overview for 2018 — https://medium.com/welldone-software/an-overview-of-javascript-testing-in-2018-f68950900bc3

9   Firefox headless browser using Selenium and Gecko driver — https://intoli.com/blog/running-selenium-with-headless-firefox/

10   SegmentIO nightmare GitHub repository — https://github.com/segmentio/nightmare

user actions (like **goto, type** and **click**) with an API that feels synchronous for each block of scripting, rather than deeply nested callbacks. It was originally designed for automating tasks across sites that don't have APIs but is now most often used for UI testing and crawling.

Under the covers, it uses Electron, which is similar to PhantomJS but roughly twice as fast and more modern. (PhantomJS is no longer supported)

1. Install Nightmare:

   a. `npmi nightmare`

2. Install Mocha and Nightmare as the 2 following dependencies

   a. `npm install --save-dev mocha`

   b. `npm install --save-dev nightmare`

3. Start scripting (below is an example that comes built in with the installation)

```
1   /* eslint-disable no-console */
2
3   var Nightmare = require('nightmare')
4   var nightmare = Nightmare({ show: true })
5
6   nightmare
7     .goto('http://yahoo.com')
8     .type('form[action*="/search"] [name=p]', 'github nightmare')
9     .click('form[action*="/search"] [type=submit]')
10    .wait('#main')
11    .evaluate(function() {
12      return document.querySelector('#main .searchCenterMiddle li a').href
13    })
14    .end()
15    .then(function(result) {
16      console.log(result)
17    })
18    .catch(function(error) {
19      console.error('Search failed:', error)
20    })
```

4. Execute the code from the installation folder or your IDE.

   a. Node "`file.js`"

```
erank@nb-erank-10-2 MINGW64 ~/node_modules/nightmare (master)
$ node example.js
https://github.com/segmentio/nightmare
```

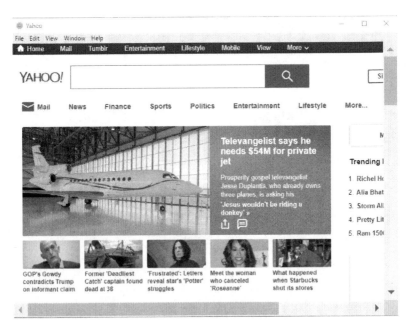

*Fig 2: **Electron** UI on which Nightmare test code is running*

Google Puppeteer Headless Testing

Puppeteer is a Node library which provides a high-level API to control Headless Chrome[11] or Chromium over the DevTools protocol[12]. It can also be configured to use full (non-headless) Chrome or Chromium.

Among the key things users can leverage from Puppeteer are the following:

- Generating screenshots and PDFs of pages

- Automating form submission, UI testing, keyboard input, etc.

- Creating an up-to-date, automated testing environment. Run your tests directly in the latest version of Chrome using the latest JavaScript and browser features.

- Capturing a timeline trace[13] of your site to help diagnose performance issues.

---

11 Google developer reference — https://developers.google.com/web/updates/2017/04/headless-chrome

12 Google chrome DevTools Protocol — https://chromedevtools.github.io/devtools-protocol/

13 Google performance capturing — https://developers.google.com/web/tools/chrome-devtools/evaluate-performance/reference

- Supports NodeJS features like async/await, callbacks and promises

As of the writing of this book, Puppeteer is the official tool for Headless Chrome from the Google Chrome team. Since the official announcement of Headless Chrome, many of the industry standard libraries for automated testing have been discontinued by their maintainers, including PhantomJS.

Puppeteer[14] includes its own Chrome/Chromium which is guaranteed to work headless. Each time you install/update Puppeteer, it will download its specific chrome version.

To get started with Google's Puppeteer[15] headless browser, you'll need to install the latest version.

Run this command: **"npmi puppeteer"**.

Once you've installed the framework, it's time to learn the supported APIs[16] and start coding!

Post-installation, one can easily learn the basic syntax of the framework. From the installation path, simply run the test code as shown below, taken from Google's developer website, with the following command: **"node ex-ample.js"**. This code snippet goes to the example.com website, takes a screenshot of the page, and saves the web page as a PDF file.

```
constpuppeteer=require('puppeteer');

(async () => {
constbrowser=awaitpuppeteer.launch();
constpage=awaitbrowser.newPage();
awaitpage.goto('https://example.com');
awaitpage.screenshot({path:'example.png'});
awaitpage.pdf({path:'Example.pdf', format:'A4'});

awaitbrowser.close();
})();
```

---

14   Google puppeteer guide — http://www.thecreativedev.com/chrome-headless-and-google-puppe-teer-with-nodejs/

15   Google Puppeteer GitHub repository — https://github.com/GoogleChrome/puppeteer

16   Google Puppeteer APIs — https://github.com/GoogleChrome/puppeteer/blob/master/docs/api.md#

Obviously, developers can leverage the large set of capabilities and APIs of this framework to develop various functional and non-functional tests as part of their development and testing activities and combine them with the larger functional and regression E2E test suites.

Here is a snapshot from the supported APIs:

- class: Keyboard
  - keyboard.down(key[, options])
  - keyboard.press(key[, options])
  - keyboard.sendCharacter(char)
  - keyboard.type(text, options)
  - keyboard.up(key)
- class: Mouse
  - mouse.click(x, y, [options])
  - mouse.down([options])
  - mouse.move(x, y, [options])
  - mouse.up([options])
- class: Touchscreen
  - touchscreen.tap(x, y)

In addition to its various testing capabilities and large API set, Puppeteer can be used with various parameters, such as specifying a Chrome OS version, executing in slow motion, and capturing console logs for debugging purposes.

SUMMARY

In this chapter, we focused on the opportunities headless web browsers offer to developers and testers as well as the best situations in which to use these kinds of tools — e.g. for unit testing, security, performance, or whenever testing with a full browser UI is unnecessary for the testing objectives. We also covered some disadvantages of these tools, including testing in parallel and across different browsers, advanced E2E testing, and testing from a user perspective.

In a growing DevOps reality where time for testing is shrinking and the number of required tests is increasing, leveraging full browsers as well as headless can be a great strategy for fast feedback and quick test execution, test efficiency, and test coverage.

CHAPTER SIXTEEN

Shifting Accessibility Testing Left

BY AMIR ROZENBERG

AMIR ROZENBERG is a thought leader in the space of agile quality methodologies. As a product director at Perfecto, he drove the core product strategy and implementation with many Fortune-1000 customers. He led initiatives in the areas of real user condition testing, accessibility, security, audio and conversational interfaces, AI/ML, IoT and medical devices etc. In addition, Amir led successful synergies with Microsoft, SmartBear, Blazemeter, Neotys, etc., to optimize value delivery to the market. Prior to Perfecto, Amir led the mobile monitoring practice at Compuware.

INTRODUCTION

In the US, nearly one in five people suffers from some form of disability (visual impairment, hearing loss, limited dexterity, etc.)[1] Ensuring applications are accessible is a practice that has been gaining attention in recent years. There are several trends driving this activity; the primary amongst these is digital transformation. Businesses are moving their interaction with end users to the multi-screen, digital front. Whether end users prefer to use — or are forced to use — an app to check their account balance or make a transfer, all users must have access. Whether or not they have been personally touched

---

1   Accessibility Guidelines — https://www.census.gov/newsroom/releases/archives/miscellaneous/cb12-134.html

by a friend or family member with a disability, developers and testers are becoming more aware of the issue. For those who need extra motivation, the growth in litigation activity associated with ADA compliance[2] is another good reason to get active.

RESPONSIBILITY AND BUDGET SHIFTING

In the past, the responsibility of accessibility testing, much like performance and security, was in the hands of a dedicated, skilled team. Testing was done manually and defects were found late, close to launch deadline. This left decision makers with a challenging decision: release the app with compliance risks or delay the launch. Often, the business impact associated with delayed launch won the argument and applications were launched with known compliance issues.

That reality is changing. Dev teams are looking to automate accessibility tests so they can occur during development, without slowing them down. While developers may not become experts in accessibility standards on day one, they are happy to learn about a defect almost immediately, fix it quickly, and learn the requirements over time. To accomplish this, an accessibility expert should mentor the team about standards, requirements, and testing. With time, minor recurring faults will be fixed by the developer; the expert can consult on severe or new ones. In summary, there is great benefit in shifting accessibility testing into the sprint.

Standards

Accessibility requirements are defined in Web Content Accessibility Guidelines (WCAG) 2.0[3] and, in the USA, Section 508 Amendment to the Rehabilitation Act of 1973[4]. Similar standards around the world are available, representing minor variations of the above. There are several levels of compliance: "A", "AA" and "AAA", from the basic to the most detailed. Most organizations are looking to comply with "AA" level requirements.

---

2   Accessibility ADA Charges — https://www.eeoc.gov/eeoc/statistics/enforcement/ada-charges.cfm

3   WCAG Guidelines — https://www.w3.org/WAI/standards-guidelines/wcag/

4   Accessibility Justice Reference — https://www.justice.gov/crt/pl-105-220-1998-hr-1385-pl-105-220-enacted-august-7-1998-112-stat-936-codified-section-504

TOOLING

Interactive testing

In terms of interactive testing, there are a few tools in the market for each type of application.

Web: Interactive testing: One possible approach would be to leverage the Google Lighthouse[5] set of tools, preinstalled in the developer toolset of the Chrome browser.

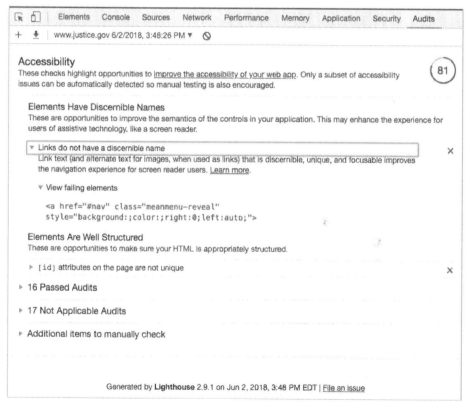

Figure 1: Google Lighthouse accessibility audit built into Chrome

---

5   Google Lighthouse Accessibility Tool — https://developers.google.com/web/tools/lighthouse/

Another approach for desktop web is to install one of the browser plug-ins such as the WAVE toolbar[6],

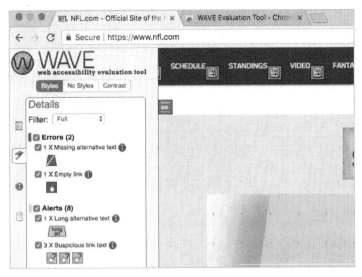

Figure 2: The free WAVE Chrome add-In Offers accessibility scan results

iOS Native apps: It is possible to conduct gestures on a device, examine the contrast visually, listen to the ScreenReader, etc. Sometimes, utilization of the Assistive Touch makes gestures easier to manipulate.

Figure 3: iOS Assistive Touch helps manual testing of accessibility gestures

---

6   Wave Accessibility Testing tool — https://wave.webaim.org/extension/

Android Native apps: Shown here, Google Accessibility Scanner is another tool that's based on built-in Android scans. This is an app that can be installed from the app store.

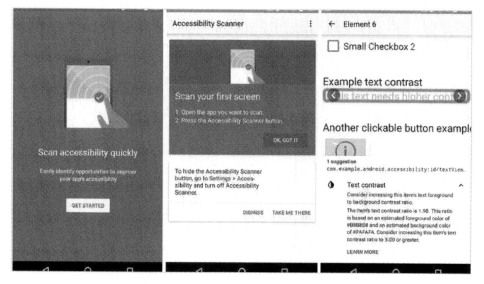

Figure 4: Google Accessibility Scanner

Test Automation

Web: There are several approaches to web testing, some based on the free (open source) version of the AXE[7] scan or its commercial counterpart, both offered by Deque. The AXE scan does a very nice job in terms of the level of detail in the report and helpfulness of the data. Each section includes the identifier of the object, criticality of the fault, which sections in the standards are relevant to this fault, a link to further explanation and suggestions, and, eventually, a summary of faults for this object. Since AXE is basically a JavaScript inject into the web page, it is very easy to integrate this code into Selenium, Gauge[8], Quantum[9], or other frameworks, and use this tool for desktop or mobile web on any platform.

---

7   AXE Accessibility Testing Tool — https://axe-core.org/docs/

8   Accessibility Testing Example (Amir's repo) — https://github.com/AmirAtPerfecto/GaugeWebAccessibility

9   Quantum with Axe Git Code Sample — https://github.com/Project-Quantum/WebAccessibilityUsingAXE

```
[
{
"id":"button-name",
"impact":"critical",
"tags":[
"wcag2a",
"wcag412",
"section508",
"section508.22.a"
],
"description":"Ensures buttons have discernible text",
"help":"Buttons must have discernible text",
"helpUrl":"https://dequeuniversity.com/rules/axe/2.1/but-
ton-name?application=axeAPI",
"nodes":[
{
"any":[
{
"id":"non-empty-if-present",
"data":null,
"relatedNodes":[

],
"impact":"critical",
"message":"Element has a value attribute and the value attri-
bute is empty"
},
…
"failureSummary":"Fix all of the following:\n Element is in tab
order and does not have accessible text\n\nFix any of the fol-
lowing:\n Element has a value attribute and the value attribute
is empty\n Element has no value attribute or the value attri-
bute is empty\n Element does not have inner text that is visi-
ble to screen readers\n aria-label attribute does not exist or
is empty\n aria-labelledby attribute does not exist, references
elements that do not exist or references elements that are emp-
ty or not visible\n Element's default semantics were not over-
ridden with role=\"presentation\"\n Element's default semantics
were not overridden with role=\"none\""
}
]
},
]
```

In addition, AXE highlights the element on the screen that's at fault:

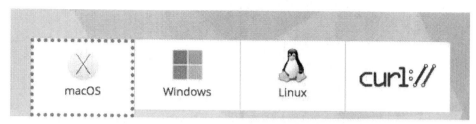

Figure 5: Highlight of element at fault from AXE web accessibility scan

iOS Native Applications: Apple offers a nice tool as part of XCode called Accessibility Inspector[10]. While not offering mapping to the standards, it does offer a detailed analysis for area such as:

- Contrast
- Hit area/element size
- Font sizes
- Missing TalkBack/ScreenReader attributes
- Image labeling
- Element duplication
- Swipe order

Each response includes a highlighted screenshot of the element at fault as well:

Issue Number: 0
Error code: 12
Short Description: Contrast nearly passed
Long Description: Contrast is not high enough for element unless font size is larger.

Thumbnail:

---

10 Apple accessibility testing on OSX — https://developer.apple.com/library/content/documentation/Accessibility/Conceptual/AccessibilityMacOSX/OSXAXTestingApps.html

Full screenshot

Figure 6: Screenshot of element in accessibility violation from iOS Scan

Android Native Applications: Beyond the aforementioned Google Accessibility Scan, Google offers a tool called Accessibility Framework[11] For Android. Similar to the iOS tool, it offers similar coverage to the above as well as detailed analysis and screenshot with highlight of the element.

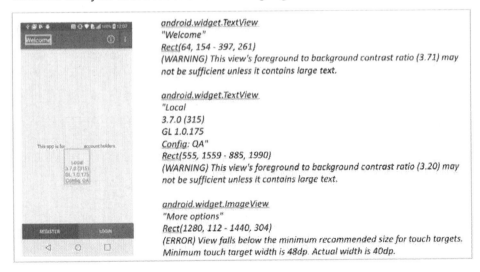

android.widget.TextView
"Welcome"
Rect(64, 154 - 397, 261)
(WARNING) This view's foreground to background contrast ratio (3.71) may not be sufficient unless it contains large text.

android.widget.TextView
"Local
3.7.0 (315)
GL 1.0.175
Config: QA"
Rect(555, 1559 - 885, 1990)
(WARNING) This view's foreground to background contrast ratio (3.20) may not be sufficient unless it contains large text.

android.widget.ImageView
"More options"
Rect(1280, 112 - 1440, 304)
(ERROR) View falls below the minimum recommended size for touch targets. Minimum touch target width is 48dp. Actual width is 40dp.

Figure 7: Android accessibility scan: unit test automation

---

11   Google's Android Accessibility Testing — https://developer.android.com/training/testing/espresso/
accessibility-checking

Developer tools

With the help of tools such as mentioned above, developers are becoming more aware of the level of accessibility of their apps and their compliance with the standard requirements. The AXE, Google's Accessibility Scan in Espresso, and Apple's Accessibility Inspector are more examples of accessibility development environments.

Android Studio shows lint warnings for accessibility issues:

Figure 8: Android Studio Lint messages for accessibility compliance

Espresso: Android offers a built-in Espresso scan tool which runs in the background of your unit test:

```
publicclassAccessibilityChecksIntegrationTest{
  @BeforeClass
  publicstaticvoidenableAccessibilityChecks(){
  AccessibilityChecks.enable();
  }
}
```

SUMMARY

It's encouraging to see the growth in awareness of the need for app accessibility (both for web and mobile) as they become the main point of interaction between users and brands. A change in both process and technology must happen to enable development teams to ensure accessibility compliance as part of their development workflows. These changes include knowledge and skills, staffing, tooling, and process. Luckily, many good tools are already in place for developers and testers to take advantage of.

CHAPTER SEVENTEEN

How to Gauge What Your Tests Are Doing?

BY THOMAS F. MAHER, JR.

THOMAS F. MAHER, JR. — best known as "T.J. Maher" — is a tinkerer, exploring ways to craft automation solutions. Back in 2015, T.J. shook the dust off his BSCS and Master of Software Engineering, combined them with his twenty years of software testing experience and his passion for writing, and launched both a software testing blog and a career in automation development. Whenever T.J. experiments with a new automation tool or technology, he blogs about the experience. On "Adventures in Automation", at tjmaher.com, he provides downloadable sample code and code walkthroughs of frameworks he has created. By 2016, T.J. became a contributing writer at TechBeacon.com, giving talks to Boston-area software testing Meetup groups. By 2017, T.J. became the Meetup Organizer of the Ministry of Testing — Boston, the Massachusetts branch of the MinistryOfTesting.com, a UK based community of software testers. In 2018, T.J. was a guest speaker at the AutomationGuild.com and the TestingGuild.com. T.J. can be reached on Twitter at @tjmaher1.

INTRODUCTION

Every software development team struggles with answering two questions:

- How can the entire team, from business analysts to developers to testers, determine how your product should behave?

- How can you gauge how your software product is truly behaving?

As an answer to these questions, Dan North came up with the concept of Behavior Driven Development (BDD)[1]. Phrasing the "testing" part of Test Driven Development (TDD) as a Behavior, it transformed BDD from a *testing* tool into a *communication* tool.

With BDD, the entire team, as a whole, can brainstorm together on how the product should (and should not) work. By breaking down behaviors into small, simple, and understandable sentences, the documentation being created can be used as a product specification, as a blueprint developers and testers can use, and as acceptance criteria the business analysts can evaluate.

Ever since Dan North and Elizabeth Keogh took this concept to Java with JBehave[2], it has spread like wildfire to many other languages. Steven Baker, and Dave Astels developed RSpec for Ruby. Aslak Hellesoy took his work on RSpec and designed Cucumber and its Gherkin language. John Ferguson Smart created a reporting framework for JBehave and Cucumber with SerenityBDD (initially called Thucydides)[3].

In this chapter, we will be exploring Gauge[4], a new BDD framework created by ThoughtWorks India. Although Gauge 1.0 just came out of beta in June 2018, it made its debut January 2015 as an open-source product. I first encountered Gauge while working on Threat Stack's Test Engineering team as a Software Development Engineer in Test. Testing involved spinning up various Linux distros on AWS instances, attaching the Threat Stack agent to monitor and detect Cloud Trail logs, verifying the correct microservice displayed the correct API output. After a proof-of-concept, Gauge was shown to handle these complexities well.

WHAT MAKES GAUGE DIFFERENT?

"What if we wanted to break away from every form of syntax and write specifications in natural language, like you'd write an email?"

---

1   Introducing BDD, https://dannorth.net/introducing-bdd/, initially published March 2006

2   JBehave 2.0 is Live, https://dannorth.net/2008/09/08/jbehave-20-is-live/, September 2008

3   JBehave.org, RSpec.info, Cucumber.io, Thucydides.info, respectively.

4   http://gauge.org

As the Gauge team asked the audience at a software testing Meetup back in 2015: What if you could create a new BDD toolset that avoided the restraining *Given/When/Then* format? One that was simpler? Customizable? These were the ideas the Gauge team presented in their "Gauge Your BDD Tests" talk[5] at vodQA, Value Oriented Discussion about Quality Analysts, a software testing conference in Hyderabad, India.

Gauge is based on Twist (2009–2015), a Java-based commercial automation framework which worked with the Eclipse IDE, built by the ThoughtWorks Studio team in Bangalore, India. With more of ThoughtWorks customers seeking open-source solutions, Gauge was created as a lightweight, cross-platform alternative.

What makes Gauge different than all the other BDD toolsets? In February 2015, Deepthi Chandramouli outlined five major points on the Google Groups for Gauge[6]:

1. Gauge is a single product that supports multiple languages across different platforms. This ensures a uniformity and consistency irrespective of which language and IDE you use to write your tests.

2. Gauge uses Markdown as the markup to author specifications. This makes it feature rich from an execution and documentation point of view.

3. Gauge's architecture is plugin based which makes it highly extensible. This means that the core product can be enhanced by adding in support for a new language, a new IDE, a customised report, external tool integration etc., all as plugins. What this means is that any features added to Gauge core automatically scale to all the supported languages.

4. Gauge has first class refactoring support both on command line and IDE. We feel that this is the extremely important to maintain a large test suite.

5. Gauge has first class parallelisation support as a core feature (in development), which applies to all supported languages".

---

5   https://www.slideshare.net/mahendrakariya/gauge-your-bdd-test-vodqa-hyderabad

6   https://groups.google.com/forum/#!msg/getgauge

WHAT PLATFORMS DOES GAUGE SUPPORT?

It is quite easy to get going with Gauge, on Mac, Windows, or Linux Machines, running in C#, Java, or Ruby, provided you have the requisite .NET framework, JDK 6+ or Ruby 2.0+ for the platform.

Gauge can be installed on[7]:

- MacOS through Homebrew
- Windows using Chocolatey or downloading the zip installer
- Linux using apt-get, dnf, or the zip installer.

Once Gauge is installed, you can install the language runner and a fully scaffolded demo project, with the project and folder structure already set up, by choosing to type into the command line either:

- *gauge install csharp*
- *gauge install java*
- *gauge install ruby*

Although we will be using Java for the purposes of this chapter, the demo projects set up for each language are all the same: Given a word, count the number of vowels, and assert that the expected and the actual count match. Tests are data-driven, with input captured in a data table with two columns, 'Word', and the expected 'Vowel Count'.

The projects can be run from the command line with *'gauge run spec'*.

Sample Output, Command Line:

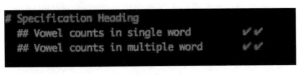

Want to see other options on the command line?
View them at manpage.gauge.org.

---

7   Gauge — Get Started: https://gauge.org/get-started.html

HOW CAN GAUGE BE USED FOR WEB APPLICATION TESTING?

To see how Gauge can be used to test web applications, let's take a look at one of Gauge's many sample projects on Gauge's GitHub site, **java-maven-selenium**[8].

Specifications: Imagine that you have a web-based bookstore application where users can log into the site, search for books, place an order, and log out. It could look something like this:

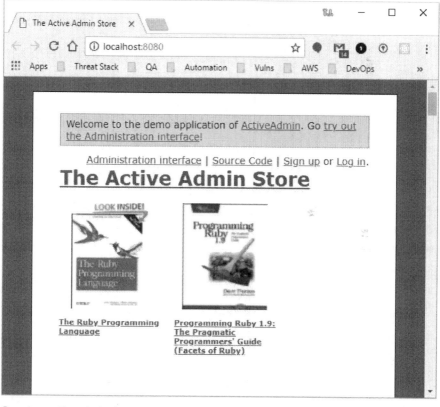

Running activeadmin-demo.war included in java-maven-selenium

---

8   GetGauge on GitHub — Java-Maven-Selenium: https://github.com/getgauge-examples/java-maven-selenium

A test case specification to place an order could look something like this:

java-maven-selenium / specs / PlaceOrder.specs

```
Place an Order
==============

* Go to active admin store

Buy a book
----------
tags: customer

* Log in with customer name "ScroogeMcduck" and "password"
* Place order for "Beginning Ruby: From Novice to Profession-
  al". The cart should now contain "1" items
* Log out
```

With Gauge, this isn't simply a specification for a feature of a product; it's a way to both organize the test code and set up the HTML or XML reports. Each element in the *.spec file corresponds to an element in Markdown, the text formatting language created by Josh Gruber and Aaron Swartz back in 2004. Specifications are "business layer test cases which can also act as your feature documentation. They are written in the business language. Typically a spec or specification describe a particular feature of the application under test", according to the official Gauge documentation[9].

- The Specification Heading, "Place an Order", at the top of the page is in H1, Header 1 format, the main header.

- The Scenario Heading, "Buy a book", is in H2, Header 2 format, a sub-header.

- Each step, written in plain English, clearly and concisely sums up, in a bullet point format, what each test will entail, step-by-step.

Concept Files: When writing a spec, readability is key. The steps referencing Login and Logout are actually rollups of a multi-step process called concepts.

---

9 https://docs.gauge.org/

"Concepts provide the ability to combine re-usable logical groups of steps into a single unit. It provides a higher-level abstraction of a business intent by combining steps. [...] They are defined in .cpt format files in the specs directory in the project. They can be inside nested directories inside the specs directory" *(Docs.Gauge.Org)*.

Below, you can see that the line *"Log in with customer name <name> and <password>"* corresponds with the specification, above. The values passed in for the name (*"ScroogeMcduck"*) and for the password (*"password"*) are inputted into the corresponding concept header.

java-maven-selenium / specs / concepts / Authentication.cpt

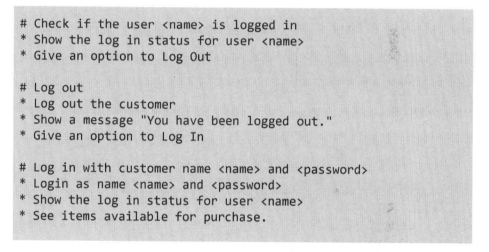

```
# Check if the user <name> is logged in
* Show the log in status for user <name>
* Give an option to Log Out

# Log out
* Log out the customer
* Show a message "You have been logged out."
* Give an option to Log In

# Log in with customer name <name> and <password>
* Login as name <name> and <password>
* Show the log in status for user <name>
* See items available for purchase.
```

Here, you can see that Log In actually consists of three steps: the action to be taken and two ways to confirm that everything is working.

Step Definitions: Each step listed in the specification corresponds to either a concept or a reusable step definition pairing the plain language of the spec with the Java, C#, Javascript, Python, or Ruby code that executes.

Example: In the **Place Orders.spec,** the login and password are initialized, fed into the **Authentication.cpt** concept, and passed into the LogIn.java step definition.

Each test is set up to be *data driven.* Enter a parameter in quotation marks in the spec, a corresponding variable name in angle brackets, and that value can now be used in that particular block of code.

java-maven-selenium / src / test / java / LogIn.java

```
@Step("Login as name <name> and <password>")
public void LoginAsCustomerDetails(String name, String pass-
word) {
    WebDriver webDriver = Driver.webDriver;
    webDriver.findElement(By.linkText("Log in")).click();
    webDriver.findElement(By.name("login")).sendKeys(name);
    webDriver.findElement(By.name("password")).sendKeys(pass-
    word);
    webDriver.findElement(By.name("commit")).click();
}
```

Here, we can see the glue that connects the spec with the step definitions, the test plan to the code that executes the test.

The name and password is fed into the Java method LoginAsCustomerDetails, which contains Selenium WebDriver + Java code which:

- Opens up a new WebDriver instance
- Finds and clicks on the link reading "Log in"
- Finds the field "login", entering the name
- Finds the field "password", entering the password data
- Finds the button "commit" and clicks on it.

Hopefully, if all goes well, the login status will show for the user. If that step passes, the test step checks that items are available for purchase. If not, that particular test would fail, and the last step would not execute.

Continue On Failure: Want the test to continue to continue to the very last step? We can add *Continue On Failure:*

```
@ContinueOnFailure
@Step("Login as name <name> and <password>")
public void LoginAsCustomerDetails(String name, String pass-
word)
```

"Gauge provides a way for language runners to mark steps as recoverable, depending on whether the step implementation asks for it explicitly. Each language runner uses different syntax, depending on the language idioms, to allow a step implementation to be marked to continue on failure".

But how did the WebDriver know how to spin up?

Execution Hooks: Like any good Selenium + Java project, setup and teardown methods are included that initialize the browser when the test suite is started and close the browser when the tests have completed. This is accomplished by using Gauge's Execution Hooks that can be executed before and after each Suite, Spec, Scenario, or Step.

- **C#:** [BeforeSuite] / [AfterSuite]
- **Java:** @BeforeSuite / @AfterSuite
- **JavaScript:** beforeSuite / afterSuite
- **Python:** @before_suite / @after_suite
- **Ruby:** before_suite / after_suite

java-maven-selenium / src / test / utils / driver / Driver.java

```java
public class Driver {
    public static WebDriver webDriver;

    // Initialize a webDriver instance of required browser
    @BeforeSuite
    public void initializeDriver(){
        webDriver = DriverFactory.getDriver();
    }

    // Close the webDriver instance
    @AfterSuite
    public void closeDriver(){
        webDriver.quit();
    }
}
```

Refactoring: With Gauge, you can refactor tests through two different mediums: through the command line and through IDE Plugins.

Let's say the word "user" was to replace the word "customer" in all official documentation regarding the step "Log out the customer". We could do a find and replace, hoping that every single instance in the spec was covered, or we could go to the command line.

> gauge refactor "Log out the customer" "Log out the user"

This will rephrase the step to match the updated terminology.

Gauge also has plugins for integrated development environments:

- Visual Studio: Plugin supports C#
- Visual Studio Code: Plugin supports JavaScript, Ruby, and Python.
- IntelliJ IDEA: Supports only Java, at the time of this publication.

Customizing Reports: The Spec doesn't simply act as a clear and concise test plan, or as way to automate. Gauge comes with a built-in customizable reporting framework, in either XML or HTML format.

If we want to provide Product Owners more detail, we can add messages that will print out in the reports:

```
@Step("Login as name <name> and <password>")
public void LoginAsCustomerDetails(String name, String password) {
    Gauge.writeMessage("Entering %s / %s", name, password);
        WebDriver webDriver = Driver.webDriver;
```

This would print out in the report:

- Entering ScroogeMcduck/password

Executing Gauge Tests: If we were to follow the instructions of the **java-maven-selenium**[10] project and download and run the *activeadmin-demo.war* file, on the **system under test** (SUT), we could go to http://localhost:8080

---

10   Once again, https://github.com/getgauge-examples/java-maven-selenium

to see the app up and running.

Let's say we had run "gauge install java", installed Apache Maven, and cloned the java-maven-selenium project. We could run the tests like so: *mvn* test

This would run all tests, including the PlaceOrder.spec we listed. It would:

- Open the Active Admin Store

- Click on the Login link

- Login as ScroogeMcduck using the password

- Place an order for a book

- Make sure that the item is available for purchase

- Log out

Reports for PlaceOrder.spec

If we wanted to drill down on logging in, which covers the Authorization.cpt concept, we would see:

SUMMARY

Like most BDD frameworks, as Agile teams, business owners, developers and testers shape the specification, they are shaping the test plan, the automation, and the reports themselves.

I found Gauge unique compared to anything I have experienced, using simple bullet points to spell out what and how things should be tested.

SECTION 3

Continuous Testing for Mobile Apps

CHAPTER EIGHTEEN

Overcoming Challenges for automating React Native Apps

BY WIM SELLES

WIM SELLES is a Test Automation Engineer based in the Netherlands. During the day he's currently under contract with Tele2, a pan-European telecom provider, where he's setting up the test automation for a new React Native app. By night, he practices his passion for front end test automation with JavaScript. He likes to create his own node.js modules to help and support (automation) engineers, and is also a contributor to multiple open source projects and an active member in multiple Gitter channels related to automation.

In recent years, he has used Appium for automating Hybrid and React Native Apps. He likes to share his automation experiences at conferences like AppiumConf London and SeleniumConf India, on his blog, and during Meetups and webinars.

You can find him blogging[1], on LinkedIn[2], and follow his tweets as @wswebcreation[3].

---

1   Blog — http://www.wswebcreation.nl

2   LinkedIn — http://nl.linkedin.com/in/wimselle

3   Twitter — https://twitter.com/wswebcreation

INTRODUCTION

React Native is gaining popularity over conventional native iOS and Android app development, gaining community support, and gaining market share. It's getting easier and easier to write brilliant apps using React Native. One codebase can be created for and used on both Android and iOS because it compiles to native Java (Android) and Swift (iOS). Specifically, React Native creates a bridge between web UI components and their native Java/Swift counterparts.

Because React Native uses JavaScript, there is no need for two development teams to maintain two platforms. There is no need to synchronize features and layouts, meaning development can go faster and companies can get more out of their budget.

Taking all the advantages of developing a React Native app into account, there should also be some advantages for testing a React Native app. However, as with almost all (web)apps, there are some pains that are associated with automating a React Native app, especially if the de facto standard Appium is used. In this chapter, the following pains around test automation with Appium for React Native apps will be handled:

- Cross-platform test automation efficiency that is attributed, e.g., to proper object identifiers.
- Appium test execution performance
- The ability to automate with mocked API's/databases (DBs) due to unreliable environments

Each pain will be analyzed and tools or code examples will be given to overcome these pains, based on my experience at Tele2.

SCRIPT ONCE, RUN ON MULTIPLE DEVICES

When writing test automation scripts for browsers, it is relatively easy to *script once and run on multiple browser and desktop combinations.* The reason is that the source code of the HTML page to be automated is the same for all browsers, meaning that one can use the same locator[4] and selector[5] to find an element in all different kinds of browsers.

The challenge is how to handle native apps. Each platform has its own language and, even when building a React Native app with JavaScript, the actual source code of the app is either native Android or native iOS code. For example, the user interface (UI) hierarchy completely differs on each platform.

iOS UI hierarchy

---

4   A locator is the way an element can be matched, for example, by class name, by id, by XPATH

5   A selector is the query string to find an element based on its locator. For example, an element can be matched based on id with the query string that matches the id attribute value

Android UI hierarchy

How can elements be located — and which selectors need to be used — if one wants to create a cross-platform test automation script?

Historically, a lot of people said, *"you should use XPATH because with XPATH you can even find a needle in a haystack."* Those people were right; XPATH is a very strong locator, but it is also a very brittle locator. XPATH tends to be error prone, completely dependent on the UI hierarchy, and extremely slow for Appium; it also leads to having two XPATH selectors for both platforms, and that's what is best avoided.

What locator should be used instead? The usage of *"accessibilityLabel"* is highly recommended[6], as the following section illustrates.

Accessibility label

Accessibility labels can be used for people who use voiceover to know what element they have selected. Voiceover then reads the string of the

---

6　For more on locator strategies, the Appium Pro newsletters by Jonathan Lipps is recommended. You can find them at htttps://appiumpro.com

accessibility label of that associated element.

In React Native, both iOS and Android possess the concept of an accessibility label. When developing a component, a developer can add an accessibility label to that component which has the same text on both iOS and Android.

Take, for example, this component, which could be a button with the visual text *'Press me!'* A voiceover on both Android and iOS will read *'Tap me!'*

```
<TouchableOpacity
 accessible={true}
 accessibilityLabel={'Tap me!'}
 onPress={this._onPress}>
 <View style={styles.button}>
 <Text style={styles.buttonText}>Press me!</Text>
 </View>
</TouchableOpacity>
```

Knowing that that the accessibility label is the same for both iOS and Android, one can use this as the new locator strategy for finding and selecting elements.

There are only a few downsides:

* sometimes the app hasn't been made accessible yet
* the current accessibility labels are not useful for testing because they are not descriptive/unique enough
* test-related code should not be packed in a production app

All 3 downsides can be overcome easily. The most important thing is, when adding accessibility labels for testing, this should only happen for a specific test build[7]. This means that when a release build is made, the actual accessibility labels must be used. It's advisable to make the components accessible with a build-specific method as shown below:

```
/**
 * If it is an automation build, add a unique test id for
iOS and Android
 *
```

---

7   For more info about making a specific build see "Preparing a React Native app", step 1

```
 * @param {string} id
 *
 * @return {object|*}
 */
function testProperties(id) {
 if (IS_AUTOMATION_BUILD) {
 return {
 accessibilityLabel: `test-${id}`,
 };
 }
 return null;
}
```

...which can be used in the mentioned component like this

```
<TouchableOpacity
 accessible={true}
 accessibilityLabel={'Tap me!'}
 {...testProperties('Tap me to!')}
 onPress={this._onPress}>
 <View style={styles.button}>
 <Text style={styles.buttonText}>Press me!</Text>
 </View>
</TouchableOpacity>
```

By implementing it this way, the 3 downsides mentioned before are overcome:

- accessibility labels for testing purposes can easily be added with 1 line of code per component

- by placing the method after the currently-defined accessibility properties, it will only overwrite the script when a specific build is used; otherwise it will use the already-defined properties

- if the component should not be accessible in production, the method will only return an accessibility label when a specific build is used — in this case an automation build — otherwise, it will return nothing

A prefix call test- is added to the accessibility labels just to ensure that they are unique.

The cross-platform accessibility label

After implementing the test properties method, it surfaced that there were some difficulties with iOS. The element could be found, yet too many elements were returned, as shown below.

Accessible component on iOS

The solution to this issue is to use *'testID'* for iOS instead of *'accessibilityLabel.'* *'testID'* is a specific property of React Native and iOS[8] to add a test property to a component. In the UI hierarchy, it will be translated to an accessibility label, but with less "pollution", and thus results in finding only one element.

Because there is only one method to handle the test properties, it becomes relatively simple to add this specific cross-platform accessibility label with this code:

```
/**
 * If it is an automation build, add a unique test id for
iOS and Android
 *
```

---

8   For iOS, *testID* is interpreted as an accessibility identifier but for Android, it's missing.

```
 * @param {string} id
 *
 * @return {object|*}
 */
function testProperties(id) {
  if (IS_AUTOMATION_BUILD) {
  if (IS_IOS) {
  return { testID: `test-${id}` };
  }
  return { accessibilityLabel: `test-${id}` };
  }
  return null;
}
```

In the end, this results in a less polluted UI hierarchy for iOS.

Cleaner accessible component on iOS

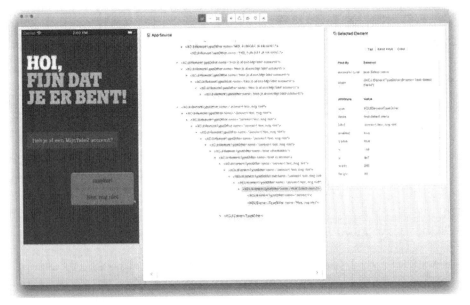

Implementation

Depending on the test framework being used — here, it's webdriver.io[9] — it is quite easy to search for elements and interact with them. Take, for example, tapping on an element. With webdriver.io, this could be written with the

---

9   http://webdriver.io/

following code (based on the touchable component from the code examples)

```
// default
browser.touchAction('~test-Tap me to!', 'tap');
// shorthand
$('~test-Tap me to!').touchAction('tap');
```

The '~' is the locator for telling the test framework that an element should be found based on an accessibility label with the selector *'test-Tap me to!'*.

With the above outlined *'testProperties'* method and the above code, a cross-platform script has been written to tap on an element for both iOS and Android with one line of code, thus meeting the requirement: *script once, run on multiple devices*.

COMPLAINTS ABOUT APPIUM EXECUTION AND/OR PERFORMANCE

One of the most commonly-heard complaints about Appium is that tests can be slow and unreliable (some even call it *'flaky'*). The question that should be asked here is "do we know why this is happening?" And, secondly, when pointing a finger at Appium, one also points 3 fingers at oneself.

It is a good idea to read the Appium Pro newsletter *"Making Your Appium Tests Fast and Reliable, Part 1: Test Flakiness"*[10] to get a good high-level overview of the technologies Appium uses. It will give the answers to this question.

But what does *"when pointing a finger at Appium, one also points 3 fingers at oneself"* mean?

Well, just try this. Point your index finger at, for example, a wall, then turn your hand over. Your middle, ring and little fingers are pointing the other way. This is also the case when talking about Appium. Just ask the following questions and try to keep the app that needs to be automated — plus Appium execution and performance — in mind:

* *Do I know my app? (the middle finger)*

---

10   https://appiumpro.com/editions/19

- *Am I focused on the feature I need to automate? (the ring finger)*
- *Do I really know my test code? (the little finger)*

Each above question will be explained using the Tele2 app as an example.

Do I know my app?

Nowadays, new apps come with a lot of animations; these are intended to increase usability and user experience (UX). Automating an app with a huge amount of animations also has a huge influence on execution times and/or performance of the tests. For example:

- using a lot of *waitForElementExists/waitForElementVisible* with high timeouts
- having *stale element references*[11]

These are just a start.

When relating this question to the Tele2 project, one can see and experience that animations have a huge influence on the execution time of the tests. Take, for example, the onboarding flow. This is the flow where Tele2 explains, in an interactive way, how the user needs to register the app with a chat-based user interface (CUI).

This CUI consists of:

- a minimum of 15 chat-bubbles
- an animation-time of 500 milliseconds per chat-bubble
- a delay of 800 milliseconds between each chat-bubble

This causes the onboarding flow to take at least 19,5 seconds (15 x 1,3s) in animations. In the 19,5 seconds of pure waiting, no further actions have yet been completed, such as selecting options, entering our credentials, and

---

11 https://docs.seleniumhq.org/exceptions/stale_element_reference.jsp

so on. From an automation standpoint, it would be highly efficient to skip these animations since it's very hard to automate and validate animations.

The investigation

The most common animations, such as delay and duration, can easily be defaulted to 0 milliseconds because they are triggered by the Animated library of React Native; it uses a timing method that updates the animated component. Because the biggest part of a React Native app is written in JavaScript, it is easy to use the same language to influence the Animated. timing method by using a stub. This resulted in two methods:

```
// The stub library that is used
const stubs = require('stubs');

/**
 * Setup the app for a specific automation build
 */
function setupAutomation() {
 if (!IS_AUTOMATION_BUILD) {
 return;
 }
 disableAnimations();
}

/**
 * Disable all animations
 */
function disableAnimations() {
 const AnimatedTiming = Animated.timing;
 stubs(Animated, 'timing', (...props) => {
 props[1].duration = 0;
 props[1].delay = 0;
 return AnimatedTiming(...props);
 });
}
```

The first method (*setupAutomation()*) is called when the app is started. It executes the most important check, namely *"Is this an automation build?"*[12] This needs to be executed first because we still want to have animation in production, only not what we are automating.

The second method (*disableAnimations()*) will use a stub to listen to the *Animated.timing.* If it is called, it will not use the given *duration* and *delay,* but rather a stubbed duration and delay which results in **no** animations and a **decrease** in execution time.

So, by just investigating our app, checking the code of the app and the core of React Native, we saved **19,5 seconds** in execution time when automating the onboarding flow. The advantage of the *disableAnimations* method is also that it is not only used for the onboarding flow, but automatically for all animated components in the app. This will save even more time when automating other features.

Side note

Keep in mind that animations are just one of the few things that can be dealt with this way. Take, for example

- loading of external libraries/components like Google maps
- using a lot of service calls to retrieve your data (see also "Increase quality by mocking your services")

and so on. Always ask the question "How does the app that needs to be automated influence the execution and/or performance of the automated tests?"

Do I focus on the feature I need to automate?

There are very few apps out there that don't use a registration process. The reason why they use a registration process is that these apps employ user data, like banking, personal data, or photos. This means that, for those apps, a lot of functionality will be behind a login screen, sometimes more than 95%.

This is also the case for Tele2. The onboarding process is needed to be

---

12   For more info about making a specific build see "Preparing a React Native app", step 1

able to retrieve the right customer data and, for example, allow the user to purchase extra data. Automating the purchase of extra data by first walking through the onboarding flow will introduce extra test dependencies which

* can be error prone.
* may cause tests to fail during onboarding because of a flaky test (environment) or other circumstances.

To prevent this, the focus should be on testing and automating the feature we need to automate, in this case the purchase of extra data, not the onboarding flow. Otherwise, the onboarding flow would become the best test feature of the app.

By testing each feature in its own scope, multiple benefits can be achieved such as:

* eliminating flakiness
* decreasing execution time
* focusing on the quality of each feature in the app

Implementing a test link screen

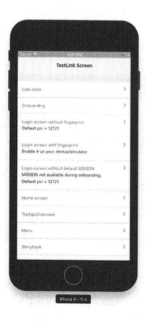

Focusing on the features that need to be automated can be accomplished by creating an option in the app to create the initial state of that feature. This can be done by creating a Test link screen that will only be shown in a specific build. On this screen, a developer and or an automation engineer will see all the states/ features in which the app can start. It will give them the possibility to focus only on that part of the app that really needs to be tested.

This test link screen gave Tele2 multiple advantages. It not only gave the developers an easy way to access a feature for fixes or creating new features, it also decreased manual and automated time to test a given feature by **15**

seconds. This is the time saved by skipping the onboarding flow.

Do I really know my test code?

Even though this question could be related to the "little finger", and might thus be seen as less important, its importance is equal to the rest of the points. Test code is also code. QAs are also developers; they produce code and software which can also contain bugs and/or flaws or produce flakiness.

I strongly recommend watching the session about flakiness by Richard Bradshaw entitled *"Your tests aren't flaky. You are!"*[13] that was given during SeleniumConf 2017 in Berlin. It touches on the following points, which are very important

- An appreciation of the skills required to design good automated checks
- An appreciation of the skills required to implement a good automated check
- How these skills differ, and how the whole team needs to be involved
- The importance of continuously reviewing automated checks for implementation, risks and value added

Based on these points, QA should also reconsider looking at their test code because the execution and/or performance of Appium may not be related to Appium; they may be related to QA-ers themselves!

INCREASE QUALITY BY MOCKING YOUR SERVICES

User experience (UX), notably poor user experience, can become a hot topic when something goes wrong in production. Even though the app has met almost all the requirements of the UX Foundation (interaction, usability, ergonomics, accessibility, performance, marketing, utility, design and so on), if one of the levels is out of balance, the complete UX is out of balance.

Take, for example, a new app that integrates with a lot of API's to retrieve user data from databases. Depending on the infrastructure, API's can have different results in response times which, in turn, can have an effect on the UX of the customer. The data sent to the app also has an effect on how the

---

13   https://youtu.be/XnkWkrbzMh0

user experiences the app, especially when the response takes too much time or leads to an app crash.

When looking at a typical app development cycle, including (automated) testing, the app is connected to a real environment regarding the API's. This could be a development, test, or staging environment which may contain different data. These different environments make it harder to test how the app responds to:

- delays
- error responses
- different data responses

Thus, it becomes harder to make a determination about that part of the quality and UX. One of the reasons for this is that it is hard to influence the APIs during test execution without bothering other teams that use the same environments and APIs.

Why mock APIs for UI testing?

A widely used approach for testing APIs is to use mocking. However, when the focus is not the API but the app, why shouldn't the app also be mocked? The reason for this question is that in most test automation cases, the main goal is to test the *functional and or visual flow of the app*, **not the integration** of all API's (that's what an integration test is for). For example, the risk of an API not working on an iPhone 8 while working on an iPhone X is very small.

Knowing that this risk is very low, the focus can be set on testing the app with mocked responses. This provides the opportunity to:

- test delays on APIs
- test different error responses
- test different data responses

Being able to test these situations will, first, give insights into how the UX will be influenced based on these conditions. Second, it will give the designers/product owners/developers the possibility to optimize the UX before going to production. And, finally, it will offer even more advantages such as

- starting to develop a feature that uses an API-contract of an API which still needs to be built or is under development
- testing the front end with consistent data for each repeatable test case — this will make the automation much more reliable
- mocked APIs are far more stable than APIs on different environments like development, testing or staging
- Set user states, such as a logged in user, without waiting for multiple seconds, thus making manual and/or test automation much faster
- Next to testing services with a long delay, services can also be tested with a minimal delay, which makes test execution much faster

Keep in mind that the app still needs to have an integration test with all APIs. This can be limited to 1 device per platform.

Mock APIs for a React Native app

Mocking can easily be integrated into a React Native app, giving developers, manual testers, and test automation engineers the advantages of what mocking offers. It's advised to set it up in a generic way so that developing, testing, and building an app for different environments can be done with little effort.

Before integrating mocking into an app, it's wise to first investigate which mocking framework suits your needs. When JAVA is a commonly used language, MockServer[14] or WireMock[15] can be used. If JavaScript is the common language, then node-mock-server[16] or the not-as-well-known ng-apimock[17] can be used[18].

In these examples, ng-apimock will be used for the following reasons:

- React Native is written in JavaScript

---

14   https://github.com/jamesdbloom/mockserver

15   http://wiremock.org/

16   https://github.com/smollweide/node-mock-server

17   https://github.com/mdasberg/ng-apimock/

18   This is just a small collection of open source mocking servers, there are more, but these are commonly used servers.

- it supports independent parallel mocking

- ng-apimock is a lightweight JavaScript module

- mocking is scenario-based so each mocked API can return different responses

- delays can easily be adjusted during manual and automated testing

- it supports dynamically loading global variables which makes the mock data easy to use, for example, with dates and times

- it has a simple UI to adjust responses/delays, so it can be used manually

- Tele2 uses it

Even though the name assumes it's related to Angular, it can also be used for all kinds of apps such as web or native.

Below, an example of the UI of ng-apimock is shown.

With this UI, manual testers can easily test the app with the responses/delays of each mocked service.

Preparing a React Native app

The first step in preparation will be to be able to build an app for each environment which will have its own configuration variables like the API_URL.

One of the tools that can help expose configuration variables in a React Native app is react-native-config[19]. It uses a simple and clean '.env'-text file in the root of a React Native app project, through which variables can easily be added and accessed in the React Native app code. For example, take this piece of code:

```
// Content of the .env file, place it in the root of the
React Native app project

API_URL=https://myapi.com
```

Accessing a variable in the React Native code can be done like this:

```
// config.js
import Config from 'react-native-config'

const apiUrl = Config.API_URL // 'https://myapi.com'
```

Each buildtype can have its own '.env' file. A file for the test environment can be called '.env.test', the file for the mocking environment can be called '.env. mocking', and so on. The only difference in the file is the value of 'API_URL'; the JavaScript code doesn't need to change.

Environment-specific builds can now easily be triggered from the command line:

```
ENVFILE=.env.mocking react-native run-ios
```

The second step is setting up ng-apimock. This can be done in 2 ways.

- Use ng-apimock as a development dependency in the React Native project
- Use ng-apimock as a standalone project (making it easier to use it either locally or in a docker-container)

Depending on the size of the project and the number of APIs, it's recommended to divide responsibilities and, thus, use ng-apimock as a standalone project.

---

19   https://github.com/luggit/react-native-config

ng-apimock comes with a readme file with instructions on how to install and set up the mock server. The only connection between the React Native app and the mock server is the URL where ng-apimock is hosted: for example, 'http://localhost:{port-number}' or a different URL on the network like 'http://example.api.com'. ng-apimock will automatically handle all API calls with correct responses that are done on 'http://example.api.com' with the selected scenario and the selected delay.

If ng-apimock won't be used during test automation, the third step can be skipped.

The third step is highly recommended and requires some coding. ng-apimock was initially made for Angular and Protractor[20] and, therefore, comes with a default interface for Protractor. To use ng-apimock with another automation framework than Protractor, a custom-made[21] interface should be made. This interface can be used during automated tests to set the state of an API (response and or delay) for that specific testcase and can be written in around 100–150 lines of code. It will hold methods like:

- *selectScenario:* select the given scenario
- *delayResponse:* set the delay time for the API so the response will be delayed
- *setGlobalVariable:* set a global variable such as the current date or time to make the response more dynamic

If mocking will be used with parallel execution, an additional adjustment needs to be made to the React Native app and to the automation framework. The reason for this is that each device on which the app is installed and tested needs to have his own unique request and response. If the response is not unique per device, a rage condition can appear and the test execution will fail. How this works and how it impacts the React Native app and the automation framework can be found in the presentation "How React Native, Appium and me made each other shine"[22] in slides 47–63.

---

20 Protractor is the de facto standard for automating Angular apps and is a widely used automation framework all over the world.

21 At the end of 2018, ng-apimock will get a new and easily-extensible interface so it can be used for multiple automation frameworks by writing only a few lines of code.

22 https://www.slideshare.net/WimSelles/how-react-native-appium-and-me-made-each-other-shine

SUMMARY

React Native technology enables organizations to develop an app for two platforms using one codebase and without the to synchronize features and layouts. In React Native apps, the developer can move faster, and the company can accomplish more within its budget. This chapter aimed to solve the three most common pains when automating a React Native app using Appium:

- cross-platform test automation efficiency
- Appium test execution performance
- the ability to automate with mocked APIs/databases

As the technology evolves and your React Native apps become more complex, it is highly recommended to follow the aforementioned best practices in order to enhance your overall testing productivity.

CHAPTER NINETEEN

Testing 101 for Next Gen digital interfaces – Chatbots

BY AMIR ROZENBERG

AMIR ROZENBERG is a thought leader in the space of agile quality methodologies. As a product director at Perfecto, he drove the core product strategy and implementation with many Fortune-1000 customers. He led initiatives in the areas of real user condition testing, accessibility, security, audio and conversational interfaces, AI/ML, IoT and medical devices etc. In addition, Amir led successful synergies with Microsoft,

SmartBear, Blazemeter, Neotys etc., to optimize value delivery to the market. Prior to Perfecto, Amir led the mobile monitoring practice at Compuware.

```
public static enum thingsToTest{
        Chatbots,
        Finger_Face_ID,
        IoT_WebConnected,
        IoT_Device_Connected,
        OTT_Devices
};
```

INTRODUCTION

Brands from every vertical are pushed to innovate in application functionality, simplicity, and for the enjoyment of their end users. As such, application scope is expanding. Examples of this change include replacing manual data entry with automated usage of sensors (ex.: camera, GPS, fingerprint), inclusion and consideration of these sensor inputs to enrich the experience (such as location-aware context, acceleration and velocity, etc.) and the ubiquity of digital applications on all screens, from web and mobile to IoT and OTT devices. This necessitates a massive test coverage matrix. In the next few chapters, we will address test approaches, with examples, for each of these areas.

NEXT GENERATION INTERFACES: ONBOARD SENSORS AND AUDIO CHATBOTS

New data entry methods and interaction schemes are driving the next generation of user interfaces. They span location and imagery sensing, acceleration, and authentication (face/touch ID), as well as new conversational interfaces. They are designed to streamline and simplify data entry, and enrich and 'gamify' the user experience in order to delight the end user. Here are some examples of using onboard sensors to create a better UX:

- Augmented/Virtual reality: location/imagery-aware games, user manuals and clothes/furniture fitting, combining real location and video feed from the camera with augmented reality content, enabling application enrichment for gaming, social and utility purposes.

Figure 1: Augmented Reality (AR) can assist with finding products in store

- Streamlined data entry and authentication: Accurate OCR technologies enable an alternative to laborious data entry. Drivers' licenses, passports, and credit card and check scanning are all great examples. In addition, advanced biometric authentication sensors enable rapid face, iris, or fingerprint authentication. This specific area is not only interesting from a security enhancement perspective; it enables new revenue streams for in-app purchases — especially those in real time gaming, where manual authentication would be inappropriate.

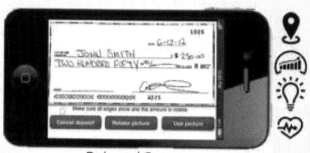

Figure 2: Leveraging onboard sensor for data entry and app enrichment

Onboard Sensors

- Textual and Conversational personal assistants: Maturation of Natural Language Processing (NLP) and AI cloud services enable human-like interaction with a smart virtual assistant. These technologies, unlike a simple Google search, can carry on an extended conversation with context. From a user perspective, interacting with a brand on the screen of my choice, at the time and place of my choice, and always getting the right answer (no haggling), is an immense benefit. The range of applications is diverse, from banking and insurance to travel, etc., whether expressing interest in getting a quote, finding account balances and transferring money, or calling customer support. Businesses can realize significant commercial benefits, both from more meaningful relationships with their end users (simply put, users are more inclined to extend conversations with human-like personal assistant) and cost savings through enabling virtual assistants in customer support scenarios.

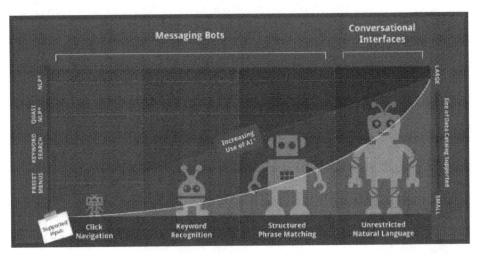

Figure 3: The positive impact of conversational interfaces on complex discussions with the brand (image source: MindMeld.com)

TESTING SENSOR-DRIVEN EXPERIENCES

Testing these interfaces on a wide variety of devices and platforms is a challenging task. Not only are these new interfaces, they are also areas of rapid innovation. Significant parts of these interactions take place at an ecosystem level rather than with your own dev team(s). Cloud providers innovate in AR and AI services, device manufacturers innovate in onboard sensor technologies and their utility at an OS level. As such, one must consider both their own innovation pace as well as ecosystem changes to ensure a continuous quality experience, both upon introduction of a new feature and/or a new device or OS.

The approach realizes the test cases, the lab, as well as the application under test, can support such automation. The latter is also called "application instrumentation": essentially replacements for operating system APIs that provide input to the app with test data from the script. It is important to note that instrumentation of an application does not require changes to the app binary. It's a wrapper that needs to be re-signed with the app.

For example, in the case of face/iris or fingerprint ID, the ideal approach would be to override the device OS APIs to simulate such events in the app through instrumentation. Essentially, when the app calls the OS to authenticate the user by a biometric sensor, the lab would circumvent the OS API call and simulate a pass/fail response. The tester then would have a range of responses: pass or fail, with relevant error codes. For example:

Auth Failed — indicates that the fingerprint was not recognized

User Cancel — indicates that the user canceled the authentication

User Fallback — indicates that user wishes to supply a fallback authentication, for example a password

System Cancel — indicates that the system canceled the authentication

Lock Out — indicates multiple failures and application should lock the account

The same approach can be taken to simulate location injection[1], image injection (simulating check scanning scenarios, for example), accelerometer injection, audio injection, etc.

Here's a sample showing how to test a fitness or navigation app without leaving the lab:

```
// Loop over the GPS data and inject it to the device
  ListIterator<String> listIterator = Locations.
  listIterator();
  while (listIterator.hasNext()) {
     MobileLocation location1 = new MobileCoordinatesLoca-
     tion(listIterator.next());
     device.setLocation(location1);
     try {
        Thread.sleep(100);
     } catch (InterruptedException e) {
        // TODO Auto-generated catch block
        e.printStackTrace();
     }
  }
..

public static void readGPSData() {
   // use the GPX file
   File f = new File ("C:\\GPS\\home_work.xml");
   DocumentBuilderFactory dbFactory = Document BuilderFacto
   ry.newInstance();
```

---

1   Sample code for simulating location change — https://developers.perfectomobile.com/display/TT/
    Test+your+navigation+app+without+leaving+the+room

```
DocumentBuilder dBuilder = dbFactory.newDocumentBuilder();
Document doc = dBuilder.parse(f);
NodeList nList = doc.getElementsByTagName("trkpt");
for (int temp = 0; temp < nList.getLength(); temp++) {
    Node nNode = nList.item(temp);
    if (nNode.getNodeType() == Node.ELEMENT_NODE) {
        Element eElement = (Element) nNode;
        Locations.add(eElement.getAttribute("Lat")+","+ eEle-
        ment.getAttribute("Lon"));
    }
}
}
```

TESTING TEXT AND CONVERSATIONAL CHATBOTS

There are two types of chatbots. The first is text-based, present in messaging applications (iMessage, WhatsApp, Facebook Messenger etc.), as well inside brands' own applications. In this type, generating full functional and responsiveness tests simply requires interacting with the virtual assistant via native or visual objects.

The second case concerns conversational chatbots: these typically live inside mobile apps. Here, testing must include some interesting scenarios beyond functional testing. One area regards responsiveness of the chatbot: in verbal communications, a long pause is awkward and leads the user to think an error has occurred. Another good idea is to test the chatbot's behavior in the presence of medium to heavy background noise. Finally, a mandatory requirement for every chatbot is to test its desired level of learning and interaction using new languages. Whereas in social applications, adoption of informal language may be desired, in other environments, this can become a problem, as Microsoft learned — the hard way — with Tay and Zo; both bots adopted racist and offensive language.

As far as the basic testing of voice chatbots goes, including their functionality, responsiveness, and background noise, one can design a test prioritization schedule, as can be seen below:

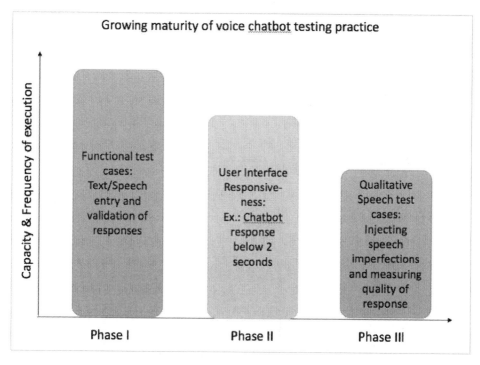

Figure 4: Prioritizing conversational interface testing

In terms of the lab itself, here's a conceptual model for establishing test automation. The lab below offers two input interfaces:

- Textual input, with the ability to convert text to audio (different genders, languages, personas, etc.), and inject these into the chatbot

- Audio input enables the ability to inject audio directly into the chatbot. This interface can prove particularly useful when emulating noise environments, voice variations, etc.

In terms of validation, a lab should offer the following interfaces:

- Textual validation: since most chatbots respond both with text and audio, basic validation can be based on visual (OCR) or native object validation, which would include a measurement for responsiveness

- Speech-to-text mechanisms can record the chatbot's vocal response, translate into text, and offer it for validation

- Finally, one might consider an audio quality mechanism to check the

quality of speech or streaming music

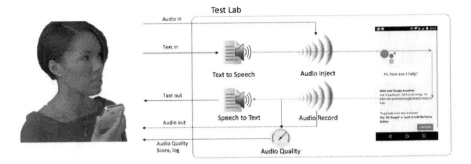

Figure 5: Conceptual chatbot testing lab

Ideally, such a lab would cater to all types of devices, chatbots[2] in and out of apps, as well as other devices such as Google Echo, etc.

The above structure would enable a novice tester to author a basic script, fundamentally based on input and output dictionaries, KPI for acceptable response time, and a representation of the basic functions.

```
    private static void setDictionary(RemoteWebDriver driver, Ar-
rayList<String> sentences, ArrayList<String> expectedResponses){
        String fileName = "";
        sentences.add("hello");
        expectedResponses.add("How can I");
        sentences.add("what is the time now");
        expectedResponses.add("the time is");
        sentences.add("find a bank of america branch near burling-
        ton massachussets please");
        expectedResponses.add("the address for bank of America
        is");
    }
// Execute the script
for (String s:sentences){
        expectedResponse = expectedResponses.get(index);
        utils.injectAudio(s);
        recordings.add(listen(driver, true, expectedResponse,15));
}
```

---

2   Testing voice chatbots GitHub code sample — https://github.com/AmirAtPerfecto/De-
    mo-voice-chatbot

```
for (String s:recordings) {
        expectedResponse = expectedResponses.get(index);
        String temp = utils.speechToText(driver, s);
        utils.speechToTextValidate(driver, s, expectedResponse);
        index = index +1;
}
```

TESTING TEXT AND CONVERSATIONAL CHATBOTS

In summary, as sprints shrink and scope grows, test automation — and having the right lab — becomes even more important. To test sensor-based functionality, application instrumentation and data sets need to be in place. With respect to text and voice based chatbots, the scope and diversity of test scenarios expand even further, mandating proper prioritization of test cases.

CHAPTER TWENTY

Pushing the Limits of Mobile Test Automation with Appium

BY JONATHAN LIPPS

JONATHAN has been making things out of code as long as he can remember. Jonathan is the architect and project lead for Appium, the popular open source automation framework. He is also the founding Principal of Cloud Grey, a consulting firm devoted to helping clients leverage the power of Appium successfully. He has worked as a programmer in tech startups for over 15 years, but is also passionate about academic discussion. Jonathan has master's degrees in philosophy and linguistics, from Stanford and Oxford respectively. Living in Vancouver, he's an avid rock climber, yogi, musician, and writer on topics he considers vital, like the relationship of technology to what it means to be human.

INTRODUCTION

Most everyone involved in mobile app testing will have heard of Appium, the cross-platform automation umbrella that offers a WebDriver-compatible interface for automation of iOS, Android, Windows, Mac, and more. Appium burst onto the scene in 2013 and has outlived many of its contemporaries and competitors over the years. This is not always due to Appium's technical superiority, but sometimes simply the breadth of its vision and the positive effects of a strong community. One other key facet of the Appium project's philosophy is pragmatism: we all know that, at the end of the day, test authors use Appium to get things done. We try to always keep a balance between (1) adherence to a standard protocol and (2) exposing features invaluable for testing that might require a bit of creativity to shoehorn into the WebDriver specification.

What this means is that while you can't do everything with Appium that you might want, you can do more with Appium than pretty much any other tool. As someone who works full time with Appium (helping run the open source project, writing tips for the Appium Pro[1] newsletter, and coming into organizations to help with Appium training or strategy as the Founding Principal of Cloud Grey[2]), I can say that there is usually a way to meet any particular automation requirement with Appium. Happily, the Appium umbrella also keeps expanding and welcoming new "drivers" (support for different automation technologies); for example, an Espresso-based driver for Android automation and an official Samsung Tizen driver, providing access to entirely new platforms or automation engines without a difference in the external protocol. This chapter embodies the foregoing reflections by diving into some specific strategies for "advanced" automation requirements or techniques: for example, performance testing or app upgrade testing.

HOW APPIUM WORKS

Before we get into the details, it's useful to know a bit about how Appium works. Even though Appium scripts are written in a particular language, Appium itself is not a library directly accessed via any language. Instead, Appium scripts rely on Appium *clients*, which connect to an Appium *server* you have running on your machine (or somewhere on the Internet, for example, at a cloud-based Appium provider). The client and server communicate via the "WebDriver protocol", which is a W3C specification for web browser testing. Appium implements this protocol (in as spec-compliant a fashion as possible), and extends it to expose mobile-specific automation behaviors. For example, the WebDriver protocol itself allows for finding UI elements

---

1   Appium Pro Newsletter — https://appiumpro.com/

2   Cloud Grey Consultancy — https://cloudgrey.io/

and interacting with them via a click. Appium adds to the set of "locator strategies" by which elements may be found to reflect the mobile situation, and also augments the library of commands available for found elements.

Appium's main goal is to be this protocol bridge between users and automation technologies (for mobile and beyond). As far as possible, Appium relies on existing automation technologies (for example, Google's UiAutomator2 or Espresso for Android, or Apple's XCUITest for iOS). We assume that, in the long run, no one will be better at producing automation tools for Android than Google, or for iOS than Apple, so we try not to reinvent the wheel. Instead, we focus on creating a highly-reliable WebDriver protocol front-end for these technologies, and ensuring that any flaws in the underlying technologies (there are many) are dealt with as gracefully as possible. Finally, we look for gaps in the underlying technologies and try to fill them by external means. For example, Google's UiAutomator2 is a library which is purely focused on UI automation; however, it's often necessary to automate higher-level device behaviors like installing and uninstalling apps. Google's ADB tool provides the facility for meeting this requirement as well as a host of other features. Appium makes these features available in the same interface by which it makes the core UiAutomator2 features available, thus presenting to the Appium user a unified front of features, knitting together whatever it needs to use under the hood in order to do so.

Fundamentally, Appium is limited by the technologies it chooses to power its array of drivers, but the community of Appium users is so ingenious that there are often interesting workarounds proposed for these limitations, which can be incorporated into the Appium layer until such a time that the underlying technology vendor chooses to fix or enhance its core tool. Some of the tips below fall into this category! And with this brief lesson on Appium's structure and purpose out of the way, let's dive into those tips. There's no space in this chapter to discuss how to set up Appium or which concepts are important for starting and running test sessions, so I will refer the reader to one of the many excellent tutorials online, or Appium's own documentation[3]. In this chapter, I will simply assume that you have Appium up and running, and are familiar with how to start and stop tests for a given

---

3   Appium Documentation — https://appium.io/

platform, device, and driver. Note that for code examples, I will use the Java language and Appium client, though the techniques will work in any language and with any Appium clients.

PERFORMANCE TESTING WITH APPIUM

Performance is an oft-neglected side of functional testing among Appium users because Appium is usually used simply to make verifications of mobile apps' functionality. Testers use Appium to check the state of an app's UI to ensure that the app's features are working correctly. Functional testing is, of course, very important, and deserves to be the primary use case for Appium, but there are other dimensions of the app user experience that are equally important and equally worthy of automated verification. One such dimension is performance. Performance is simply how responsive your app is to the user; this notion of "responsiveness" can be cashed out in terms of a variety of proxy factors, from network request time to CPU and memory usage.

Mobile apps (more so than desktop apps) often run in tightly-constrained environments when it comes to system resources. Mobile apps which over-utilize system resources can create a bad experience not only for users of the app in question, but can also cause problems for the system as a whole, shortening the battery life or causing other applications to run slowly. Engaging in performance testing is a way to be a good citizen of the app ecosystem, not just to ensure the best experience for your own users.

Fortunately, Appium provides access to all kinds of interesting performance data via its API on both Android and iOS. Because the tools available for performance data gathering on these systems are different, there is unfortunately no way to present the data in a uniform fashion, but at least the data are there! Let's explore how to specify what you're interested in and retrieve it on both of the mobile platforms.

PERFORMANCE TESTING ON ANDROID

Building on the wealth of information that comes via a call to adb dumpsys, Appium provides a succinct overview of all aspects of your app's performance via the getPerformanceData command. The client call is simple:

```
driver.getPerformanceData("<package>", "<perf type>", <time-
out>);
```

In this example, `<package>` is the package of your App Under Test (AUT), or any other app you wish to profile. `<perf type>` is what kind of performance data you want. There is another handy driver command (getSupportedPerformanceDataTypes) which tells you which types are valid. At the time of writing, they are: cpuinfo, memoryinfo, batteryinfo, and networkinfo. Finally, `<timeout>` is an integer denoting the number of seconds Appium will poll for performance data if it is not immediately available.

We don't have the space to explore all these types of profile data, so let's focus on a simple example involving memory usage. One problem encountered by many apps at some point in their history is, of course, a memory leak. Even though Android apps are run in a garbage-collected environment, they can still cause memory to be locked up in an unusable state. It's therefore important to test that your app is not using increasing amounts of memory over time, without good reason or beyond a certain known-good threshold.

Let's construct a simple test scenario as an example of how we might check this. All we need to do is open up a view in our app, take a snapshot of the memory usage at that point, and then wait a pre-determined amount of time. We subsequently take another snapshot, and assert that the memory usage indicated at the second snapshot is not unreasonably greater than that indicated at the first snapshot. In essence, we're making the assertion that our app isn't using increasing amounts of memory while, theoretically, doing nothing. It's a simple memory leak prevention test. Let's construct an example based on the sample Android ApiDemos[4] application:

```
List<List<Object>> data = driver.getPerformanceData("io.ap-
pium.android.apis", "memoryinfo", 10);
```

What we get in the call here is a set of two lists; one list is the keys and the other is the values. We can bundle up the call above along with some helper code that makes it easier to query the specific kind of memory info we're looking for (of course, in the real world we might make a class to hold

---

4   Android API Demos App — https://android.googlesource.com/platform/development/+/master/
      samples/ApiDemos

the data):

```
private HashMap<String, Integer> getMemoryInfo(Android-
Driver driver) throws Exception {
    List<List<Object>> data = driver.getPerformance
      Data("io.appium.android.apis", "memoryinfo", 10);
    HashMap<String, Integer> readableData = new Hash
      Map<>();
    for (int i = 0; i < data.get(0).size(); i++) {
    int val;
      if (data.get(1).get(i) == null) {
 val = 0;
    } else {
 val = Integer.parseInt((String) data.
         get(1).get(i));
    }
    readableData.put((String) data.get(0).get(i),
       val);
    }
    return readableData;
}
```

We now have a HashMap we can use to query the particular kinds of memory info we retrieved. For our purposes, we're going to look for the totalPss value:

```
HashMap<String, Integer> memoryInfo = getMemoryInfo(driv-
er);
int setSize = memoryInfo.get("totalPss");
```

What is this value, anyway? "PSS" means "Proportional Set Size". According to the Android dumpsys docs, this is a measurement of an app's RAM use that takes into account sharing pages across processes. "Any RAM pages that are unique to your process directly contribute to its PSS value, while pages that are shared with other processes contribute to the PSS value only in proportion to the amount of sharing. For example, a page that is shared between two processes will contribute half of its size to the PSS of each process." In other words, it's a pretty good measurement of the RAM impact of our app. There's a lot more to dig into here, but this measurement will do for our case.

So far we have the magic method that gets us the value we want; at this point it is trivial to hook up an Appium example that calls this method at two different points and then asserts on the (lack of) difference between the values at those points. Of course, memory usage might indeed increase validly in the specified duration, so we may not want to assert that no increase at all happened, only that we didn't increase beyond a certain multiple of the first snapshot, for example.

That's it for Android — definitely check out the other types of app profile data available, like CPU usage or how the app affects battery state!

PERFORMANCE TESTING ON IOS

Performance testing for iOS apps is, unfortunately, not as straightforward as for Android because the performance data generated during an iOS test session can only be delivered in a proprietary Apple format, viewable in the Instruments utility distributed by Apple alongside Xcode. Thankfully, we can at least trigger the capture of this data programmatically via Appium so it can be stored as part of a test artifact in a CI environment and reviewed. In terms of what kind of data we can get, Instruments comes with a number of built-in analyses and measurements. If you open up the Instruments app on your Mac, you're greeted with a list of these:

These are the various measurements it will be possible to initiate using Appium, so you will need to examine this list for ideas about what you might want to measure for your app and make sure to read Apple's docs carefully if you want to know more about what each one does. In this chapter, we're going to work with the "Time Profiler" instrument. As I mentioned above, since we're using Appium, we don't need to click on anything in the Instruments app itself, so it can safely be closed until we need to view a performance report.

The way iOS profiling works with Appium is with two commands: one to start the profiling and one to stop it and dump the data out to us for viewing. These commands are available as of Appium 1.8, via the mobile: command interface:

```
driver.executeScript("mobile: startPerfRecord", args);
// here: do some stuff in the app that you want to profile
String b64Zip = (String)driver.executeScript("mobile: stopPerfRecord", args);
// here: convert the base64-encoded zip file to actual file
data on your system
```

We use the `mobile: startPerfRecord` and `mobile: stopPerfRecord` commands to signal to Appium when during our script we'd like the profiling to occur. There is one caveat, however: for performance recording to work, we need to have started the Appium server with the --relaxed-security flag. This is because Instruments can gather data from the system as a whole, not just the AUT. It's therefore a security risk to expose potentially sensitive system information to Appium sessions running from a remote client, for example, in the context of a cloud Appium host.

What about the args parameter to these methods? What should it look like? The "start" method takes an argument object with three fields, for example:

```
HashMap<String, Object> args = new HashMap<>();
args.put("pid", "current");
args.put("profileName", "Time Profiler");
args.put("timeout", 60000);
```

These correspond to:

1. pid: Which process we want to attach to ("current" is a handy shortcut to refer to the AUT, which is probably what we're interested in. By default,

all processes will be profiled if we don't specify anything, potentially filling the resulting profile data file with lots of extraneous noise).

2. profileName: Which kind of instrument we want to run (in our case, the Time Profiler).

3. timeout: a number of milliseconds after which the performance trace will stop on its own. These trace files can get pretty huge, so this is an important parameter to remember.

For the "stop" method, the only argument we care about is profileName, whose value should match exactly what we passed in to the "start" call, so Appium knows which (of potentially multiple) traces to stop. And what about the value of stopPerfRecord? What's b64Zip supposed to mean? What Appium returns when we stop performance recording is actually an "Instruments Trace Document", which happens to be a directory from the perspective of the macOS filesystem. Since directories are impossible to send in string format, Appium zips up this .trace directory and hands it back to the client script in base64 encoding. To be able to access this data after a test session, we have to teach our Appium script to decode it and write it into a zipfile on our system, with code like the following:

```
File traceZip = new File("/path/to/trace.zip");
String b64Zip = (String)driver.executeScript("mobile: stop-
PerfRecord", args);
byte[] bytesZip = Base64.getMimeDecoder().decode(b64Zip);
FileOutputStream stream = new FileOutputStream(traceZip);
stream.write(bytesZip);
```

At this point, we'll have a nice little trace.zip file sitting at the specified location on disk. We can now simply unzip it and double-click it to open the trace file up in the Instruments viewer, which greets us with a screen like this:

In this GUI, we can explore the threads that were active during the profiled portion of our Appium test and see which routines that thread spent most of its time in (via the stacktrace snapshots taken by the profiler). This can help us to find CPU-hungry areas of our app, which we might decide to offload to a worker thread to improve the user experience, for example. There are all kinds of considerations and potential avenues for improvement based on the data gleaned from these trace files, but that is outside the scope of this brief section. As mentioned above, you might want to consider dumping one of these zip files pre-emptively for any test that runs in your CI environment, so you can always go back to a failed test and see if there were any performance issues that might help explain what went wrong.

ACCELERATING TEST EXECUTION WITH DEEP LINKS

One of the most common exasperations we encounter in functional testing (yes, even functional testing with Appium) is that functional tests can be slow. There is a sort of fundamental "speed limit" which we are forced to obey, coming from the underlying technologies. If Appium's iOS driver is built on XCUITest, and XCUITest takes X seconds to execute an action, then that is how long it will take Appium, at a minimum (not to mention the slight overhead of Appium's HTTP model on top of that).

So, this is a fact of life, but it's not one we should be willing to live with, especially given that most of the steps of any given functional test are often devoted merely to setting up state for the actual verification. It's very common, for example, for much of the functionality of a mobile app to be hidden behind an authentication barrier, such as a login screen. In order to test scenarios having to do with authenticated features, it's therefore necessary to have a login step at the beginning of each test. But even navigating to and filling out a login screen and waiting for the authentication to occur over the network could take an egregiously long time. It's not out of the question to say that logging in to an app could take 20 seconds by automating the UI itself, as we are typically habituated to doing with Appium. This is frustrating enough when developing a test, but when you multiply the login step by the number of tests in your build which require it, you often end up with a much bigger waste of time. With only 50 authentication-requiring tests, you end up with north of 15 minutes of wasted build time. This is very significant and should not be acceptable to any of us!

Thankfully, while we can't usually override the speed limit and make individual functional test steps (clicks, keystrokes) themselves go faster, we can sidestep the whole problem by finding an alternate method for setting up state for our application. After all, that's what we care about; we don't care about testing the login function of our app dozens of times over in each build. We only need to validate it once! In every other case, we are conceptually in the clear if we can find some other means to set up the test preconditions without going through the UI.

We can accomplish this in a truly cross-platform way on both iOS and Android with something called a "deep link". Deep links are special URLs that can be associated with specific apps. This association happens when the developer of the app registers a unique URL scheme with the OS. From then on, whenever that URL is tapped or otherwise triggered, the app will come alive and will be given the opportunity to parse the URL that spawned it, thereby doing whatever it wants with the URL.

To resolve the problem of setting up login state I described above, we'd thus need some kind of special URL that, when our app is opened with it, is interpreted as a login attempt. In this special launch case where the app has been started with this special URL, it will be directed perform the login behind the scenes and simply redirect the app to the correct logged-in view, without needing even to show a login UI in the first place! Of course, all this logic must be added to the app itself; it has nothing to do with Appium. The app developer needs to understand the URL schema, write the code that parses it and performs the login behavior, and register the URL scheme pertaining to the application. Exactly how this is done is an app development question and beyond the scope of this chapter. There are plenty of tutorials online for adding deep link support to your iOS or Android app.

For now, let's imagine we have correctly implemented this app-level feature, and can successfully leverage a URL of the form:

```
yourapp://login/<username>/<password>
```

In other words, we are in a position where, with your app installed on a device, we can tap that URL (or otherwise trigger it), and your app will start up, parse the URL for the "controller" ("login"), and the username and password data, and finally attempt a login with that data. All that remains is to figure out how to trigger the URL with Appium (since there's no human user around to type that URL into the nav bar in Safari, for example).

It's easy: just use driver.get. Since the Appium client libraries just extend the underlying WebDriver clients, we can use the same command that Selenium WebDriver would use to navigate to a browser URL. In our case, the concept of URL is just ... bigger ... than the concept of a URL in the browser! So, let's say we want to log in with the username appium and the password isAwesome. All we have to do is construct a test that opens a session with our AUT, and runs the following command:

```
driver.get("theapp://login/appium/isAwesome");
```

As we said before, it's up to the app developer to build the ability to respond to URLs and perform the appropriate action with them. And you probably want to ensure that URLs used for testing are not available in production versions of your app, so as to prevent real users from stumbling onto them. Despite all this effort for the app developer, it's definitely worth building these kinds of shortcuts into your app for testing. Being able to set up arbitrary test states is the best way to cut off significant portions of time off your build. In our initial example of 50 tests requiring a logged-in state, we could easily turn that 15 minutes into something more like 2–3 minutes.

Time savings is not the only reason to build shortcuts like these. Reliability is also a key factor. When running through the steps of logging in via the UI dozens of times, the chance that any individual step might fail is heightened. This means that your test might fail even before it reaches the stage of verification, which is a recipe for flakiness. Taking shortcuts whenever possible can also help dramatically increase the stability of your build by reducing the number of functional steps your tests have to take to do their job.

TESTING APP UPGRADES

One common requirement for many testers goes beyond verifying the functionality of an app in a single version, considered alone. This is because your team is shipping new versions of your app to customers on some (hopefully frequent) basis. Your existing users are therefore *upgrading* to the latest version, not installing it from scratch. As an example of the kind of issue testers should care about: most apps store some kind of existing user data in some kind of data structure, which might change from version to version. This data would then need to be migrated for the app to work correctly, and simply running functional tests of the new version alone would not be sufficient to catch these cases. Instead, we need to have a test scenario that specifically checks the upgrade case.

Happily, this can be managed within Appium for both iOS and Android. While the technique is purely cross-platform, the individual commands are not (at this stage) because Appium is experimenting with newer, more reliable app management commands for iOS, but these have not yet officially taken the place of the old commands, and so are accessible only via the executeScript interface we saw above. In the case of either platform, the Appium test steps are the same:

1. Start a session with the old version of your app
2. Verify the appropriate user/UI state
3. Stop the old version of the app
4. Install the new version of the app
5. Launch the new version of the app
6. Verify the new user/UI state is as expected

Essentially, we walk through the same process a user would, only we use Appium's app management commands rather than some app store. Let's take a look at how it's done for each platform.

APP UPGRADES FOR IOS

On iOS, we utilize three special methods. These are made available as part of the "mobile:" interface within executeScript, because (as I mentioned above) they are newer and the Appium project is incubating them in this way:

```
driver.executeScript("mobile: terminateApp", args);
driver.executeScript("mobile: installApp", args);
driver.executeScript("mobile: launchApp", args);
```

This set of commands (1) stops the current app (which we need to do explicitly so that the underlying automation technology doesn't think the app has crashed on us), (2) installs the new app over top of it, and then (3) launches the new app.

What do the args look like for each of these commands? Each one should be a HashMap that is used to generate simple JSON structures. The terminateApp and launchApp commands both have one key, bundleId (which is of course the bundle ID of your app). installApp takes an app key, which is the path or URL to the new version of your app. (The path/URL to the old version would have been included as the app desired capability, used in conjunction with other desired capabilities to launch your Appium session).

For example, let's say that the bundle ID of my app is com.test.app. And let's further stipulate that I have paths to two versions of my app (version 1.0.0 and version 1.0.1) saved in String objects appropriately named APP_V1_0_0 and APP_V1_0_1. In this case my code would look as follows:

```
// we already used APP_V1_0_0 to start the Appium session
HashMap<String, String> bundleArgs = new HashMap<>();
bundleArgs.put("bundleId", "com.test.app");
driver.executeScript("mobile: terminateApp", bundleArgs);
HashMap<String, String> installArgs = new HashMap<>();
installArgs.put("app", APP_V1_0_0);
driver.executeScript("mobile: installApp", installArgs);
// we can just reuse args for terminateApp
driver.executeScript("mobile: launchApp", bundleArgs);
```

All these commands correspond to steps 3, 4, and 5 of our overall upgrade flow. What are not pictured here are the app-specific verifications we would need to make to ensure that the upgrade went as planned. That, of course, is up to you and the idiosyncrasies of your app!

APP UPGRADES FOR ANDROID

Fortunately, on Android, this whole process is even simpler than on iOS! This is for two reasons. First, we don't have to use the executeScript ("mobile: *") interface; instead, we can use first-class client methods. Second, on Android, we don't have to worry about stopping the old version of our app before installing the new version. Installing the new version will stop the old version for us automatically. So, what do we need in terms of Appium code? Just these two methods:

```
driver.installApp("/path/to/apk");
// 'activity' is an instance of io.appium.java_client.an-
droid.Activity;
```

```
driver.startActivity(activity);
```

This set of commands replaces the existing app with the one given in the path (or URL) as the argument to installApp, and in so doing stops the old version of the app from running. It then starts up the new version of the app using the Android-specific startActivity command, which can be used to start any app and any Android Activity available within that app. For our purposes, we're not using it to launch a different app; we're using it to launch the same app (but now the freshly-installed new version of it).

The only complexity here is that the argument to startActivity must be an instance of the Appium client's special Activity class. There is a separate Activity class because there are a number of options that can be passed to this method. We're only interested in the basic ones for the purposes of app upgrades, so we can simply create and use our Activity object as follows:

```
Activity activity = new Activity("com.test.app", "MyTes-
tActivity");
driver.startActivity(activity);
```

That's basically it! As above for iOS, these methods correspond to steps 3, 4, and 5 of the requirements for testing app upgrades. The rest of the steps are up to you to implement based on the state of your UI that represents a functional upgrade experience.

SUMMARY

In this chapter we've taken a look at three less common (but still very useful) automation goals which can be satisfactorily achieved using Appium. Of course, Appium is up to the challenge of "basic" automation (finding elements, tapping on them, verifying text labels, and so on). What makes Appium special is not its ability to do these basic tasks but its huge array of methods that assist in all levels of automation. While there will always be some features that lie out of reach for technical reasons, or might be a bad idea for other reasons, our overall approach with the Appium project is to figure out what useful functionality we can offer to users and to do so in as spec-compliant and reliable a way as possible.

If you haven't given Appium a try, it's worth considering as you begin your next automation project. It's not the right tool for every app and every team, but it's got a broad enough feature set and an experienced enough community to help you meet most, if not all, of your beyond-the-browser automation needs.

CHAPTER TWENTY-ONE

Stabilize Your Espresso Tests with Static Data Feeds

BY GREG SYPOLT

GREG SYPOLT (@gregsypolt) is Director of Quality Engineering at Gannett I USA Today Network, a Fixate IO Contributor, and co-founder of Quality Element. He is responsible for test automation solutions, test coverage (from unit to end-to-end), and continuous integration across all Gannett I USA Today Network products and has helped change the testing approach from manual to automated testing across several products at
Gannett I USA Today Network. To determine improvements and testing gaps, he conducted a face-to-face interview survey process to understand all product development and deployment processes, testing strategies, tooling, and interactive in-house training programs.

INTRODUCTION

Your user interface is straightforward but the feeds are regularly changing, causing endless failures with front-end Android automated testing. Your content feeds have no problem rendering on the Android device, but the pain point is that the dynamic feed changes in the app every time it's launched, which is unpredictable for testing. Once you do away with the concept of dynamic data feeds and shift to static entities, you see that testing will stabilize — and there is hope.

This chapter focuses on how to stabilize unreliable Espresso test scripts, also known as "flaky" tests. It will cover how to use Espresso to write concise, elegant, and reliable Android UI tests using a static data feed for testing.

To be explicit: testing dynamic data feeds is essential but much more effective when pushed down the pyramid stack to the API layer.

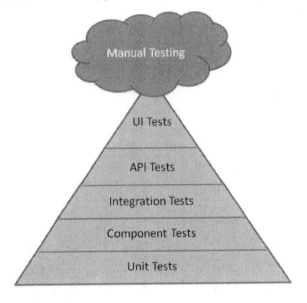

ELIMINATING ONE FLAVOR OF FLAKE FROM TESTING

If you know anything about user interface (UI) automated testing, you know that it's very difficult and frustrating at times.

The battle with unreliable tests, aka flaky tests, is one that never will end. A test should consistently pass if no code changes are deployed. Test flakiness occurs in many flavors; in our case, we are focused on stabilizing dynamic feeds throwing a monkey wrench into the software delivery process by causing false positives. The screenshot below illustrates the randomization of feeds when launching a mobile native app; in this case, only the 'video' feed appears in the view. If your test suite is expected to test other types of feeds such as blogs, photos, etc. after the app is launched, there is a strong possibility these tests will fail.

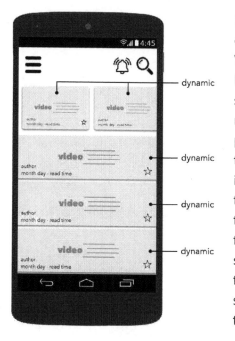

I feel this solution could be a game changer for you: shift to static entities. Why should you use static feeds with Espresso tests? The purpose of using static feeds is that the desired content is readily available and it is more natural to pin content in a specific position to run tests efficiently. The screenshot below illustrates pinning specific feeds upon the initial launch to help stabilize our testing. This method does not guarantee the removal of all flakiness since the static feed is still making endpoint calls to your staging environment; it does ensure the feed will exist when launching the mobile native app under test.

Once you're familiar with developing Espresso test scripts, you are ready to learn how to feed your Android app with static feed JSON files for testing.

THIS IS HOW IT WORKS

You can find thousands of apps in the app store — all have one thing in common. Do you know what it is? They all serve various types of data feeds which are rendered as content in the mobile app. In order to predict what kind of data will be rendered in the app under test, it must be configured with static feeds.

Here are the steps for creating a static feed by identifying the content that you want to include in the static feed for testing. The link below provides the JSON data for a photo blog post on a mobile device.

Example: https://api.<site-cdn>.com/mobile/<version>/<type>/photo-blog?-consumer=android&api_key=<api_key>

<version> = version of the api feed	<type> = home front, photo blogs front, etc.

We need to create a new JSON file within the Android app repo. Here is a possible location where you can put the new JSON file to stabilize testing: cd my-android-app/blogs/src/androidTest/res/raw. Now, we need to copy the static feed URL from above into the new JSON file: home_photo_blog.json.

Android Studio makes it easy to build and run your app to pick up your static feed changes. With the project open, click *Build > Make Project* from the Android Studio menu bar.

Now you are ready to configure your testing suite for static feeds. Every Android app must have an AndroidManifest.xml file. The android:name is optional; we are declaring the *TestMyApplication* class which includes the method to insert static feeds.

```
<application
 android:name=".ui.activity.TestMyApplication"
 ...
      ...
</application>
```

Go to class *TestMyApplication* method *getStaticFeedMap* to insert the feed from above.

```
public class TestMyApplication extends MyApplication {
 ...
 ...
 public Map <String, Integer> getStaticFeedMap() {
 Map <String, Integer> staticFeedMap = new Linked
HashMap<>();

 staticFeedMap.put("mobile/v5/home/1?", com.android.
blogs.test.raw.home_video_blog);
      staticFeedMap.put("mobile/v5/home/1?", com.android.
blogs.test.raw.home_photo_blog);
 ...
 ...
```

We want to create a custom test runner to declare the *TestMyApplication* class with the static feeds, disable animations, screen unlock, keep screen awake, and anything else to help stabilize the tests. You can find many examples by Googling *'custom test runner android espresso'* to extend the AndroidJUnitRunner.

It's really that simple to create consistent static data that we can pin in the desired position. We can continue to manipulate data easily as needed for all testing. Now, when executing the 'photo-blog' test, it renders the feed from your JSON file. Is this the single, optimal solution for flaky or unreliable tests? No, it's not! It's only eliminating one flavor of flake.

SUMMARY

We should run Android Espresso tests against a controlled environment to assure the assertions receive the expected behavior. Based on my experience, I can safely say that it requires significant effort to develop a robust UI testing ecosystem for native mobile apps. This concept is simple; it assists, stabilizes, and removes flakiness, but it requires several well-thought-out static-feed JSON files in the project. Any time the app makes a network request from the test, the request is intercepted and mapped to the appropriate static feed JSON file.

Finally, as I mentioned above, this strategy is not guaranteed to remove all flakiness. The greatest advantage of this solution is that it ensures the feed exists when launching the mobile native app whereas the production version renders random dynamic feeds.

CHAPTER TWENTY-TWO

DevSecOps: Reality or collection of buzzwords?

BY AMIR ROZENBERG AND BRIAN REED

BRIAN REED — As NowSecure's Chief Mobility Officer, industry veteran Brian Reed brings over a dozen years' experience in mobile, security and risk, including Good Technology, BlackBerry, ZeroFOX and BoxTone. With more than 25 years driving customer value through innovative solutions and strong go-to-market strategies, Brian is a noted authority who brings unique insights with a global track record of success scaling startups and mid-size organizations. Brian is a graduate of Duke University.

AMIR ROZENBERG is a Senior Director of Product Management at Perfecto Mobile — the leading digital, Cloud, and automation company. He is responsible for the core product strategy of Perfecto. Amir has pioneered many practices to extend the company's offering across the whole application life cycle. Amir has extensive experience in the digital industry with expertise in areas including infrastructure, applications, application delivery, and monitoring. Mr. Rozenberg has led many successful synergies with technology partners to optimize the value delivery to Perfecto's customers. Prior to working at Perfecto Mobile, Amir was head of the mobile monitoring practice at Compuware. Prior to Compuware, he induced the

founding of Adva Mobile, a direct-to-fan mobile marketing startup, and held various leadership positions at Groove Mobile, Nextcode Corp., and others.

INTRODUCTION

Security, privacy and vulnerability to hacker attacks is top-of-mind these days. Over 85% of public app store applications on the Apple App Store and Google Play violate one or more of the OWASP Mobile Top 10 Risks (NowSecure). According to NowSecure, 80% of Android apps lack basic obfuscation, allowing attackers to reverse engineer the app. Over 18% of iOS apps transmit sensitive data (credentials, IMEI, location, MAC address etc.) insecurely. With the proliferation of open source and third-party libraries/components in apps, the risk continues to grow. In the age of Agile, the organizational tendency for many has been to blow past the uncovered security vulnerabilities in effort to meet the speeds that business demands. We will examine various activities, offer best practices, and explain how to pragmatically embed these into secure development activities and the DevOps toolchain.

INTRODUCTION TO SECURITY THREATS

The following diagrams describe the key threats and vulnerabilities found for websites by industry (source: WhiteHat) and in mobile apps (source: NowSecure):

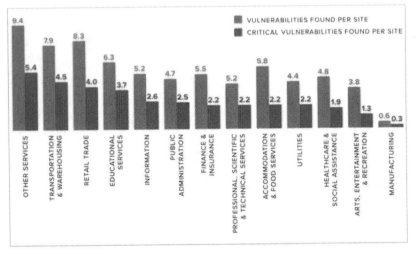

Figure 1: Vulnerability profile by industry — DAST, Source: 2017 WhiteHat Security Application Security Statistics Report

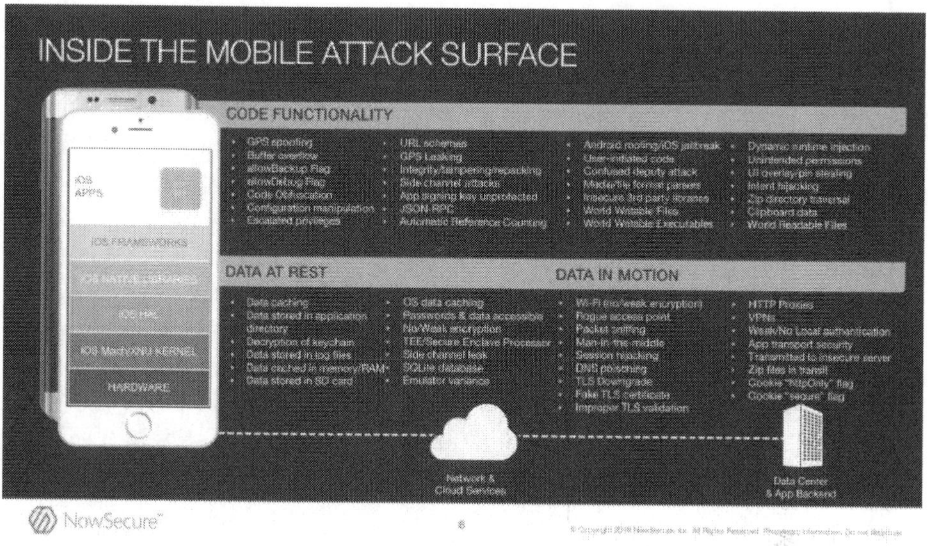

Figure 2: Mobile Attack Surface courtesy of NowSecure

DEVOPS-FRIENDLY SECURITY TEST APPROACHES

There are a myriad of tools and approaches that can be used for testing and ensuring the security of mobile apps. When looking to optimize for speed and lowest risk, consider choosing a mix of technologies at each stage of the development process to detect and remediate security issues earlier and faster.

- IDE Code scanners — Well-integrated security approaches begin with the developer, coding in real time. IDE (IntelliJ, Eclipse, Visual Studio etc.) plugins scan code (in the background) for potential SQLi and thousands of other potential risks. The scan typically leverages a set of continuously updated rules representing industry standards and recent security vulnerabilities. Their ability to highlight code and offer a contextual remediation approach means that as developer is creating code, they immediately become aware of the risk and can fix it in real time. This introduces a new level of efficiency for developers, compared to latent feedback and extended time remediating a security defect when left to late-stage security testing cycles.

- Static source code scan (SAST, 'White-box testing') [Gartner Definition] technology analyzes an application's source, bytecode or binary code for security vulnerabilities, typically at the programming and/or testing phases of the software development life cycle (SDLC). The objective of the static scan is to scan the code of the app for key vulnerabilities such as unencrypted application data, residual log files in the app folder, imperfect file cleanup after app deletion, insecure data storage, etc. Such scans can scan the source code or binaries. Typically, solutions are available in a cloud-SaaS environment or on-prem. Can be launched manually or, in some cases, tools plug into DevOps toolchain to automatically run after code commit and before build. The challenge with SAST is the high number of false positives which can require time consuming manual investigation.

- Software Composition Analysis (SCA) Scans: Start with scanning the 3rd-party libraries and OSS that you use to build your apps. While open source libraries increase productivity, those also introduce risk. More than 80% of organizations use 3rd-party and open source libraries that are vulnerable (Source: Sonatype). Open source code scans build an inventory of open source libraries, scan them using a bank of known vulnerabilities, and provide a report. Advanced vendors, such as Sonatype, proactively inform their customers once a vulnerability[1] has been found that might affect an SDK or open source code in their app.

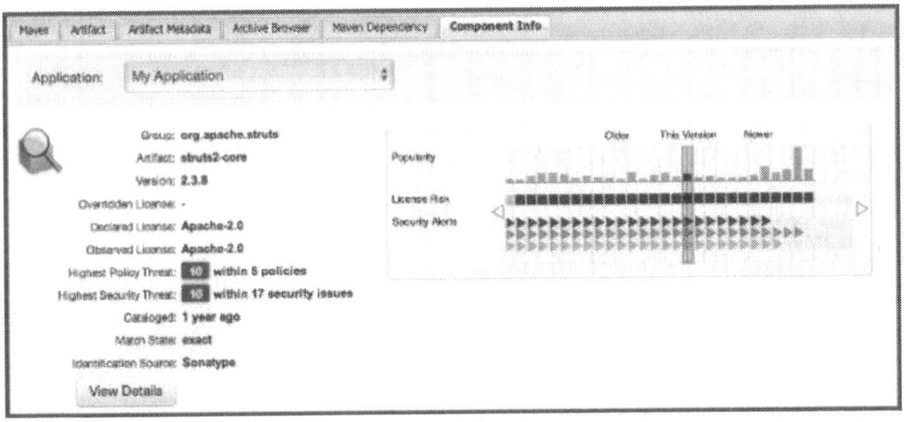

Figure 3: Open source vulnerability report (Source: Sonatype)

---

1   Sonatype list of vulnerabilities — https://blog.sonatype.com/2015/11/why-nexus-rocketed-beyond-60000-installs/

* Dynamic scan (DAST) [Gartner definition] technology analyzes applications in their dynamic running state during testing or operational phases. It simulates attacks against an application and analyzes the application's reactions to determine whether it is vulnerable. Dynamic scans are conducted while the app logic is being exercised from an end user perspective, in various setups (different devices, locations, connectivity and networks, etc.) On web, this testing approach is rather straightforward on live sites or sandbox emulators, but is much more difficult on mobile. For mobile, dynamic scans typically require the device to be jailbroken/rooted, although NowSecure also offers Jailed testing on iOS using the NowSecure Gadget. DAST solutions are available as services-backed software, managed services, and standalone software. Some software-only solutions meet the need of fast testing in <30mins so they can be plugged into the DevOps toolchain for automated testing of every build. Tests involving dynamic scans typically cover data at rest, data in motion, endpoint connections, and more, and can exercise the internally written code as well as embedded third-party and open source code for a more complete view of mobile app vulnerabilities. Dynamic scans can simulate client-side injection, dynamic code downloading, attempts to disassemble the app, method swizzling etc., while simultaneously scanning the app's network traffic. The latter would examine insecure data transmissions, proper certificate validation and certificate pinning, downgrade attacks, etc.

Report Summary				Export Report
FINDINGS SUMMARY				
IMPACT	CVSS	TITLE	ANALYSIS	CATEGORY
⚠ HIGH	7.7	Man-in-the-Middle Attack	DYNAMIC	NETWORK
⚠ HIGH	7	Certificate Validation / Hostname Verification	DYNAMIC	NETWORK
⚠ MEDIUM	6.5	HTTP Requests	DYNAMIC	NETWORK
⚠ MEDIUM	5.3	Cookie `httponly` flag	DYNAMIC	NETWORK
⚠ MEDIUM	5.3	Cookie `secure` flag	DYNAMIC	NETWORK
⚠ MEDIUM	5.3	Sensitive Data: Device Info (HTTP)	DYNAMIC	NETWORK
⚠ MEDIUM	5.3	App Transport Security	STATIC	NETWORK
⚠ LOW	1.6	Certificate Pinning Bypass	DYNAMIC	NETWORK

Figure 4: Sample report for dynamic code scan by NowSecure

- Interactive scan (IAST) [Gartner definition] need to insert definition. IAST is an emerging category of scanning where security testing code is built into the application by including 3rd-party vendor test libraries, then security tests are run in combination with QA and functional tests. Imagine the simplicity and consistency this can potentially bring to the DevOps pipeline. The benefits include the ability to combine the two testing types; some developers are concerned about the performance load and risk of including yet more code to be maintained. Today, the only vendor with IAST support specifically for mobile is NowSecure but others may add it in time.

- Crowd-sourced community scans: in addition to formalized, automated security scans, there are vendors, such as BugCrowd, HackerOne, and more, offering access to independent security researchers and hackers, The benefit is that hackers are likely updated with the latest hacking techniques. Much like crowd testing in the context of functional coverage, the hackers-for-hire approach cannot be automated. This methodology, dependent on human manual testing, clearly does not lend itself well to an agile or DevOps process and typically is used in other areas.

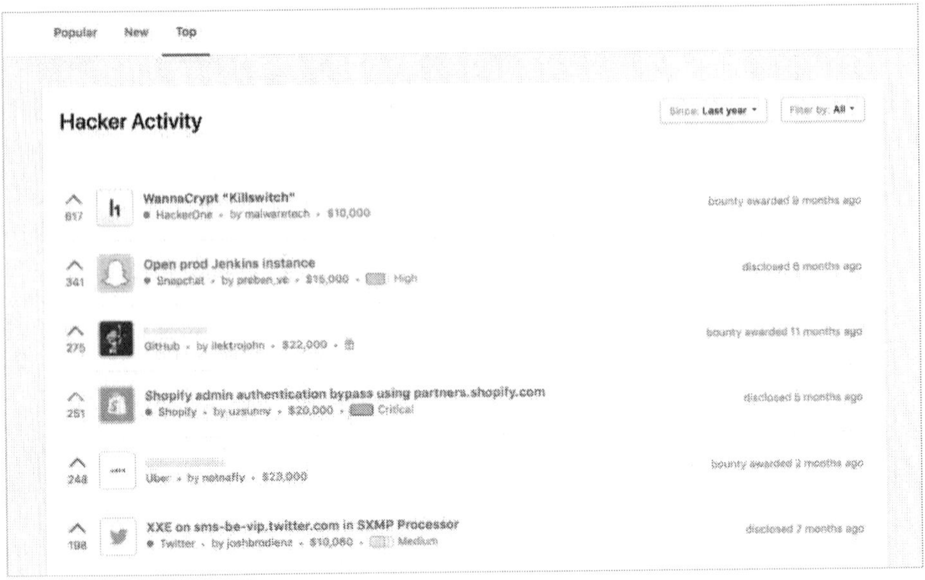

Figure 5: Hacker productivity model (Source: HackerOne)

- Continuous threat awareness and defense in production: Runtime Application Self-Protection (RASP)[2] is a security technology that is built into an application and can detect and prevent real-time application attacks in production. RASP prevents attacks by "self-protecting," or reconfiguring automatically without human intervention, in response to certain conditions (threats, faults, etc.)

SUMMARY: DEVOPS'ING IT ALL TOGETHER

- Identifying and tracking security vulnerability risks CVSS[3] is an industry-standard methodology to evaluate vulnerabilities by risk leverage tools that identify CVSS scores and then, with a vulnerability management approach, you can track trending and remediation over time and detect in-sprint which issues require immediate attention for improvement.

- Use a multi-layered approach with consistent regular scanning in the DevOps pipeline

  - Ideally this includes SCA before using components, IDE security code plugins, SAST post-commit pre-build, DAST and/or IAST post-build every day, and generating tickets back into issue-ticketing systems. In addition, where necessary, such as high-risk critical apps, adding pre-release certifications: red/green, go/no-go. The key is automation and integration everywhere. Testing at each step reduces vulnerabilities, enables faster fixes, lowers costs, and ultimately, builds security in.

  - CI connectors: Proper security practices mandate recurring, unattended execution of various security scans. This means integration with key CI components. As mentioned, at the coding stage, in-IDE code scanners will highlight risky code. When the developer commits the code into the repository, Jenkins integration can automatically trigger a static scan of the binary. Then, Jenkins can trigger loading the apps onto devices and backend servers and launch a set of tests that will include dynamic scans. As a result, from coding to commit, smoke and nightly regression tests can include security scans such that developers gain insight into new defects within minutes.

---

2   RASP Technology — https://www.veracode.com/products/runtime-protection-rasp

3   CVSS Technology — https://www.first.org/cvss/

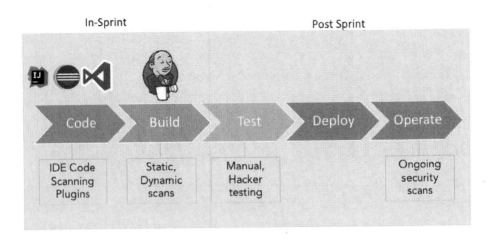

Figure 6: CI orchestration of security testing

- Security insights on app quality dashboards:

The theme of this chapter involves including security testing in Agile sprints or, daily in the DevOps pipeline, to increase developer efficiency. When a defect is uncovered late, or even in production, developers spend expensive time finding the root cause, then undoing and redoing code.

In the same manner, security testing needs to happen more frequently; security scores and risks need to become apparent on application health dashboards. This way, team leads can direct investment in-sprint on a daily basis to address areas of concern.

Relevant resources for further reading

- Gartner 10 Things to Get Right for Successful DevSecOps
- OWASP mobile top 10
- Devops.com

CHAPTER TWENTY-THREE

Complete Guide for Testing iOS Native Apps Using XCUITest

BY OREN BILGORAY

OREN BILGORAY is the R&D Director at Perfecto, leading the developer tools agenda along with his talented team. Oren brings over 6 years of experience in mobile OS (Android, iOS, Blackberry) and Web, specializing in building Enterprise Software using Agile and DevOps methods. Oren holds a B.S. in Computer Science.

INTRODUCTION TO XCUITEST

According to Apple's documentation[1] — *"UI testing gives you the ability to find and interact with the UI of your app to validate the properties and state of the UI elements*

*UI tests rests upon two core technologies: the **XCTest** framework and **Accessibility.***

- * **XCTest** provides the framework for UI testing capabilities, integrated with XCode. Creating and using UI testing expands upon what you know about using XCTest and creating unit tests. You create a UI test target, and you create UI test classes and UI test methods as a part of your project. You use XCTest assertions to validate that expected outcomes are true.

---

1   Apple's definition of UI Testing — https://developer.apple.com/library/content/documentation/DeveloperTools/Conceptual/testing_with_xcode/chapters/09-ui_testing.html

XCTest is fully compatible with both Objective-C and Swift.

- **Accessibility** *is the core technology that allows disabled users the same rich experience for iOS and macOS that other users receive. It includes a rich set of semantic data about the UI that users can use can use to guide them through using your app. Accessibility is integrated with both UIKit and AppKit and has APIs that allows you to fine-tune behaviors and what is exposed for external use. UI testing uses that data to perform its functions.*

Creating UI tests in source code is like creating unit tests. You create a UI test target for your app; then XCode creates a default UI test group and implementation file for you with an example test method template in the implementation file. When you create the UI test target, you specify the app that your tests will address.

UI testing works by finding an app's UI objects with queries, synthesizing events and sending them to those objects, and providing a rich API enabling you to examine the UI objects properties and state to compare them against the expected state."

"UI testing differs from unit testing in fundamental ways. Unit testing enables you to work within your app's scope and allows you to exercise functions and methods with full access to your app's variables and state. UI testing exercises your app's UI in the same way that users do without access to your app's internal methods, functions, and variables. This enables your tests to see the app the same way a user does, exposing UI problems that users encounter.

Your test code runs as a separate process, synthesizing events that UI in your app responds to"

Why XCUITest?

- XCUITest gives you the option to test your application in the same way that users do.
- Your test code runs as a separate process.
- Official Apple framework

XCUITest vs Appium

- Appium is an open source project and XCUITest is an Apple framework
- Appium supports many languages (C#, Java, Javascript...) and XCUITest supports only Swift/Objective C.
- Appium is fragile because it is affected by changes made by Apple. XCUITest is Apple's framework.
- With XCUITest, tests run faster and are more stable.
- XCUITest has a built-in recorder

XCUITest vs XCTest

XCTest is Apple's official framework for writing unit tests of classes and components at any level.

XCUITest is used in the industry in conjunction with **XCTest,** along with additional classes (such as **UIAccessibility**), for authoring UI tests.

XCTest test scenarios are bundled within the application itself. XCUITest tests, however, are packages in a separate IPA file. XCUITest communicates with Accessibility APIs and not objects themselves.

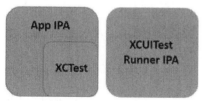

Usually, XCTest is designed for unit and performance tests to test specific code or measure the performance of specific code.

XCUITest offers the ability to test an application like a real user; it is designed for functional and UI tests.

Write your first test – create and run a very simple test

You can write XCUITest scripts in both Swift and Objective C.

Create UI testing target

If you have an existing project and would like to add automated UI tests to it, you first need to create an iOS UI testing target. This is how you do it:

Go to "File -> New -> Target".

Choose "iOS UI Testing Bundle" and click "Next".

Choose your team, application target and click "Finish".

Create UI test file

If you already have UI testing target, you need to create UI test file. In your XCode project, go to "File -> New -> File..."

Then choose "UI Test Case Class" and "Next"

On the next screen, give a name to your Class and choose your coding language.

Then choose where to save your tests and click "Create".

```
import XCTest

class ExampleXCUITest: XCTestCase {

 override func setUp() {
 super.setUp()

 // Put setup code here. This method is called before the invo-
 cation of each test method in the class.

 // In UI tests it is usually best to stop immediately when a
 failure occurs.
 continueAfterFailure = false
 // UI tests must launch the application that they test. Doing
 this in setup will make sure it happens for each test method.
 XCUIApplication().launch()

 // In UI tests it's important to set the initial state - such
 as interface orientation - required for your tests before they
 run. The setUp method is a good place to do this.
 }

 override func tearDown() {
 // Put teardown code here. This method is called after the in-
 vocation of each test method in the class.
 super.tearDown()
 }
```

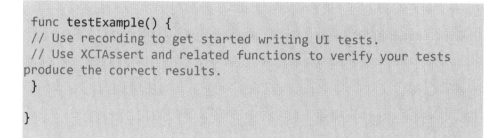

```
func testExample() {
// Use recording to get started writing UI tests.
// Use XCTAssert and related functions to verify your tests
produce the correct results.
 }

}
```

You can see that we have a new class that inherits from the XCTestCase class.

We have 3 methods:

- **setUp** — Provides an opportunity to reset the state before each test method in a test case is called.

  Here you can see "XCUIApplication().launch()," which will launch the application before every test.

- **tearDown** — Provides an opportunity to perform cleanup after each test method in a test case ends.

- **testExample** — Example for test function. Please remember that your test methods should always start with the "test" word, otherwise they will not run.

Let's just add an assertion and run the test:

```
func testExample() {
// Use recording to get started writing UI tests.
// Use XCTAssert and related functions to verify your tests
produce the correct results.

XCTAssert(true);
}
```

To run the test, users have a few options:

1. Run all the tests in your project via "Product -> Test".

2. Run only the UI tests bundle; from the test navigator, click on the play button that is relevant to your tests.

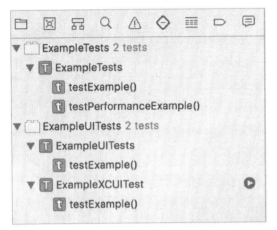

3. You can also run your specific test via the play button near your test code

```
30
     func testExample() {
32        // Use recording to get started writing UI te
33        // Use XCTAssert and related functions to ver
34
35        XCTAssert(true);
36    }
37
```

After the test run, users will see the result:

```
30
     func testExample() {
32        // Use recording
33        // Use XCTAssert
34
```

You can also go to the "Test Navigator," right click on the test, and "Jump to Report".

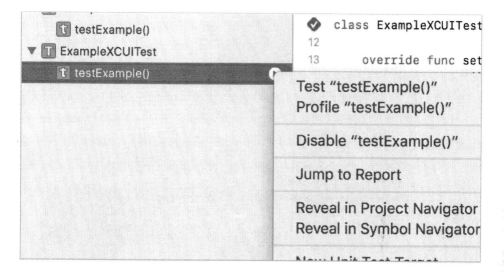

There, you will find a report about your tests.

XCODE RECORDER

The UI recorder can give you a good starting point for your test; however, it cannot guarantee reliable, continuous test code.

How to use the recorder?

To start recording, go to the line in the test where you want to add code from the recorder and click the record button at the bottom.

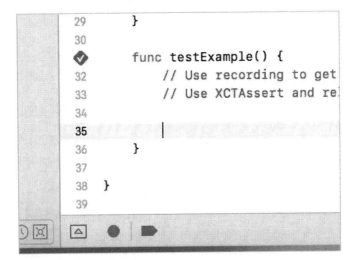

Once you click the button, the application will be launched on the simulator or device, depending on the target you selected in XCode. From here, every operation that you will do in the application will be recorded and the test will be generated.

```
30
     func testExample() {
32       // Use recording to get started writing UI tests.
33       // Use XCTAssert and related functions to verify your tests produce the correct results.
34
35
36       let app = XCUIApplication()
37       let textBox1LabelTextField = app.textFields["text_box_1_label"]
38       textBox1LabelTextField.tap()
39       textBox1LabelTextField.typeText("text box 1")
40
41       let textBox2IdentifierTextField = app.textFields["text_box_2_identifier"]
42       textBox2IdentifierTextField.tap()
43       textBox2IdentifierTextField.tap()
44       textBox2IdentifierTextField.typeText("text box 2")
45       app.buttons["button_identifier"]▾.tap()
46       app.staticTexts["Label"].tap()
47
48
49   }
50
51 }
```

The above code, generated by the UI recorder, simply inserts text into 2 texts boxes and performs a click on a button and on a label.

The UI recorder prefers to identify objects by their accessibility identifier/label because it is more stable to use these "IDs" then to rely on the hierarchy.

In the image below, you can see that XCode allows the ability to choose how to identify the button — either by accessibility identifier or by accessibility label — because my button has both. It is highly recommended to add accessibility identifiers/labels to your objects.

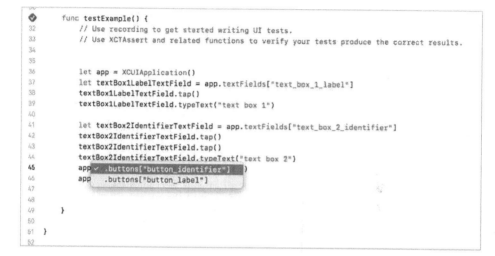

Why not only use the recorder?

The recorder can help you to build your test easily and to identify your objects. Sometimes the decisions that the recorder makes are not stable enough; you should go over your code to verify the identification of your elements.

Also, you should add waits/retries to your code to make your test cases more stable.

Accessibility Inspector

Because XCUITest is based on Accessibility, it means that we can use all its tools, such as Accessibility Inspector, which can give us some information to help build our scripts.

To open the Accessibility Inspector, go to XCode -> Open Developer Tools -> Accessibility Inspector.

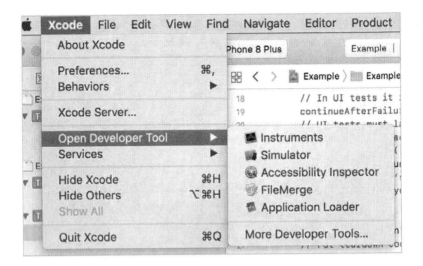

Launch your application on the simulator/device and change the target in the Accessibility Inspector.

Now, click on the inspect element button and then on the element that you want to reveal.

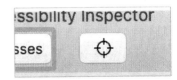

After choosing the element, you'll see all the accessibility properties of the element. You can see the hierarchy, the accessibility label, and the identifier of your element.

Then, you can write code that uses these properties to find the element.

```
func testExample() {

        let app = XCUIApplication(bundleIdentifier: "com.apple.
        Preferences")

        app.launch()

        app.staticTexts["General"].tap()

}
```

XCUITest APIs overview and querying elements

XCUITest provides several ways to identify your elements[2]. XCUIElement

---

2   XCUITest Element Query Documentation — https://developer.apple.com/documentation/xctest/
    xcuielementquery

conforms to XCUIElementTypeQueryProvider[3] and offers test developers with functions to identify elements, such as "firstMatch", "buttons", "windows", etc.

Finding the first matching element

As Apple says in its documentation, using the firstMatch property is recommended when users know that there can only be one possible match for an element query. When calling firstMatch, XCTest stops traversing your app's accessibility hierarchy as soon as it finds a matching element, speeding up element query resolution.

Declaration

```
var firstMatch: XCUIElement { get }
```

XCUIElement interactions

Per Apple documentation[4], on macOS, XCUIElement provides keyboard- and mouse-like interactions such as typing, hovering, clicking, and scrolling. On iOS, XCUIElement provides gestural interactions such as tapping, pressing, swiping, pinching, and rotating.

Here are a few examples of interacting with UI Elements on iOS using XCUITest

To **type** a string into an Element, use the below declaration

```
func typeText(_ text: String)
```

To send a **tap** event to a hittable element, use the Tap function or one of the below declarations

```
func tap ()
```

---

3 XCUITest Element Query Provider Documentation — https://developer.apple.com/documentation/xctest/xcuielementtypequeryprovider

4 XCUITest Element documentation — https://developer.apple.com/documentation/xctest/xcuielement

Tapping and Pressing	`func doubleTap()`
	Sends a double tap event to a hittable point computed for the element.
	`func press(forDuration: TimeInterval)`
	Sends a long press gesture to a hittable point computed for the element, holding for the specified duration.
	`func press(forDuration: TimeInterval, thenDragTo: XCUIElement)`
	Initiates a press-and-hold gesture, then drags to another element.

To perform a set of **iOS gestures** on the app under test, use declarations from the below range.

Among the options supported, there are swipe left, right, up, and down, pinch, and rotate. Users can also find information on working with UIPicker-View, Sliders, and more, in the API documentation.With respect to UI testing,

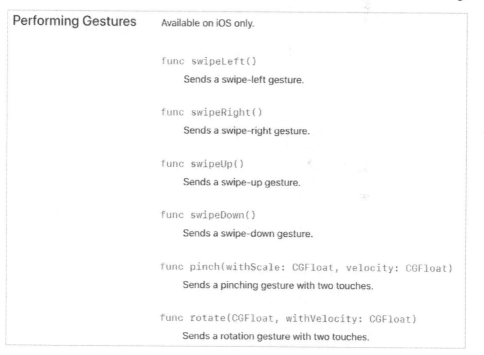

Performing Gestures	Available on iOS only.
	`func swipeLeft()`
	Sends a swipe-left gesture.
	`func swipeRight()`
	Sends a swipe-right gesture.
	`func swipeUp()`
	Sends a swipe-up gesture.
	`func swipeDown()`
	Sends a swipe-down gesture.
	`func pinch(withScale: CGFloat, velocity: CGFloat)`
	Sends a pinching gesture with two touches.
	`func rotate(CGFloat, withVelocity: CGFloat)`
	Sends a rotation gesture with two touches.

XCUITest provides the ability to take screenshots from the application under test using the XCUIScreen[5] class. To leverage the class, use the following declarations:

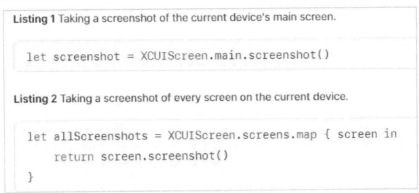

Listing 1 Taking a screenshot of the current device's main screen.

```
let screenshot = XCUIScreen.main.screenshot()
```

Listing 2 Taking a screenshot of every screen on the current device.

```
let allScreenshots = XCUIScreen.screens.map { screen in
    return screen.screenshot()
}
```

ASSERTION METHODS

XCTest provides multiple options for assertions[6]. To validate your expected behavior of the test with respect to the actual behavior, leverage the XCTAssert[7] method:

```
let resultView = app.otherElements["view_result"]
let viewExists = resultView.waitForExistence(timeout: 10)
XCTAssert(viewExists)
XCTAssert(app.staticTexts["Result for Xcode term"].exists)
```

The **XCTAssert** class offers a few assertion types:

1. **Boolean** — such assertions validate that a condition is True or False

```
func XCTAssert(_ expression: @autoclosure () throws -
> Bool, _ message: @autoclosure () -
> String = default, file: StaticString = #file, line: UInt= #line
)
```

---

5   XCUIScreen declaration — https://developer.apple.com/documentation/xctest/xcuiscreen

6   Recommended article on using XCTest assertions — https://medium.com/@danielcarlosce/some-good-practices-for-xcuitest-807bfe6b720d

7   Apple XCTest assertion formal documentation — https://developer.apple.com/documentation/xctest/boolean_assertions

2. **Nil and Non-Nil** Assertions

```
func XCTAssertNil(_ expression: @autoclosure () throws -> Any?,
_ message: @autoclosure () -
> String = default, file: StaticString = #file, line: UInt= #line
)
```

3. **Equality** and **Inequality** Assertions — checks whether 2 values are equal or not

```
func XCTAssertEqual<T>(_ expression1: @autoclosure () throws ->
T, _expression2: @autoclosure () throws -> T, _ message:
@autoclosure () -
>String = default, file: StaticString = #file, line:UInt = #line
) where T :Equatable
```

4. **Comparable and Value Assertions** — compares 2 values to determine whether one is larger than the other

```
func XCTAssertGreaterThan<T>(_ expression1: @autoclosure
() throws -> T, _expression2: @autoclosure () throws ->
T, _ message: @autoclosure () -
>String = default, file: StaticString = #file, line:UInt = #line
) where T :Comparable
```

5. **Error Assertions** — checks for expressions throwing an error

```
func XCTAssertThrowsError<T>(_ expression: @autoclosure ()
throws -> T, _message: @autoclosure () -
> String = default, file: StaticString = #file, line: UInt =
#line, _ errorHandler: (Error) -> Void = default)
```

6. **Failing Unconditionally Assertions** — reports a failure immediately and unconditionally

```
func XCTFail(_ message: String = default, file: StaticString =
#file, line:UInt = #line)
```

Using the XCUIApplication Class with iOS Apps

The XCUIApplication class[8] serves as a proxy for an application that can be launched and terminated.

---

8 XCUIApplication documentation — https://developer.apple.com/documentation/xctest/xcuiapplication

Working with this class is straightforward and allows test developers to initialize a proxy to the app, get its state, launch the app as-is or using arguments, and terminate it, as stated above. There are differences between the Launch and Activate methods of an iOS app — Launch will terminate an existing instance of the app, while Activate will simply launch the app if it's already running.

Creating an Application Proxy	`init()`
	Creates a proxy for the application specified as the "Target Application" in Xcode's target settings.
	`init(bundleIdentifier: String)`
	Creates a proxy for an application associated with the specified bundle identifier.
	`init(url: URL)`
	Creates a proxy for the application at the specified file system URL.
Launching the Application	`func launch()`
	Launches the application.
	`var launchArguments: [String]`
	The arguments that will be passed to the application on launch.
	`var launchEnvironment: [String : String]`
	The environment variables that will be passed to the application on launch.
Activating the Application	`func activate()`
	Activates the application.
Terminating the Application	`func terminate()`
	Terminates any running instance of the application.

Jenkins Integration

Integrating XCUITest to run from within Jenkins CI can be achieved with Gradle plugins[9]. This is how Perfecto enables customers to execute their XCUITest/XCTest tests.

---

9   Perfecto gradle plugin for XCUITest execution — https://developers.perfectomobile.com/display/PD/Integrate+With+Jenkins

RECOMMENDED DOCUMENTATION AND REFERENCES

XCUITest iOS localization and I18N testing	https://medium.com/xcblog/ios-localiza-tion-and-internationalization-testing-with-xcuit-est-495747a74775
Apple UI Testing documentation	https://developer.apple.com/documentation/xctest/user_interface_tests
XCUITest testing in the cloud with Perfecto	https://developers.perfectomobile.com/display/PD/Test+Frameworks+Support
Getting started with XCUITest	http://blog.novoda.com/getting-started-with-xcuitest-framework-for-testing-ios-apps/
Apple UI Testing guidelines	https://developer.apple.com/library/content/docu-mentation/DeveloperTools/Conceptual/testing_with_xcode/chapters/09-ui_testing.html
Getting started with XCUITets and Swift	https://medium.com/@johnsundell/getting-started-with-xcode-ui-testing-in-swift-ac7b1f5101e5
UI Testing cheat sheet	http://masilotti.com/ui-testing-cheat-sheet/
Network stubbing options for XCTest	https://medium.com/xcblog/network-stubbing-op-tions-for-xctest-and-xcuitest-in-swift-2e0dcce9a37d
Apple iOS UI Testing tutorial	https://www.shinobicontrols.com/blog/ios9-day-by-day-day2-ui-testing
iOS UI Testing Gotchas	https://www.bignerdranch.com/blog/ui-testing-in-xcode-7-part-1-ui-testing-gotchas/
iOS Dev Directory	https://iosdevdirectory.com/

SUMMARY

This chapter covered the basics of the XCUITest UI test automation framework for iOS native app testing and provided a sample overview of supported APIs. Leveraging this framework for iOS white-box testing can be highly beneficial for test engineers and developers; the fact that the Appium cross-platform test automation framework uses this solution is also an advantage to practi-tioners. While powerful, XCUITest for iOS, as with Espresso for Android, cannot provide complete end-to-end testing capabilities; therefore, test automation teams need to take advantage of the benefits of these frameworks while complementing them with Appium or similar tools to get full test automation coverage that includes functional testing outside of app context, advance UI, performance testing, and much more.

SECTION 4

Advancing Continuous Testing

SECTION 4 INTRO

By this section in the book I have covered the fundamentals of continuous testing and dive deep into leading mobile native and web app testing techniques. The future of CT is most likely to change the way tests are being authored, managed and executed. IN the following section I collected some key insights from experts in AI and ML to start planting the seeds for the future of CT. My personal POV on what will be the role of the modern tester in the era of ML and AI are in this blog: http://continuoustesting.blog/the-role-of-a-modern-tester-in-the-era-of-machine-learning-ml-and-artificial-intelligence-ai/

CHAPTER TWENTY-FOUR

Using AI to solve the Quality/Velocity Dilemma

BY OREN RUBIN, CEO, TESTIM.IO, HTTP://TESTIM.IO

OREN RUBIN, the founder and CEO of Testim.io, has over 20 years of experience in the software industry, building products for developers at IBM, Wix, Cadence, and Testim.io. In addition to be a busy entrepreneur, Oren is a community activist and and the co-organizer of the Selenium-Israel meetup and the Israeli Google Developer Group meetup. He has taught at Technion University, and mentored at the Google Launchpad Accelerator.

INTRODUCTION

Just like autonomous cars, which suse software to drive without human input, autonomous testing is the notion of using software to assist us with testing our applications. With respect to test automation, it specifically relates to the aspects of authoring, maintenance and risk management. Autonomous testing will transform the way software is developed, making quality assurance so seamless that engineering teams will only be limited by the speed at which they code. Having said that, Tesla's first car wasn't self-driving but the user experience significantly improved with each release, as was the case with its "Autopilot", which was also AI based. The same holds true for software testing.

This chapter will discuss how AI will help us solve the tradeoff between faster time-to-market and flawless user experience, specifically focusing on functional end-to-end testing. According to multiple sources, this is the biggest bottleneck in software quality, which is evidenced by the growth in front end development. Stack Overflow's 2018's survey* shows that 37.8% of developers claim to be "front end" and 48.2% claim to be "full stack". This trend shows that critical business logic now resides on the front-end side of the application, making it even more complicated to test before release.

Why is E2E testing still a nightmare for most teams?

1. **Skillset** — It's harder to find an automation engineer than it is to find a full stack developer. Plus, let's just say it:

   - Developers do not want to spend much time on testing.
   - Coding is challenging for manual testers, and only a few succeed in making the transition.

2. **Test authoring is slow** — Spend a few minutes and troll the online communities, user groups and forums. Some have suggested that to create a good/stable test takes as long as to develop the feature. I would have to agree with them. We all see companies that release features without having automated tests for them.

3. **Test maintenance sucks** — This is probably the most overlooked parameter: 30% of a tester's day is spent on tedious maintenance of flaky tests, e.g. every time you change the UI the tests might fail and need fixing.

So, how is AI going to help with all of this?

The holy grail of testing would be autonomous testing, where tests are authored, maintained, and diagnosed automatically. Just as Tesla's cars are not completely autonomous, test automation isn't quite autonomous yet either. However, with the help of AI, we've made great strides in speeding up authoring time as well as reducing maintenance and repair time.

Before we explain how AI is going to help us solve the E2E nightmare, let's outline the 4 different levels of assistance and how each level will get closer to truly autonomous testing.

- **Level 0 — Manual Authoring —** You write and maintain everything yourself.

- **Level 1 — Teach by example —** Machines help you to author quicker and improve the stability of the tests.

- **Level 2 — Semi-Autonomous —** Machines author and maintain the tests by observing humans' usage of the app. Some human assistance will be required.

- **Level 3 — Fully Autonomous —** Machines build tests for you, and also auto-maintain the tests

How do each of these levels apply to E2E testing? E2E Tests are made up of four elements (for convenience we'll ignore the teardown, which is hardly used).

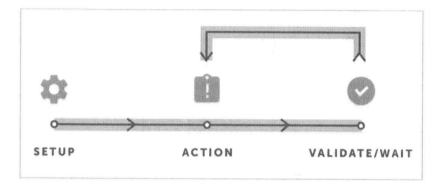

ACTIONS

Most E2E/UI tests comprise at least one action on the user interface. An action can be a click (for web apps), a finger tap (for mobile), scroll, entering text, etc.

Level 0 – Manual Authoring:

Regular coding is level 0 as we get no machine assistance while we author everything from scratch and need to maintain the tests upon every UI change.

This stems from the assumption humans have to read the entire source code (including the locators), thus making the locators short and simple. Query languages, such as CSS-Selector and Xpath, used to locate elements in the app's UI,h focused on a single or fixed amount of properties in the UI, are too rigid to handle changes. Those are denoted as *static locators* through the chapter.

For years, numerous attempts to record & play back user interactions simply failed and lost adoption. Although most code was generated for you, the limitation of static locators was the root cause of failure. They failed much more frequently than with tests written by humanst, especially developers, as they had more internal knowledge of the app they could use to author better selectors.

In addition, with the underlying technology, no reuse was generated (nor any other computer science design pattern implementation), leading to more maintenance.

Level 1 – Teach by example:

When we shift away from static locators, which break once the app changes, we can think of new locator strategies and even let machines decide on strategy. AI can handle hundreds of locators, prioritize them, score them by understanding which are good and stable, and which are not. Besides the sheer volume of properties they can handle, the nice thing is that machines are not biased, which can favor attributes other than class, id, or text.

What makes AI so great is that it can learn from past executions, making your test more stable after a set of examples (executions in our case). At Testim. io, after executing (hundreds of) millions of tests across hundreds of companies, we were able to find new strategies that are relevant to all projects. So, if you're using Angular.js, React.js, Vue.js, etc., you already get a head start using our tool as we already know which parameters are good and which are bad for these projects, e.g. knowing that the data-ember-action property has low scoring in all projects.

Another amazing part is that manual testers can now author E2E tests and they only need to train the system once. On every action the tester makes (e.g. click), the system can introspect the entire DOM (similar in native mobile/desktop apps), extract the information (attributes), and process it (generate locators). Although it doesn't require coding, the user still needs to know basic engineering as they'll still need to reuse (e.g. group the actions set-username, set-password, and click-login and name it "login"), and possibly pass in parameters if the value differs in each call.

Behavior Driven Development (BDD) Support: BDD was designed to enable the shift-left paradigm, where you test as early as possible, even as early as the product definition. This would lead to product specs being tested by different stakeholders, including Devs and QA. In reality, we don't see this a lot, but do sometimes see teams use tools like Cucumber to write the specs in natural language (usually English) and then connect those sentences to actions in another platform which knows how to automate the UI (e.g. Selenium).

In this case, we can use AI to try to locate the elements automatically, i.e. by looking at the properties of each element in the UI, the system can guess which element fits best (e.g. extract from the sentence "set username to Dave" that we're looking for an input which has a property that best matches "username" and set the value to "Dave"). This will still include a lot of human interaction in large apps comprising many elements on the screen.

Visual Driven Development: the notion of authoring a test out of the app's visual design mocks is not new (e.g. Sikuli), but was considered unstable, as pixels are just one property and are very fragile. However, since the system can now improve from every execution, it merely needs to see the app once and extract all the properties related to the element, thus not counting on the visual aspects anymore. The advances in computer vision in the last decade may lead to a point where this will be feasible.

Level 2 – Semi-Autonomous:

This means the system authors the tests by connecting to production or staging environments and observes how humans interact with the app. This means either real users (on production) or staging (while QA/dev/product interact in one of the development cycles). The big improvement at this level, compared to the previous one, is that AI can help with the clustering of these actions and can understand that some actions are repeatable, thus converting them into reusable user scenarios (comprising a groups of actions).

For example: if we take a shopping website like Amazon, this would include the "login", "logout", "add to cart", "checkout", and other scenarios.

As we expect to see only happy paths being suggested, testers will still author more tests for edge cases.

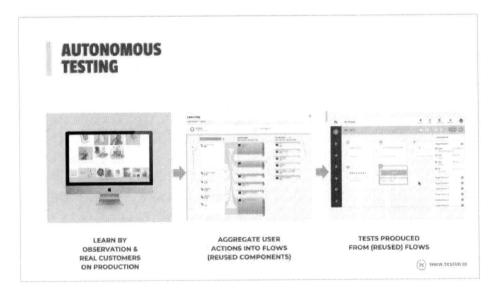

Level 3 – Fully Autonomous:

Fully autonomous means the authoring is done by the system as well and no human intervention is needed (with the exception of login credentials). This is also "monkey testing" as the app randomly clicks and gets to different states of the application. Although this is simple for some forms, it is extremely difficult for some apps (imagine an application like Paint, which comprises an empty canvas and the user can add rectangles and drag them around. To automatically understand that an overlap is an interesting case is hard, and assuming the expected result should be that the last rectangle added is on top is even harder (and actually impossible, since the product team could have chosen otherwise).

"WAIT-FORS"

As almost all of today's apps are asynchronous, and as humans we don't just click on elements, consciously or not, we wait until we see something on the screen before we continue clicking. Today, most platforms support implicit waits, which means waiting for the element to be visible before performing the action on it. In many cases, we need to wait for a specific state, i.e. something else to load first and appear on the screen (e.g. populate a dropdown with a list which was dynamically requested from the backend).

Although there is no big difference between a wait-for and a validation (both fail if we don't reach a specific state), we decided to split into two sections.

Level 0 — Manual Authoring: We are at level 0 today, and we rarely even give attention to this unless our tests start failing. I personally have seen many testers adding "sleep for X seconds" where not only this makes the tests flakey (as staging environments might be much slower as we usually only test the functionality not performance). Adding those random sleeps can also affect the speed of which the tests are done.

Level 1 — Teach by example: A system observing humans interacting with the app can reveal things that consciously are harder to conclude. This might be waiting for element to be visual or even a network request to return and to be processed.

Level 2 — Semi-Autonomous: This is very similar to the actions section, though the system can look at several tests failures and suggest steps to be inserted into the tests.

Level 3 — Fully Autonomous: We believed this can achieved fairly easily, as the system can add random delays between execution and train automatically.

VALIDATIONS

After we have performed the actions needed, we want to validate whether we reached the intended state. There are three paradigms: the 1st involves making a text validation at the DOM level (e.g. string compare, regex, etc.), the 2nd is to validate CSS properties (e.g. height, color, distance from another element), and the 3rd regards the rendered pixels.

Text validation and *element style* refer to validating that a specific element in the UI has a specific value; pixel validation is referred to as taking a screenshot and comparing the entire screen — or a portion of it (e.g. an element) — to a baseline comprising the expected result.

Style validation visually tests the state of visual properties. The Galen framework is an example of such a validation typen. For example, you can validate that the width of an element is 10px, or 10% from the neighbor element.

Level 0 — Manual Authoring: Most companies are still at this level, where validation still requires a lot of manual effort. This is usually done by extracting text from the UI and comparing via some function, e.g. the equals method or an ad hoc regex.

Both *style validation* and *pixel validation* were considered cumbersome and fragile; practitioners recommended to avoid these approaches.

For pixel validation, this stems mostly from:

1. Display adapters are non-deterministic in nature and generate a slightly different result for each execution. These changes, caused by anti-aliasing and subpixel shifts, are almost unnoticeable by the human eye and ignored by the brain.

2. Sometimes, taking a screenshot of the entire page actually validates too much (every text, every color, every location), causing high maintenance, especially if the page changes frequently.

For *style validation,* since there were numerous validations on each page, it created a lot of maintenance

Level 1 — Teach by example: The current focus is on pixel validation, with computer vision showing great improvements, resulting in many fewer false positives. At this level, humans are still needed to filter out noise, such as marking regions comprising random values (e.g. today's date).

TDD: as enhancements in computer vision continue, it will be easier to specify how far from the designer-created baseline we are willing to go and have it remain part of acceptance tests. This is also where style validation can come back and shine; this might be generated directly from design editing software (e.g. Photoshop) and added to the test.

Level 2 — Semi-Autonomous: We are getting closer to solving level 3 with automatic maintenance for validations. For example, if you change your logo, which affects a 1000 UI screens, we can figure out that it's a single universal change, which is either a bug or not, but we don't need to review over 1000 screenshots and approve each of them.

Level 3 — Fully Autonomous: Deep learning can help us automatically understand whether a page looks good or not with regard to structure, font size, and alignment. It will still be nearly impossible to automatically know the answer for results. For example, it will be hard to determine whether the result of 2+2 should be 4 or not (as it depends on the base).

SETUP

This refers to the starting state of the app prior to the actions which modify the state.

Level 0 — Manual Authoring: Today, a lot of tests fail as unexperienced testers fail to keep the initial state of the application in mind. This is still a big pain for most companies and every company authors its own ad hoc code, e.g. populating the DB with some fixtures data.

Level 1 — Teach by example: Although in some systems it seems relatively easy to dump the DB and restore it before each test run, this will start failing the second you start running tests in parallel. The only thing possible is to have some optimizations which look at the database and see what minimal projection is needed to run the tests. This can't be used for load testing and might also be problematic as it may cause false negatives. This shouldn't be used for full acceptance tests but merely for speed optimization in early stages.

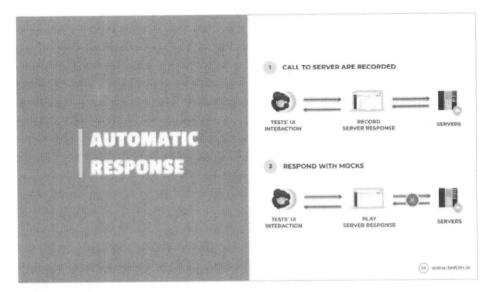

Level 2 — Semi-Autonomous: Given that the system observes the network and saves the communication between services and components of our app, it can create mocks to enable faster testing. For example, if a code change happened only on the front-end side, we might want to replace setting up a server and a database and have each call to the server (or between some microservices) be mocked and replaced with the saved data. This is especially useful when we want to generate a case were the server returns an error and verifies that an error message is shown to the user. This will still require human intervention but AI may help with dynamic content that we would understand and, ideally, automatically replace (alter the response).

Level 3 — Fully Autonomous: Model Based Testing is very mature and is a great way to generate test cases — especially the data required for each test. What hinders its popularity is that humans are required to model the entire application under test and ROI decreases dramatically; therefore this is a rarely used method. The system, with the help of AI, can understand the apps' relationships between objects/services/components and automatically deduce the model, thus making it easier to generate tests automatically.

This seems very challenging and sounds far-fetched; however, in the near future, we expect to release a semi-autonomous version which observes humans and makes it easier to understand these interactions.

RISK MANAGEMENT

At the end of the day, Quality Assurance is about the customer. Whether it's protecting their data, ensuring a flawless user experience, or testing software functionality, we are managing risk. One method I see companies take to reduce functional testing risk is code coverage, and, although I'm not a huge fan, it's better than nothing. The only question I have is: "is this the right indicator?" Let's revisit the notion of connecting your production environment and apps to your testing cycle. I already pointed out that this will resolve the authoring challenge; however, the most important thing to pay attention to here is that it will give us the scenarios that we should really be testing (at least for regressions). It is important to look at which critical scenarios are required for the business to succeed and which scenarios occur more than others.

We want to at least test what our customers are going through and, hopefully, we'll speak less in terms of code coverage and focus more on user coverage.

SUMMARY

We believe that AI will help to achieve Autonomous Testing, which will eliminate the quality/velocity dilemma many software companies face every day. In terms of quality, it will become easier for teams to maximize user coverage by connecting the authoring of tests to production apps and mapping to real user flows. In addition, this will give us the ability to take a risk-based approach to enable better data-driven decisions. So far, the big innovation for us at Testim is leveraging AI to proactively fix issues through self-healing mechanisms and drastically reduce maintenance time for our customers. In terms of improved velocity, we make it easy for our customers to author more user scenarios in a shorter time frame. This not only helps teams find bugs faster, but they release faster since they have a better safety net they can count on. The future of software quality has become brighter with autonomous testing.

CHAPTER TWENTY-FIVE

Functional Test Automation with AI

BY JASON ARBON, CEO, TEST.AI

JASON ARBON is a test nerd and currently the CEO of test.ai, where his mission is to automate the testing of the world's apps with AI. He has also been the director of product and engineering at Applause.com/uTest.com. Jason previously held engineering leadership roles at Google (Chrome/Search) and Microsoft (WindowsCE, SQL Server, BizTalk, Bing). He also co-authored the books: How Google Tests Software and App Quality: Secrets for Agile App Teams. In his spare time, Jason likes to read up on AGI and consciousness and is working on a new personalized search engine. Note that this chapter outlines the basics of how to Build AI-based test Automation Systems, and test.ai has filed patents for specific implementations of these concepts.

INTRODUCTION

Software testing is about to be transformed by Artificial Intelligence (AI) and Machine Learning (ML). While other aspects of software engineering have improved dramatically in the past decade, software testing still looks much the same. Testing hasn't changed much because testing requires human judgement, manual activities, domain knowledge, and empathy for the end user — all of these require human-level intelligence. AI is a way to build software that can replicate human judgement. The resurgence of AI as a field, combined with affordable computing, means that AI can be applied to some of the most challenging aspects of automated testing and deliver AI-assisted testing for humans.

AI is a broad category of software including machine learning where the software is 'trained' to do basic tasks with or without human instruction. AI even includes work on Artificial General Intelligence (AGI) — the work to construct conscious, even superintelligent machines. This chapter is humbly focused on those parts of 'AI', particularly machine learning techniques, that can be practically applied to common software test automation tasks.

Of all professions, software testing is the ripest to be automated via AI. Most applications of AI are really pattern matching. Today, AI is being applied to many fields, from radiology, to driving cars, to making hair appointments over the phone. These applications use the output of the AI training process and apply that to specific problems, such as analyzing MRI scans, recognizing a stop sign and stopping a car, or composing conversations with hair stylists. These are problems which consist of inputs and comparing the outputs to expected results. Testing is another matter altogether, though, as the basic processes of software testing are similar to the processes used to train AI. Testing is fundamentally an AI training problem. The good news is that since the processes are so similar, all the money spent today on infrastructure and researching AI training techniques is really an investment in AI test automation.

Testing is fundamentally the process of applying inputs to an application/system-under-test, observing the outputs, and checking those outputs against the expected values. (See Figure A)

Fig. A: System testing

Training AI Systems is very similar to testing. Instead of applying inputs and measuring outputs to an application under test, AI systems apply inputs to the neural network (or other model) and measure the outputs from that model. AI training systems also compare the output of the neural network with the expected value (training data). This looks very similar to testing. It *is* testing. (See Figure B)

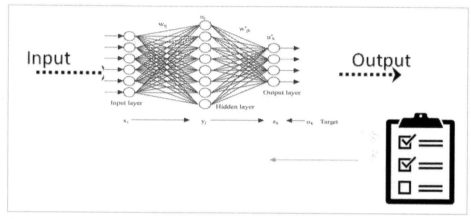

Fig. B: AI Training is very similar to testing

Not only is AI training similar to testing, but most testing activities consist of quick visual inspections to determine what to do next, or to determine whether the application's functionality is correct. Modern AI is great at solving such quick-twitch judgment calls. Even better, the AI can be trained on the judgement of not just one tester, but on the collective wisdom of thousands of smart testers, and have all that brainpower encoded in the machine.

"Pretty much anything that a normal person can do in <1 sec, we can now automate with AI..."

—Andrew NG, Twitter[1] Stanford CS faculty. Former head of Baidu AI Group/Google Brain.

Test automation is a combination of testing best practices and software development, so it is often as time consuming and expensive as application development. There are many types of testing. The most painful today is UI (User Interface)-based functional regression testing, as the application is

---

1   Twitter, Andrew Ng, https://twitter.com/AndrewYNg/status/788548053745569792

constantly changing and the test code needs to drive another application, not just an API (Application Programming Interface) or call a function (Unit Testing). UI test automation is fundamentally composed of four major tasks:

1. Test definitions
2. Screen and element identification
3. Test step sequencing
4. State verification

Below, we explore how each of these aspects of test automation can be written with an AI-first approach. For each test automation task, we'll also explore how AI improves the following aspects of testing:

1. Efficiency of test development
2. Reliability of test execution
3. Reduced cost of maintenance
4. Re-use of test artifacts across platforms and applications.

Lastly, the sum of all these improvements in test automation will usher in a new world of software testing. Ultimately, most test automation will be centralized thanks to re-use and AI. Most test cases will already be written for an app — before it is even implemented. And most importantly, AI-powered test automation means competitive benchmarking in quality is finally possible. AI won't just make test automation better, faster, and cheaper, it will fundamentally revolutionize the testing profession and help standardize measures of quality as the same 'test' can now be performed on different platforms and even different applications.

AI TEST DEFINITIONS

Manual test cases are often written in human language, as their purpose is to describe the test for people to read and execute. Most test case definitions, however, are written in procedural code, or long winding paths of poorly written Python or Java test scripts. This approach is less than ideal:

1. Only programmers can create or modify the tests
2. Test code is difficult to write, test, and debug

3. Most of the code written is for test case setup and tear down — not the test.

4. Test code must be manually updated when the application changes

The astute reader may be thinking of the Cucumber test framework. On the surface, Cucumber tries to tackle this test definition problem so that tests can be constructed in a human-like language and then executed by a second system or model of the application. The reality is that Cucumber projects often fail because they still have the same problems of procedurally coded tests. The Cucumber tests need a few programmers to connect the human-like language of the test definition to executable code that drives the application. We'll see below how AI can do all that magic for humans.

"Cucumber is not a tool for testing software. It is a tool for testing people's understanding of how software (yet to be written) should behave."
—Aslak Hellesoy, Creator of Cucumber, Hacker News[2]

AI test cases need to be written in some sort of language. Ideally, these test definitions should be abstracted from the application's implementation as far as possible to make the test case execution flexible and reusable. The test definition should also be human-readable so both machines and humans can work from the same test case definition and be free from the need to know or bother with programming languages for test creation or execution. At this point, the best candidate for such a test case definition format is the Abstract Intent Test (AIT) language, which conveniently has "AI" in its acronym. This format is an open standard and actively worked on by the AI for Software Testing Association (https://www.aitesting.org).

AIT borrows from the learning of Cucumber and its Gherkin[3] language as it is designed for human readability and often used by designers or product managers to specify the functionality of an application. AIT just adds some additional syntactic sugar to the steps of a Gherkin scenario so that it is readily readable by machines. AIT enables test definitions to be as precise or as general as the test author likes. Steps that are left out, or obvious, are performed by the AI automatically. For those steps that are specific and

---

2   Hacker News, Aslak Hellesoy, https://news.ycombinator.com/item?id=10194242

3   Gherkin, Wikipedia, https://en.wikipedia.org/wiki/Cucumber_(software)#Gherkin_language

necessary for the test, the AI will execute those steps exactly as declared by the test author.

The full AIT language specification is beyond the scope of this chapter, but a simple example should suffice. Here is simple AIT defined for executing a test case against a search engine, searching for the word 'Gradient', and verifying that a search result with the word 'Gradient' is returned.

```
Test Name: Search for Gradient
Description: Perform a simple, single word, web search for
the term "Gradient"
Tags: "Single_Word", "Search"

Step: Get To Search
StepType: Navigation
Labels: "Search Button"

Step: Enter Search Text
StepType: TextInput
Text: "Gradient"
Labels: "Search Box"

Step: Execute Search
StepType: Action
Action: Tap
Labels: "Search Button"

Step: Verify Result Appears
StepType: Verify
VerificationString: "Gradient"
Match: 3
Labels: "Search Result"
```

The reader, without programming knowledge, can easily determine that this is a test case that searches for the word "Gradient" and verifies that there is a result with the word "Gradient" in it. Let's walk through each step quickly and note a few things.

The Test Name and Description are straightforward in meaning. The "tags" field is a way to organize and search for tests when there are large numbers of tests.

The "Get to Search" test step does just that. It is a step of type 'navigation', which tells the AI to 'find the search page' and we'll start the test from there. The AI looks through the app for any element that can be classified as 'search page'. The magic of this step is that we can tell an AI, just as we would a human, to 'start the test on the search page'. Because the mechanics and specifics of how to do this aren't specified in code, or in exact steps, we are leaving it to the AI (or human) to figure out how to get there. If we had to specify the exact buttons or links to click to get to the search page, the test would 'break' every time that part of application changed. We'll discuss how this magic works later.

The "Enter Search Text" step is a TextInput step. It instructs the person or AI to put the text "Gradient" into the "Search Box". How does the AI know what a search box is without knowing the magic ID, XPATH, CSS Selector, etc., of the search box element? That magic is described below. The beautiful thing here is that the test author doesn't have to know anything about the implementation of the application. The AI, just like a human, should be able to figure out how to find the search box and enter the text.

The "Execute Search Step" executes the search by clicking on a button called "Search Button". Again, the magic of how the AI knows it is a search button is described later.

The "Verify Result Appears" step verifies that there is a search result with the word "Gradient" in it. The AI looks on the page for things that are called 'Search Result' and scans each of them for the presence of the word "Gradient". The match clause specifies that for this step to count as a passing test, this matching of the word "Gradient" must appear in at least 3 test result objects on the page.

Here, we have defined a test case that is human-readable, doesn't require a programmer, and promises that there is a whole lot of AI magic to convert such high-level steps into an automated test case.

It should also be noted here that this test case doesn't have a lot of things required for most test automation: It is missing things like magic IDs, CSS selectors, accessibility labels, or XPATHs to find element. It is also missing any platform-specific code. The same test could run on a mobile device or a web page. Most interesting is that this test case also doesn't mention the actual application. This test could run on any search engine or application with search functionality. AIT test cases are, by design, written to be platform and application agnostic. Given the right human or AI test execution, this test can be reused everywhere; it need only be written once in the world.

AI-powered testing means that test cases are also quick to write, with no programming knowledge needed, and can magically execute test cases across platforms and applications — just like a human could. The same test case can deal with very different user interfaces, numbers of steps, platforms, and apps.

Now that we can define the ideal test case for execution by AI (and humans), let's get into the nuts and bolts of how to get AI to magically execute all these AIT test cases for us.

AI SCREEN AND ELEMENT IDENTIFICATION

A key aspect of test automation is the ability to identify elements in an application. Test automation needs to find elements to interact with them via taps, swipes, and text input. Test automation also needs to find elements to verify the correct output or results of a test case: for example, finding the search result item and verifying that it is the expected result by examining the text description of the link.

When humans test an app, they can readily identify what type of screen it is, e.g. search, login, profile, etc. Humans can also do a very good job of determining if a button is a search button, or if a textbox is a search box, or if an image is a picture of a product. People can even readily identify screens and elements in applications they have never seen before, even if the buttons are a bit larger, a different color, or different position on a page, because the person has likely seen similar objects in other apps. Much like people are trained to recognize basic application screens and elements, we can teach machines to do the same.

To teach an AI how to classify a screen or element we need lots of training data. Training data is simply a large set of examples of, say, search buttons. Some may be small, some large, some red, some blue, but we need lots of examples. Many will have the word 'search', or 'go', in the text of the button. Most will be centered, or on the right-hand side of the application, and often in the middle or top near the search text box. We humans know this intuitively, we just need to give lots of examples to an ML model to 'learn' to recognize search buttons too.

So how to get a large corpus (set) of training data? There are three steps. First, write a crawler bot that will download thousands of applications (or browse websites) and take screenshots of everything. Second, break down the screenshots into individual images of buttons, text boxes, images, etc. Third, you need to get the labels to train the AI. Labeling is the process of naming each individual image with a label such as 'search_button', 'product_image', or 'shopping_cart_button'. We now have a set of training data to teach the machines to think like human testers.

How do you get labels for hundreds of thousands of images? Amazon's Mechanical Turk is a common solution. You can pay people pennies per label. Simply send the service a list of images and define the job as 'please pick one of the following that describe the picture' (see Figure D). Posting this type of job is pretty easy.

Fig. D: User Interface for Mechanical Turk Labeling

Now, powered with a bunch of training data, which is simply a large set of images that are labeled, we just pass this data to some machine learning infrastructure such as TensorFlow or SciKitLearn Python libraries, etc. The detailed mechanics of doing that is beyond the scope of this chapter but, basically, you just put all the images and labels into a giant array and call a function to, say, 'train'. The AI starts by randomly guessing the correct label for each element. When it is right, it tries to remember how it was configured. When it is wrong, it reconfigures (changes its internal connections) and tries again. In practice this happens hundreds of thousands of times until it can get most labels for elements correct.

Next, feature values need to be computed. Machines cannot really 'see' images so we need to translate things that humans can see into numbers between 0 and 1 so the computer can 'see' them too. You can think of features as a function that takes the image and document object model as an input and then returns a value between 0 and 1. A few feature examples that have proven to be useful in test automation:

Features for Elements:

- **%Height:** determine the height of the image in pixels and divide that value by the max height of the device's screen. This results in a value between 0 and 1, representing the relative height of the image.

- **%Width, X, Y, Area,** etc. (same as % Height)

- **Average Color:** Look at every pixel in the image. For each pixel determine the different Red, Green and Blue (RGB) components which are values between 0 and 255. Then, for each color, divide that value by 255 to normalize the numbers to a value between 0 and 1.

- **Text match:** Run Optical Character Recognition (OCR) on the image to extract any possible text. For interesting values such as 'Login', or 'Allow', create a separate feature that sends a 0 or a 1 depending on whether that text is present in the image.

- **Text length:** Like text match, but length of string divided by the maximum expected string length.

Features for Screens:

- **Number of Elements:** Number of total elements on the screen. Simply count the number of elements on the screen and divide by a maximum number of screen elements expected (e.g. 1000).

- **Average Color:** (see above)

- **Number of Elements By Type:** Number of buttons, text boxes, images, etc.

If you think about how you determine what a screen or element is in your own mind, you may realize that your brain is doing very similar things. E.g., login screens usually have only a few elements, often 'blue', and often only a single button, whereas a product listing page might have hundreds of images, one text box, and only a couple buttons, and be mostly white. Computing these features and passing this data to the AI training systems enable the AI to 'see' similar to how humans see the screen. AI might even learn some patterns or hints that we humans don't even notice. A production system might include hundreds of these 'features'.

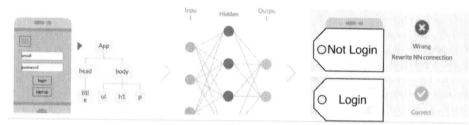

Figure E. Example of AI Training for a Login Screen

Now, these vectors of feature values for each image, along with its correct label (training data), are passed to the AI training system. A high-level view of the training process follows:

1. A randomly configured 'Brain' is generated

2. The system presents each image and its 'feature values' to the neural network and measures whether the network guesses the correct label.

   a. If the label was correct, the network is 'reinforced' that the current configuration is a good one.

   b. If the label was incorrect, the network is 'changed' in hopes that next time it will guess correctly.

3. The system repeats this process hundreds of thousands of times until the network has 'learned' to produce the correct results.

After 24 hours of computation on high-end machines, the AI training system generates a neural network that can now take the input of an image and suggest the correct label for that screen or element. Just like a human can. Perhaps better than a human. Testing the correctness of such a system is also out of scope for a quick chapter on the topic, but essentially, the brain is tested using a separate set of images that were not used in training and then tested to see how accurately the brain, like a human brain, performs on those new images. This AI approach is known as supervised learning as we have supervised the learning of the system by giving it many examples and letting the machine learn to reproduce the same output as the humans.

With all this work, we now have an alternative way of identifying parts of an application. Remember, traditional non-AI software automation finds elements by hardcoded searches in the application for a magic accessibility or other ID value, XPATH, or CSS Selectors. AI-based element identification, however, finds elements just like the human brain.

The AI-based approach to identifying elements is far more complex to set up but it has two distinct advantages versus traditional methods:

- **Speed:** The engineering time it takes a human to write the code to identify an individual element can be several minutes. With an AI trained on thousands of different elements, the time to identify an element is less than a second and can be done at runtime. This represents a 10X development speed/cost improvement. Moreover, these AI classifiers can be shared between app teams, so only one or a few people on the planet need to build these classifiers and everyone else can benefit.

- **Robustness/Maintenance:** A key problem in test automation today is that the applications are constantly changing. The color, size, location, or text of a search button may change and break test code, but to the eye of a human, or well-trained AI, the search button still looks like a search button, whereas traditional element identification will fail with even minor changes to the application. AI-based identification keeps working and doesn't require maintenance.

It is worth noting that the trained AI is the collective knowledge of all people and testers that contributed to the training set of images and labels. When the AI is trained on hundreds of thousands of images with labels from hundreds of different people, it has seen more search buttons than most humans ever will in their lifetime. This means the AI might just be smarter than any single tester at identifying elements in applications.

AI TEST STEP SEQUENCING

A test case is a sequence of steps: a series of inputs and outputs. Find the search screen, enter text in the search box, click the search button, then verify the search results seem relevant to the query. We've seen how AI can be trained to identify the individual parts of an application such as search boxes and buttons; now we need to teach it to accomplish a task that is a series of steps.

Traditional test automation expresses test step sequences in procedural code such as Python or Java. Each step is hard-coded, step-by-step[4], to interact with elements in the application. Procedural code for test steps is problematic in three ways:

1. **Test automator needs to know how to program.** There are a limited number of competent programmers in the world and they are expensive. Generally speaking, test engineers are not the most experienced engineers, nor do they produce beautiful test code.

2. **Time to develop tests.** Programming is labor intensive. Programming is, ironically, manual in that each line of code must be hand crafted and it also needs to be tested.

3. **Brittleness/maintenance.** The biggest issue with procedural code is that if the flow/structure of the application changes, the test automation breaks. Often it breaks at the exact moment the team looks to the automation to verify that the application still works. A/B testing, redesign, interstitial dialogs, etc. can appear during execution and break the expectations of the procedural code.

---

4   New Kids On the Block, "Step By Step", https://www.youtube.com/watch?v=ay6GjmiJTPM

So, let's explore ways to motivate an AI brain to build and execute these test case step sequences for us.

The following approach is borrowed from the work of Google DeepMind and OpenAI teams and how they teach each machine to play video games. Again, all this AI work is really just test infrastructure. Playing video games like Mario Brothers are sequences of steps like running, jumping and spinning. People learn to play Mario Brothers by playing around a bit. If they run into a mushroom, they power up. If they run into a coin, they get more points. The humans are rewarded and punished into learning how to play the game correctly. By analogy, paths through a video game look a lot like the paths taken in an app by an automated test case. Just think of training an AI to automatically navigate the application along the waypoints that constitute a test case instead of walking through the levels of a game. This general AI method is called reinforcement learning. The details are beyond the scope of this chapter, but the astute, curious, clever reader can find a lot more details on how Google's DeepMind team uses reinforcement learning to play Atari games[5].

Playing games is fun but executing test cases is geekily-amazing. To teach an AI how to execute the test steps you want, we need a 'map' of the application, equivalent to a game's level design, and we need to place 'coins' or rewards on this map to encourage the AI to follow the path we want. Then, we let the AI train on thousands of attempts to walk around and explore the map of the application, learning how to execute the path we want it to achieve to maximize its reward.

The map of the application, aka 'AppGraph', is critical to the training of an AI to execute test cases. The map is a simple graph view of the various states of an application. One node may be the home screen, another node may be the search screen. Lines between the nodes represent ways to get from one page to the other, e.g. clicking the search button on the home screen takes the user to the search result screen state. Once we have a map of the application, which can be generated by classic link-following or checking methods[6], we can begin to train the AI bot to accomplish the testing task.

---

5   Google DeepMind Atari Reinforcement Learning, https://deepmind.com/research/publications/
    playing-atari-deep-reinforcement-learning/

6   Google Link Checker, https://developers.google.com/adwords/scripts/docs/solutions/link-checker

HOW TO TRAIN AI TO EXECUTE A SHOPPING CART TEST CASE

Let's explore how to teach an AI to accomplish a basic test case. For a sample test case, let's verify that the application still has a shopping cart. First, we assign a start state (the home screen), and also set a reward for reaching the first step (the shopping cart in this example). We also set the 'game score' to zero to begin. The rules of the game are simple:

1. The AI bot can step from one state to any other state in the app graph.

2. If the AI bot takes a step that doesn't contain a reward, the bot is penalized one point.

3. If the AI bot takes a step and lands on a state that contains a reward, it gets 100 points.

To train the AI, we let it take thousands of attempts at walking through the graph to accomplish the testing task which, in this case, is to get to the shopping cart. Once the AI has been trained to get to the shopping cart, the process begins again to train it to get to the next reward state, which is the next test step state we want the bot to take in sequence.

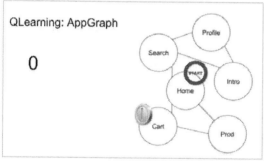

Figure E: Graph of App with Reward at Cart Page

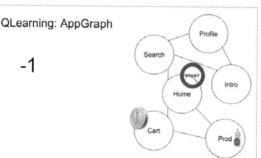

Figure F: Bot takes step to a product page, loses one point.

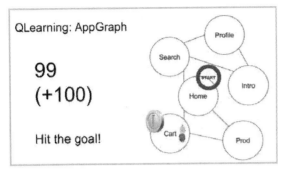

Figure G: Bot takes step to cart page, where the reward lies. Bot's net score for this path is 99.

In the figures above, the bot found a pretty good way to get to the cart page, but it isn't the optimal path. On a later training run, the bot may find how to click the shopping cart icon on the home page to go directly to the cart page, which would give it a score of 100 for that path, which is higher than the 99-point score it got for going through the product page first on the way to the cart. The AI training process does this thousands of times for each step in every test case. The training process produces a 'heat map' of how to navigate the app graph in search of the next test step. This is the 'brain' of the reinforcement training.

There are three powerful implications of this approach to 'teaching' an AI how to accomplish a test sequence versus traditional hard coding of steps:

1. **No code.** No human programmers were harmed in the construction of this test case. There is no code to be written. The AI training process reads in the test step sequences desired in the AIT and trains an AI to execute those steps in sequence

2. **App change resilience.** The AI learns many ways to get to the cart page. If the default path is removed in a future build of the application, the AI brain, just like a human brain, can use other ways to still find the cart and execute the test case despite app changes.

3. **Cross-application.** Each app can have a different graph structure but the process of training an AI brain to execute the same high-level test is the same, meaning this approach to step sequencing will work on all apps.

Important to note, and easy to miss, is the ability of AI-based test sequencing to take the test execution to a particular place (state) in an application without specifying all the steps to get there. So, only the steps needed to execute the test need to be specified. Ironically, the less specific a test case definition is, the more robust, efficient, and reusable it is.

Figure H is a demonstration of the same test case 'Search for the string "Gradient"', trained and executing across different applications (Bing, Google, Yahoo, and YouTube), and across different platforms (Android and Desktop Web).

Fig. H: Test Execution Report for Search Test. Cross-platform and Cross-application.

The AI-based approach to test sequencing eliminates the need for crafting hard coded steps in procedural code. The AI approach is not only better, cheaper, and faster. The bots have effectively done most of the work that humans do today. The Singularity is near...

BENCHMARKING

Software quality, performance, etc., has traditionally been '# of the tests we have bothered to write so far, x% of them passed' or 'we are better than yesterday'. Neither of these answers to quality seems very sophisticated, engineering-like, or confidence-inspiring. However, with the arrival of test cases that execute both cross-platform and cross-application, we can now answer the quality question with a number relative to other apps, relative to a benchmark.

AI means it is finally financially feasible to not just automate your own applications, but those of your competitors and see how the two stack up. Which app has a faster login page? Which app is missing a particular functionality? Which app fails login tests in production less often?

Figure I shows the performance of search page loading times across several mobile apps. This data was gathered during the test execution above. Google itself would probably be surprised by the results, as even they don't have the time to write traditional UI regression tests for competitive apps. Benchmarking quality can be motivating to organizations to increase their focus on quality as a competitive advantage.

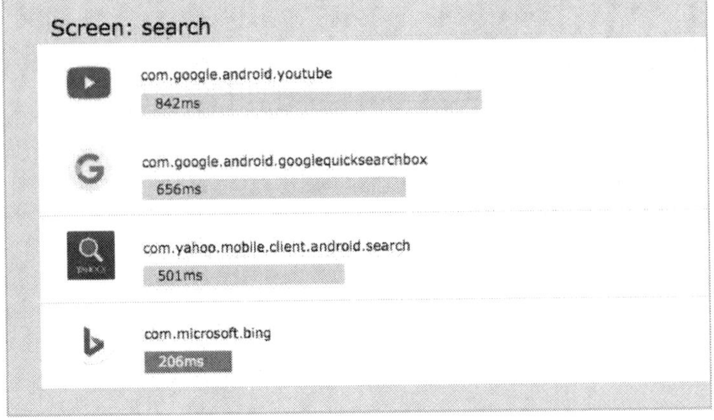

Fig I: Relative performance of mobile app search pages.

Figure I is a rendering of real test results of the very AIT test case defined above, running cross-platform and cross-application. Not only does AI-powered test automation work today but it also delivers insights into the behavior of applications. Notice how Bing takes far more steps to accomplish a search versus the Google app? Notice that Yahoo's app design means that searching for something takes only two steps and bests Google's design in user efficiency?

CENTRALIZATION OF TESTING

AI-powered test automation is here. Even in its early form, AI-first approaches to testing are already beating traditional procedural code-based approaches to test definition, element selection, and test step execution. This is the first time that test artifacts are truly reusable — not just across platforms, but across different applications. The test search test case we've been exploring above need only be written once. If the first engineer to write the 'Search for "Gradient"' test case worked at Google, theoretically, with zero porting work, the same test could be leveraged by the team at Bing. AI means teams can now collaborate and share test artifacts. Previously, most every test was rewritten from scratch by every app team. Maybe AI will encourage testers to be more social now that they have an icebreaker — reusable test artifacts.

Better, what if there was a global repository of test cases for shopping carts, login tests, maps, that every app team in the world could leverage with zero code. This means that if you started your own search engine app from scratch today, an automated test suite for that application already exists before you started building it. Instant-on test coverage. The ultimate in Test Driven Development (TDD) where tests are written before the application is coded.

AI-Powered test cases are a step-function in software testing as the test artifacts are now truly reusable. The implication of this is that if testers shared their AIT test cases, test.ai, among others, can execute AIT defined test cases; there really only needs to be one global repository for most automated testing.

Sure, there will always be unique and corner-cases that need test development, or even demand human intervention, but the next wave of app teams won't have to start from scratch on the basic tests every time and can focus on the app-specific, and differentiating features of their app. AI-powered testing should finally free engineers from the mundane and let them focus on the hard problems. That was the original promise of software test automation with procedural code, but the implementation proved to be less than adequate.

SUMMARY

We've explored just one approach to applying AI to software test automation. AI and machine learning are core technologies that can be applied in a nearly infinite array of ways to many different testing problems. Unsupervised learning is applied at Concur to automatically identify servers are acting oddly. Ultimate Software is using AI to generate additional test cases by learning from existing test cases. King (of Candy Crush fame) uses AI to automatically test new level designs. Many testing vendors are, right now, figuring out how to integrate AI because they don't want to be left behind. Others are so motivated that they claim to be using AI before they know what it means. All this is evidence that AI will transform software testing — whether we like it or not.

AI for software test automation is real, it's here, and it is running on real world apps today. Many testers will be in denial. Many testers are intimidated or confused by "AI". Many testers ask if their automation or manual jobs are in peril. Many will say "it can't perform this edge case", or that they are too invested in the procedural testing world to change. By analogy, cars were initially noisier, more complex, more expensive, couldn't travel well on muddy roads, needed gas, and even ran over humans, but you don't see many horses around town anymore. AI is just as transformational a technology for the testing profession as cars were to transportation. We are in the early days of figuring out how to apply AI to testing but the revolution has begun. Regardless of what people want to believe, AI for software testing is here today and it will rapidly transform what we know as test automation in the coming years.

CHAPTER TWENTY-SIX

Testing 101 for IoT-enabled Applications

BY AMIR ROZENBERG

AMIR ROZENBERG is a thought leader in the space of agile quality methodologies. As a product director at Perfecto, he drove the core product strategy and implementation with many Fortune-1000 customers. He led initiatives in the areas of real user condition testing, accessibility, security, audio and conversational interfaces, AI/ML, IoT and medical devices etc. In addition, Amir led successful synergies with Microsoft, SmartBear, Blazemeter, Neotys etc., to optimize value delivery to the market. Prior to Perfecto, Amir led the mobile monitoring practice at Compuware.

```java
public static enum thingsToTest{
        Chatbots,
        Finger_Face_ID,
        IoT_WebConnected,
        IoT_Device_Connected,
        OTT_Devices
};
```

TESTING IOT-ENABLED APPS

IoT devices, which aim to solve real-world problems with embedded connectivity, are proliferating at a stunning pace. By 2020, this market is expected to exceed $1.7 trillion with over 200 billion connected devices. Beekeepers, for example, distribute colonies to remote locations, optimizing pollination and honey creation. IoT sensors save significant time and investment, reporting the maturity of the hive for honey harvesting. The value is demonstrable as IoT finds its way into many areas of our lives. At the same time, market pressures are driving brands to accelerate new features to market. As an example, devices and services associated with fitness accessories see new features introduced frequently. Development teams must adapt to the growing scope of development and test coverage in a shrinking timeframe.

Compliance plays a big part

Considering the difference between passive devices (such as fitness trackers) and proactive ones (insulin pumps), one needs to incorporate standards compliance into their test plan. Devices invariably communicate data to backend systems, such as the medical 'backbone', which connects patients with healthcare professionals and insurance vendors. HIPPAA specifies the security of data transmissions and sharing. FDA regulations are applicable to Class-C proactive devices such as insulin pumps. One must account for these regulatory requirements in the test plan, consider submission and approval schedules, etc.

Divide and conquer

The task of ensuring the overall quality of an IoT application might seem beyond reach. However, breaking the problem down can lead to interesting conclusions. Consider the application architecture, the IoT device at the front, a mobile device, and the backend.

IoT device manufacturing typically follows an embedded software development lifecycle. The hardware is tested on its own; the firmware is tested using a home-grown desktop simulator. Then the whole unit is tested. Hence, release cycles for the IoT unit are long, with limited realistic potential to shorten them. In the medical space, since compliance is of primary importance, predictability of test and certification phases is challenging.

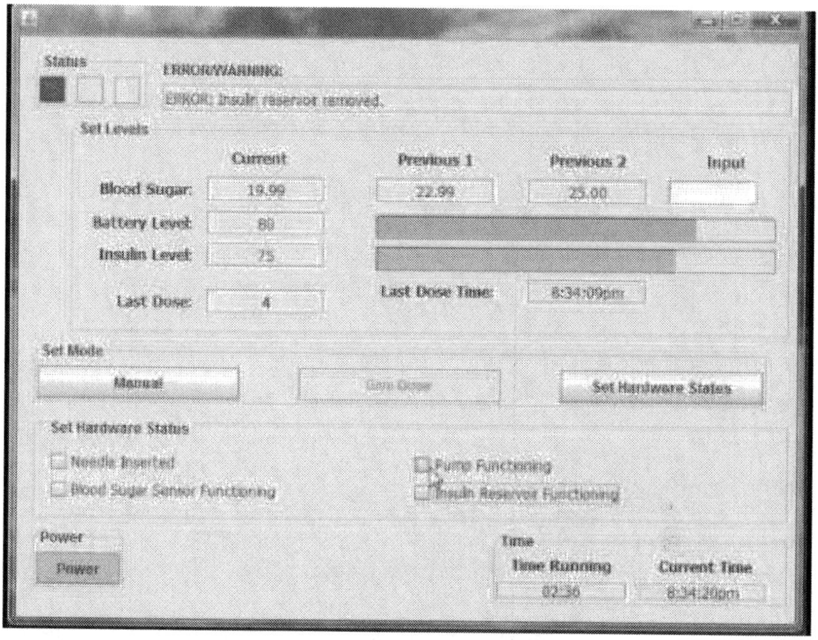

Figure 1: Insulin pump test simulator

Figure 2: Example application
for diabetes patients

Next, one must consider the mobile device/ application. The device offers two functions: connect the IoT unit to the web and inform the user with useful (sometimes critical) information. This information might include alerting the user they need to use their inhaler, tracking overuse of medicine, etc. Correlating patient vitals over time and with the consumption of medicine could lead to altering a course of treatment and assisting research globally.

While mobile devices do not change often, operating systems and applications do. Testing an application in presence of different data sets from the IoT unit is key. Test automation and virtualization are critical to achieving quality and velocity in the mobile app/device.

Finally, we need to look at web-based infrastructure, storing, processing, and sharing data from the IoT unit and the mobile app accordingly. These environments must be tested for compliance, resiliency, etc.

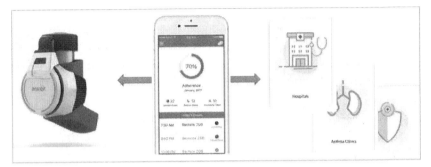

Figure 3: IoT-Enabled application architecture

Virtualize

In a complex environment, the key to predictable success is to insulate teams and deliverables. Independent teams accelerate and progress faster, each at its own pace. Thus, two ingredients are required: virtualization and frequent integration. Virtualization will allow mobile app development independent of the IoT unit development cycle. A proper means of simulating various transmissions and exchanges of data sets between the IoT unit and the mobile device/app is needed. Using automation, the app team will then be able to test the app against many versions of firmware and hardware of the IoT unit.

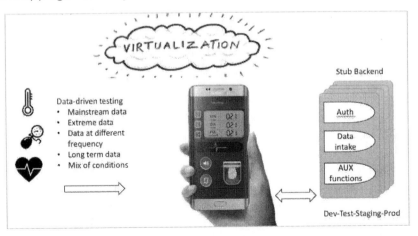

Figure 4: Service virtualization used to test IoT, BLE-Enabled apps

FUNCTIONAL TESTING VS. RADIO TESTING

Many IoT units are making use of Bluetooth Low Energy (BLE) technology to communicate with mobile devices. While testing of both functionality and BLE radio transmissions is part of the test plan for all these devices, in the case of an insulin pump, testing radio transmissions is mandatory with any mobile device.

Hence, one can split the functional testing into a phase of its own. Typically, it is estimated that functional testing entails over 90% of the overall test plan, and therefore is a great candidate for test automation. In terms of testing the application in the presence of data sets, there are ways to instrument the application such that HTTP packets transmitted from a BLE simulator will be processed as if they come over the BLE channel. Such a software-based solution is scalable, reliable, and consistent.

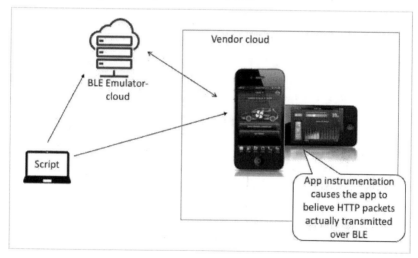

Figure 5: Possible lab solution for IoT functional testing

In terms of testing radio transmissions, there are a number of approaches that can be taken. Practically speaking, there are a limited number of BLE chipset manufacturers in the market. Therefore, a lab with a few BLE dongles (encompassing some of those chipsets) can offer a nice solution. Simulation using a cloud lab could be based on open source BLENO[1] server and BLE

---

1 Bleno technology — https://github.com/noble/bleno

sniffer. In this way, effective test automation can be achieved. The downside of this approach is scalability problems due to radio interference. While there are estimates in the market regarding interference from closely-spaced BLE devices, there is no practical evidence as to the actual limitations of such a lab.

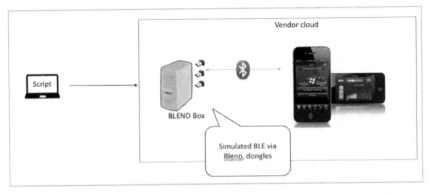

Figure 6: Possible solution for a lab that offers BLE radio transmission testing

Another approach is to have an on-prem lab, possibly part of a cloud solution, where representative real devices connect to real units or dongles. Such an approach is fairly easy to set up and it follows compliance regulations for the vendor. Naturally, this approach does not lend itself well to scalability as the on-prem lab will require setup and maintenance resources of its own.

WEB-CONNECTED IOT DEVICES

These days, it is possible to control your car remotely from an app: turn it on, control the lights, unlock, etc. Home automation (such as NEST and others) also offer web-based applications that connect mobile apps and home automation systems. The main distinction is that the IoT device is connected directly to the internet; this connectivity scheme is not based on BLE.

In such a scenario, one can fully separate IoT device testing, as described earlier, and mobile app testing. The E2E testing can be done, for example, between a scripting PC, the mobile device in a lab, and a car simulator that resides on the vendor side.

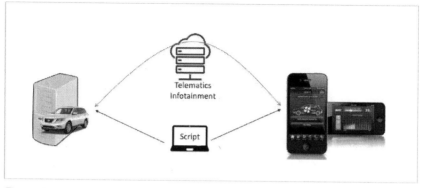

Figure 7: Testing IoT web-connected devices

SUMMARY

IoT-enabled applications are growing rapidly in number, creating new and significant challenges for dev and test teams. These are complex architectures that commonly include the IoT unit, a mobile device, and backend infrastructure. This challenge can be difficult to address. However, dividing the larger problem into different system components — and carefully evaluating what really needs to be tested at any given stage — can help build the right solution and process, and, eventually, lead to a high quality, compliant product.

As always, proper reporting solutions need to be in place to offer fast feedback to the developer.

CHAPTER TWENTY-SEVEN

Testing Rich-Media Apps and Over-the-Top (OTT) Devices

BY AMIR ROZENBERG

AMIR ROZENBERG is a thought leader in the space of agile quality methodologies. As a product director at Perfecto, he drove the core product strategy and implementation with many Fortune-1000 customers. He led initiatives in the areas of real user condition testing, accessibility, security, audio and conversational interfaces, AI/ML, IoT and medical devices etc. In addition, Amir led successful synergies with Microsoft, SmartBear, Blazemeter, Neotys etc., to optimize value delivery to the market. Prior to Perfecto, Amir led the mobile monitoring practice at Compuware.

```
public static enum thingsToTest{
        Chatbots,
        Finger_Face_ID,
        IoT_WebConnected,
        IoT_Device_Connected,
        OTT_Devices
};
```

TESTING RICH-MEDIA APPS AND OVER-THE-TOP (OTT) DEVICES

"OTT video is video transmitted via the Internet that bypasses traditional cable/linear distribution." (Forbes)

Rich media experiences are proliferating to increase end-user engagement. As mentioned earlier in this book, conversational interfaces already are paving the way to a future of personalization and customization. In the video media space, new experiences are also being introduced. Naturally, traditional video streaming brands (Netflix, Hulu, the NFL, etc.) are finding new engagement and revenue streams in mobile apps. Taking this concept even further, retailers are now offering video snippets containing product information, how-to and troubleshooting help, reviews, etc.

Whether you're sitting in a flight trying to watch a movie with intermittent delays, trying to make a product purchase decision based on a how-to video, or watching the Super Bowl, sensitivity to the video quality is high.

 Millennials are 2x more likely to be focused while watching video on their smartphones vs. on TV

Source: Google and IPSOS

QUALITY OF VIDEO STREAMING

Naturally, every application associated with OTT requires great functional testing for account management functions, content discovery, and other functions.

Video streaming has been around for a while; it is now being served on many more devices, operating systems, wireless networks, etc. Consideration needs to be given to whether the stream is rights-protected (DRM). A robust, automated testing and monitoring solution is needed to ensure high quality.

From an algorithm perspective, there are two approaches to score the Video Quality Analysis (VQA): Mean Opinion Score (MOS) and Differential MOS (DMOS). MOS reflects a computational score for video quality that normally would be perceived by the human eye. MOS detects black video, frozen video, tiling/macroblocking, blurriness, and other types of video distortion. A good solution will capture video and, using VQA, generate metrics on every frame of the video with heuristic algorithms to assess the quality of each. DMOS conducts a similar process, but in comparison to another feed.

In many cases, with live content, vendors are forced to use the MOS method. In other cases, where the content is pre-recorded, DMOS is possible. In some live-content cases, it is possible to compare the live stream of a relatively reliable source (for example, a web stream) to another which is the one under test (for example, mobile device on a cellular network).

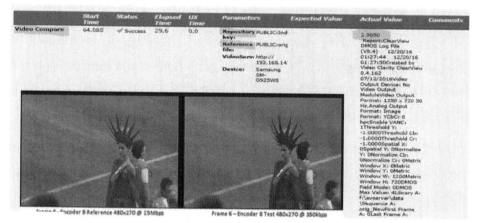

Figure 1: Example VQA report

From a solution architecture perspective, let's consider a lab built in the following manner:

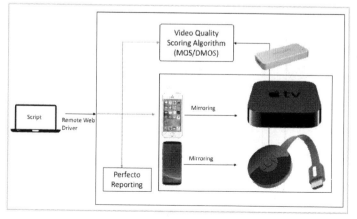

Figure 2: Video Quality Testing Lab Setup

In this setup, devices are part of a lab, connected and fully operational. The test script would navigate the app, through content and pages, and would get to the video content. Once played, the video content would be mirrored to the Chromecast/Apple TV device(s). Note that by mirroring, the stream is not set up directly from the streaming server to the Chromecast/Apple TV, but rather from the server to the mobile device, and from there to the Chromecast/Apple TV. Next, the HDMI output would be connected to a video capture card and, from there, to a VQA server to determine the score. As mentioned, this setup could be used for testing as well as production monitoring.

FUNCTIONAL TESTING OF DEVICES IN A HOME ENVIRONMENT

Modern home entertainment setups enable in-home streaming between the set-top-box (STB) and devices in the home. Functions on mobile devices include changing channels on the STB, setting up video recordings, etc. In addition, providers have different licensing schemes for how many devices at home can stream content concurrently. Such setups can be tested using a lab like the one above with an STB added to it.

Figure 3: Mobile app controlling the Set Top Box

FUNCTIONAL TESTING OF OVER-THE-TOP (OTT) DEVICES

The introduction of smart home entertainment devices and systems such as Fire TV, Roku, Apple TV, and others, has established yet another screen, one which is very attractive to advertisers, content providers, gaming companies, retail etc.: the big TV screen. Take Fire TV, for example; it can load apps from the Google app store, users can log in, play games, buy products, etc. Furthermore, users can explore video content and consume it on the big screen. In an effort to drive adoption and usage, Amazon announced their intent to establish cross-app streamlined authentication. In other words, those devices are yet another front to the brand's digital strategy.

From a testing perspective, these devices are very similar to mobile devices containing mobile apps; they both have a functional testing component and, as some apps do, they also have a video streaming component.

For example, one common use case for Fire TV is exploring content, downloading and logging in to apps, etc.

Figure 4: Functional testing of Fire TV

```
...
        capabilities.setCapability("model", "Fire TV");
        AndroidDriver driver = new AndroidDriver(new URL(host),
        capabilities);
...
// Navigate content
        driver.findElementByXPath("//*[@text=\"Your Videos\"]").
        click();
        PerfectoUtils.ocrTextCheck(driver, "Videos", 30, 99);
// measure user experience timer: how long it took it to load?
        long homeTimer = PerfectoUtils.getUXTimer(driver);

        driver.findElementByXPath("//*[@content-desc=\"Sneaky
        Pete - Season 1, Prime\"]").click();
        driver.findElementByXPath("//*[@content-desc=\"Seasons &
        Episodes \"]").click();
        driver.findElementByXPath("//*[@text=\"Season 1, Episode
        1\"]").click();
// let it play
```

As this script shows, navigation through apps and content can be done with standard Appium, and then switch over to VQA testing with the methods mentioned earlier.

SUMMARY

The modern application landscape is rapidly expanding to offer new, compelling experiences to end users: new devices, new services and new experiences. A business needs to be continuously aware and proactive in adopting these approaches to maintain leadership in their space. Test coverage must take into consideration all the various potential combinations, and in light of shorter agile sprints, prioritize accordingly. Robust test automation must be built to support this acceleration and proper reporting solutions need to be in place to offer fast feedback to the developer.

CHAPTER TWENTY-EIGHT

Using Mock Test Data as Part of Continuous Testing

BY UZI EILON

UZI EILON is the CTO at Perfecto Mobile. He joined Perfecto in 2010 after a fifteen-year career as a software developer and manager at IDF, Netrialty, Comverse, and SanDisk. Over the past seven years, Uzi has grown the company by managing expanding R&D teams and leading Sales Engineering teams. His fields of expertise include mobile application testing, automation tools, defining customer projects, and on-board-

ing, plus bringing Agile methodologies into the equation. Uzi Eilon speaks regularly on behalf of Perfecto Mobile at events, such as AnDevCon, Star-West, HP Discover, and ongoing technical webinars.

INTRODUCTION

Data is a key part of testing as it affects the accuracy, complexity and quality of tests.

In some cases, **controlling the data** is a basic requirement for successful test execution and the best way to control the data is by using a mock server. Especially when teams are trying to enhance velocity and get greater test coverage as part of their continuous testing efforts, using this type of tool can definitely enhance overall test productivity.

A "mock server"[1] is a software that communicates with an app and provides predefined data along with responses for specific requests.

The most common reasons for using and objectives of using mock servers are:

- **Data integrity in the test environment** — in many test environments, the test data that is generated from production becomes a subset, and after few test executions by different teams and test iterations, the data may become corrupted and not reflect the production data structure. Mock servers allow teams to control the full data entity and ensure that the response data is accurate and contains all relevant data.

  Industry example: A business logic role in an insurance company does not allow active users in the system without a connected policy; however, quite often, in the test environment, there are cases with users that have such a state.

  Logging in to the system with such accounts can crash the app and prevent it from finishing their 'happy path' regression testing.

- **Better validations** — to have strong validations, teams need to be able to predict the data being used for transaction validation.

  Industry example: A banking app needs to cover a test that transfers money between accounts; the account balance changes constantly during the test and, without visualizing the data, the transfer validation is not predictable or reliable.

- **Simulate uncommon scenarios** — tests should validate different states in an app; in most cases it's not easy to manipulate backend data to mimic such unique scenarios.

  Industry example: In a car app, mock servers might be necessary to test the **"low air pressure"** feature; this would otherwise be difficult for teams to simulate.

- **Integration and sync between components** — in agile development, not all components are developed together. In some cases, one component is ready but another is not. The mock server plays a key role in such cases and is used as a stub to provide data to the app under test.

---

1 Wikipedia definition for MockServer — https://en.wikipedia.org/wiki/MockServer

MOCKSERVER – HOW TO START?

Step 1: Define the scenarios

Before starting with implementation, users should define the requests from the app and the mock server's responses.

The definition should contain the request structure and parameter values.

In this example, we use a "bank application" and, after the login, the app sends random requests to cover a list of transactions and balance validations.

Request:

```
http://ec2-34-234-65-172.compute-1.amazonaws.com/random/
```

Response:

```
action1:966 action2:442 action3:361 action4:309 action5:941
action6:583 action7:302 action8:582 action9:490 total:4976
```

We want to use the mock server in order to control the field total

Step 2: Choose a mock server

There are large numbers of mock servers in the industry; some are open source and others are commercial.

For this example, we will use the MockServer[2] open-source tool.

Step 3: Install MockServer

This server provides different methods of executions; in the following example, we select the JAR method. To use it, download the jar and execute the following command:

```
java -Dmockserver.logLevel=INFO -jar ~/Downloads/mockserv-
er-netty-5.3.0-jar-with-dependencies.jar -serverPort 1080
```

---

2   MockServer Open Source tool — http://www.mock-server.com/

Step 4: Set up MockServer

The basic traffic between the client application and the back end looks as follows:

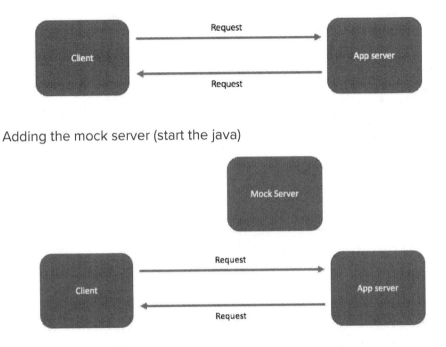

Adding the mock server (start the java)

Under the mobile device's WIFI settings, configure the client to use the mock server as a proxy.

Enter the new mock server proxy into the "Proxy host name" and use port 1080

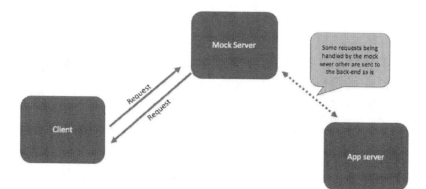

Step 5: Configure the required transactions.

The mock server contains two components:

- Request matcher
- Response actions

The matcher gets the requests and verifies if they need to be handled by the mock server or if they should be sent to the original address.

If the user configures the mock server to handle the request, it is sent to the response action that generates the relevant data, then it is sent back to the client.

To configure the mock server (ad-hoc) based on test requirements, an HTTP call with the relevant data needs to be sent to the mock server (request matcher) before the app sends the request.

In this example, we are trying to control the balance data ('total' value in the response).

Review the following JSON file named **test**:

- The role for the **request matcher** (`httpRequest` part) if request is `":"/random`.

- The action for the **response actions** (`httpResponse`) — send HTTP 200 back with the body of total 12345

```json
{
    "httpRequest":{
    "path":"/random/"
},
    "httpResponse":{
    "body":"total:12345",
    "statusCode":200
    }
}
```

Send the JSON to the mock server (part of the automation script)

```
curl -v -X PUT "http://MOCK_SERVER_IP:1080/expectation" -d
@test
```

In the next client request ,the expected balance should have a total of 12345

Test Scenarios Examples Using MockServer:

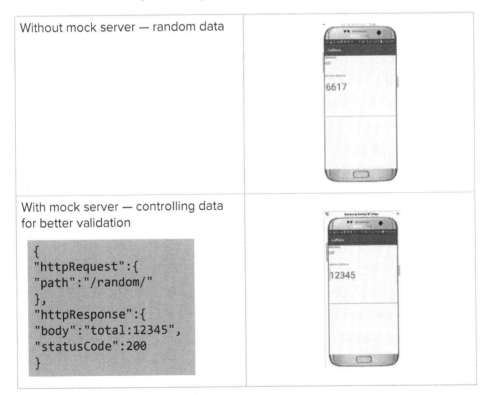

Without mock server — random data	
With mock server — controlling data for better validation	

Response invalid data

```
{
"httpRequest":{
"path":"/random/"
},
"httpResponse":{
"body":aaaaaa:12345",
"statusCode":200
}
}
```

Application crash

Control the HTTP response code	The expected result is a pop-up with "cannot connect to the system" but the application crashes again
```{ "httpRequest":{ "path":"/random/" }, "httpResponse":{ "statusCode":404 }```	

```
{
"httpRequest":{
"path":"/random/"
},
"httpResponse":{
"statusCode":404
}
```

SUMMARY

Mock servers allow developers and testers to execute end-to-end tests and, in addition, to be able to control the test data for better validations and test management.

Such servers also allow teams to perform boundary tests and extend their overall coverage.

Mock servers can improve overall test suite quality and increase coverage. The correct continuous testing phase in the DevOps pipeline in which to leverage mock servers it is when the version is stable in the **pre-prod stage.** Please refer to Chapter 8: 'Guidelines for Matching Testing Tools to Your DevOps Pipeline' for more details into the test coverage guidelines.

A few closing tips:

- There are a few configurations for MockServer. They can be used to handle requests before or after connection the back end — check which are relevant for your requirements.

- To support **HTTPS,** the server certificate should be configured on the mock server

- After sending a request to the mock server, the request matcher will handle **only** the next request; therefore, before **each test,** users should send the data to the mock server.

- Timeout, time to live (TTL), caching — MockServer supports all these different timing configurations; these parameters affect your apps but are very hard to test. During performance improvements, these parameters can change (not related to the version release). Use the mock server to verify the different timing behaviors for every version.

Special thanks to the technical reviewers of this book!

Mike Lyles is a Director of QA & PM with over 20 years of IT experience in multiple organizations, including Fortune 50 companies. He has exposure in various IT leadership roles: development, PMO, and testing. He has led various teams within testing organizations: functional testing, environments, SCM, TDM, performance testing, test automation, and service virtualization.

Mike has been an international keynote speaker at multiple conferences and events, and is regularly published in testing publications and magazines. You can learn more about Mike at www.MikeWLyles.com where you can also find his social media links and connect with him there.

Alan Page has been a software tester for over 25 years, and is currently the Director of Quality for Services (and self proclaimed Community Leader) at Unity Technologies. Previous to Unity, Alan spent 22 years at Microsoft working on projects spanning the company – including a two year position as Microsoft's Director of Test Excellence. Alan was the lead author of the book "How We Test Software at Microsoft",

contributed chapters for "Beautiful Testing", and "Experiences of Test Automation: Case Studies of Software Test Automation". His latest ebook (which may or may not be updated soon) is a collection of essays on test automation called "The A Word: Under the Covers of Test Automation", and is available on leanpub.